A History of Naval Aviation
WINGS OVER THE SEA

A History of Naval Aviation
WINGS OVER THE SEA

David Wragg

ARCO PUBLISHING, INC.
New York

Published by Arco Publishing, Inc.
219 Park Avenue South, New York, N.Y. 10003

Copyright © 1979 by David Wragg

Printed in Great Britain

Library of Congress Cataloging in Publication Data

Wragg, David.
  Wings over the sea.

  1. Aircraft carriers—History. 2. Naval aviation
—History. 3. United States. Navy—Aviation—
History.
I. Title.
V874.W73 1979   359.8'3   78-21853
ISBN 0-668-04626-0

Contents

Acknowledgements

I should like to thank all of those, too numerous to list, in the various navies and air forces, museums, shipbuilders and aircraft manufacturers, who have helped me by providing information and illustrations, and whose enthusiasm for the subject has been of considerable assistance in the writing of this book

Fleet Air Arm Museum
Imperial War Museum
National Maritime Museum
Library of Congress
Musée de L'Air
Newport News Shipbuilding & Dry Dock, USA
Ministry of Defence
US National Archives
Australian War Memorial
South African Air Force
Naval Photographic Centre, Washington D.C.
US Coast Guard
Royal New Zealand Air Force
Italcantieri
Hawker Siddeley Aviation
Vosper Thornycroft Ltd (British Shipbuilders)
Embraer, Brazil
McDonnell Douglas, St Louis
Foto Pozzar, Trieste
Shorts, N. Ireland
Royal Australian Navy

For Sally my wife

1 Faltering Steps

Of all the developments associated with airpower, that of having aircraft land on or take off from ships is perhaps the least easily identifiable as being the inspiration of any one individual. The idea is fundamental to the whole concept of naval aviation, and the logic is obvious; clearly it is better that aircraft should accompany the fleet to sea rather than have to travel from a shore base to provide air support, and it is highly desirable that aircraft should be taken by the fleet to wherever they might be needed for offensive or defensive purposes. This is the basis of 'organic airpower', of having aircraft under the control of surface forces to act as their eyes, ears and teeth.

Many early visionaries and pioneers saw flight in terms of ships taking to the air for commerce and war, but it was not until the American Civil War that a coal barge, the *G. W. Parke-Curtiss*, was used to transport and tow observation balloons for the Unionist Army. A few years earlier, in 1856, HMS *Assistance*, while searching in the Canadian arctic for the ill-fated Sir John Franklin expedition, had despatched messages by small balloons, giving the ship's position to survivors. The messages were attached in bundles to a slow fuse, and released as the fuse burnt down.

Dreams of flight finally achieved reality in 1903, the year in which the French Lebaudy brothers built and tested the first successful and truly practical airship, their famous Lebaudy No. 1 or *Jeune*, and the American Wright brothers made the world's first true powered heavier-than-air flights in their *Flyer I* biplane.

Others claimed to have achieved powered heavier-than-air flight before the Wrights, but it has long been generally accepted that theirs were the first flights in history in which an aircraft had lifted itself and its pilot off the ground under its own power and without any downhill assistance, and had sustained itself in flight, eventually landing on a point no lower than that from which it took off. Two other aircraft, the *Flyer II* and *Flyer III*, were produced and flown by Wilbur and Orville Wright in 1904 and 1905, while they attempted to interest a cynical world in the validity of their claims. Recognition came only slowly. The British Army certainly took an early interest, but it was not until September, 1908, that the United States Army became involved in trials with a Wright A machine, and by that time the Wrights had spent two years without attempting further development, disappointed and disheartened at the lack of recognition accorded their achievement.

One rival of the Wrights deserves mention. Samuel P. Langley started experiments in powered heavier-than-air flight with a series of tandem-wing monoplane models, launched from the roof of his houseboat moored on the Potomac River. In 1903 he used the same system to launch his full-sized aeroplane, the inappropriately and oddly named *Aerodrome A*, which fouled the launching apparatus on two attempts at flight, both times depositing itself and its hapless pilot, Charles Manly, in the river. Langley's supporters have always contended that but for his launching mishaps

Langley's *Aerodrome A* waits to be launched from the roof of his houseboat on the Potomac River

he could have beaten the Wrights into the air. However, although the Wrights' other rival, Glenn Curtiss, later rebuilt the *Aerodrome A* and flew it successfully, this was possible only after extensive modifications by Curtiss, who was attempting to discredit the Wrights. In fact the *Aerodrome A*, built with a $50,000 grant from the United States Army, not only lacked three-dimensional means of control, necessary for a true aeroplane, but was also under-powered.

After the five years or so of natural hesitation that followed the Wright brothers' first historic flight, the navies of the world were not slow to take up the challenge of the aeroplane. Their reasons for doing so were those which had already commended the aeroplane and airship to many army commanders—the compelling and constant need to be able to extend the field of vision and to have some idea of enemy movements.

Inter-service rivalry acted as a spur to progress, although it could have the opposite effect. It was not uncommon during the early days for officers to have to pay for their own flying tuition, while in some countries patriotic and wealthy citizens donated aircraft to the armed service of their choice. Commercial flying schools would train an aspiring pilot for as little as £35, (then about $150), and an ambitious aircraft manufacturer would not present too unhelpful or costly a front to a young officer interested in learning to fly, simply because his sales prospects improved if he could claim that the army or navy of a particular country already contained officers able to handle his aircraft.

It was the British who were first to establish an air branch for maritime duties. Purists might, with justification, argue that subsequent events lose for the United Kingdom the distinction of having the longest continuous tradition of naval aviation, but the fact remains that the British Admiralty rose to the occasion ahead of its counterparts elsewhere. In 1908 United States Navy representatives were present at Fort Myer, Virginia, to see Orville Wright conduct a series of trials with the *Flyer III* and Wright A biplanes, but they took no definite action. On the other hand, the estimates for the Royal Navy in 1909 included the princely sum of £35,000 ($175,000) for an airship.

The French were not far behind. In

Glenn Curtiss flying the modified Langley *Aerodrome A* in 1914

1910 the Service Aéronautique was formed, with Henri Farman and Voisin aeroplanes, which were soon supplemented by Blériot and Nieuport types. Russia also took steps towards forming an air element for the Imperial Russian Navy in 1910.

In 1911 the Royal Swedish Navy was amongst the first to receive an aeroplane, a Blériot, from an air-minded benefactor. The Japanese, with two Maurice Farmans and a Curtiss seaplane, and the Germans, with two Curtiss seaplanes, had to buy their aircraft in the normal way. These developments, and the real progress of individuals in the United States Navy, spurred Congress into voting funds for aircraft for the USN that same year. The following year, the Royal Norwegian Navy followed the example of its next-door neighbour and accepted a plane, in this case a Rumpler Taube monoplane from Germany, donated by a private individual. The Royal Danish Navy bought its own first aircraft, an Henri Farman.

Brazil was able to form the first South American naval air arm in 1913, while the Royal Hellenic Navy was equipped with aircraft in 1914, and assisted by the British in training pilots and mechanics.

To these few pioneers scattered across the globe was entrusted the awesome responsibility of making naval aviation not only work but actually contribute something of value to the conduct of warfare at sea. It was a question of exploiting the full potential of aeroplane and airship, and of bringing aeroplane and warship together, not to mention discovering just what the potential of flight could be for naval aeronauts.

At first there was the added spice of competition, a notable example being that between the United States Navy and a merchant shipping line. November, 1910, saw a Canadian, McCurdy, waiting to fly his Curtiss biplane from the Hamburg–America liner *Pennsylvania*, while a young USN officer, Lieutenant Eugene B. Ely, was hoping to fly his Curtiss biplane from the light cruiser USS *Birmingham*. Ely had the backing of Glenn Curtiss himself, and, even more important, of Captain Irvin Chambers, USN, who was entrusted with consideration of such schemes on behalf of the Navy Department, and who also helped smooth the way for Ely's contemporary,

Eugene Ely makes his second take-off from a ship, flying his Curtiss biplane from the USS *Pennsylvania*

Ellyson. Both Ely and McCurdy had launching platforms constructed over the forecastles of their respective ships.

While both men managed to avoid creating the kind of tension which was soon afterwards to become associated with attempts on the speed record and other pioneering competitive efforts, they were certainly aware of each other, and an atmosphere of impatience naturally developed. Their respective camps, if that is the right word, had their fill of excitement, although the general attitude of the aviators themselves seems to have been on the lines of 'let's get on with it'.

It was eventually decided that Ely should make his attempt during the afternoon of 14 November, while the USS *Birmingham* steamed at 20 knots into the wind. The impatient Ely had rather different ideas. As soon as the anchor was raised, at 15.16 hours, and during the short pause before the ship got underway, he started the engine of his frail machine and gave the word to the ground crew for it to be released. Trundling forward along the eighty-foot long launching platform, the aircraft could not quite gather sufficient speed to become airborne on leaving the platform. It fell towards the water below the bows of the ship, with Ely feverishly trying to gain control and speed after leaving the platform. He just managed to make it, but not before the aircraft had hit the water once and damaged the propeller. Regaining control, he flew on and landed safely at Willoughby Spit, just two-and-a-half miles away and rather less in distance than he had originally hoped to fly.

At one time, NASA made considerable play of using married men on America's space missions, on the assumption that they would be more cautious than their unmarried colleagues. Certainly, Ely didn't let an attractive young wife deter him from risking his neck.

For the crew of the USS *Birmingham*, the whole event was cause for excitement, in spite of the short and explicit signal to the shore: 'Ely's just gone.'

The British were far from dilatory at this time. In 1910, the Royal Aero Club put two Short biplanes at the disposal of Royal Navy officers wishing to learn to fly. However, it seems that there was no great rush to get airborne, perhaps because many young and ambitious officers had no wish to ruin their career prospects through association with a novel concept which they thought higher authority might regard as eccentric.

Higher authority, if it ever had such ideas, had shed them, and was anxious to convey the message to its subordinates. That December, the Commander-in-Chief at the Nore, Admiral Sir C. C. Drury, drew the attention of his officers to the availability of the aircraft, based at Eastchurch on the Isle of Sheppey, describing them as biplanes 'of the most modern type, fitted with Gnome motors', and stating that they were placed at the disposal of naval officers 'at all times and without charge'. In fact, there were only two conditions attached to this offer, the first being that any damage be made good, and the second that the officers concerned should become members of the Royal Aero Club.

Further encouragement followed immediately. King George V approved an Order in Council giving a daily allowance to naval airmen amounting to six shillings for officers, half-a-crown for chief petty

officers, petty officers and leading seamen, and a florin for able seamen. Ordinary seamen were obviously not expected to be involved.

On the other hand, the British medical paper, the *Lancet*, was somewhat less encouraging. It published an article about the blood pressure of aviators, recommending that they keep to a low and steady altitude! Correspondence in *Flight* magazine about aerial attack was concluded by a deep-thinking correspondent who warned that in a future war the crew of an enemy aircraft might be inclined to drop bombs on a town or village from which they were shot at! Not quite right.

The distinction of making the first landing on a warship went to Ely. Again the ship was at anchor, in spite of an earlier intention that she should be steaming into the wind. The decision on this occasion was that of the ship's captain, Captain Pond, who felt that there was insufficient room in San Francisco Bay for his ship, the cruiser USS *Pennsylvania*,

After his first landing aboard a ship, Ely also took off from the USS *Pennsylvania*, making a round flight

Eugene Ely at the controls of his aircraft

to steam into the wind. A slight mist and the presence of a number of other vessels anxious to be around for the great occasion no doubt had a bearing on this decision. This was on 18 January, 1911, just two months after Ely's first dramatic take-off.

There was an air of festivity about the whole occasion. Ely took off from Selfridge Field, an army camp just outside San Francisco, at 10.45, and flew low over the city and the warships in the bay, keeping contact with the USS *Pennsylvania* in the mist by listening for the sounding of the ship's siren. A contemporary account explained how he flew slowly past the cruiser and on for 'some hundreds of yards, before circling back and then rising slowly toward the stern of the vessel to settle finally on a platform built over the stern. His landing was assisted by the first primitive arrester-wire system, with wires strung across the platform and kept in position by a 100-lb sandbag at each end. One eyewitness estimated his speed at about 40 mph, and he landed on the fifty-foot-wide platform, taking just sixty

of the 130 feet allowed for his landing run, at 11.01 exactly.

The siren of the USS *Pennsylvania*, which had acted as a navigational aid, now signalled success, and the message was echoed by the sirens of the other ships in the bay, and by the cheers of their crews.

Captain Pond entertained Ely to a lunch in his honour. An hour afterwards, Ely took off from the USS *Pennsylvania*, still at anchor, 'at high speed', this time making only a gentle dip toward the water before climbing steadily and circling the ships in the bay. He returned to Selfridge Field, flying over San Francisco at the then not inconsiderable height of 2,000 feet, and on landing was cheered by the officers of the 13th US Infantry Regiment, which was in camp there.

Against this steady progress in the United States, the Royal Navy had the humiliating experience of seeing its first airship, officially known as 'Naval Airship No. 1' and named, perhaps with tongue in cheek, the *Mayfly*, destroyed at Barrow Yard before it could make its maiden flight. Worst of all, the destruction was not due to any natural disaster. Finding the airship to be rather heavy, the British set about lightening the structure, but only succeeded in weakening it to the point of sudden and total collapse!

However, it was during 1911 that the Royal Navy received the first pilots from Eastchurch. The first four were Lieutenants A. N. Longmore, R. Gregory and Charles Rumney Samson, RN, and Lieutenant E. L. Gerrard, of the Royal Marine Light Infantry. Others followed, including Sub-Lieutenant F. E. T. Hewlett, RN, who had the distinction of having received his instruction from his mother—a woman of some character who flew in poor weather wearing sabots, a type of wooden clog!

head of the French Military Aviation Department, who lost little time in devising his own tests for officers wishing to be selected for aviation duties. His tests included a flight of at least a hundred kilometres across country, a flight of at least two hours' duration, another of more than 300 metres (about a 1000 feet), and one of at least ten metres per second. On the introduction of these requirements, there were no less than fourteen army officers and two naval officers, Lieutenants Biasson and Delage, suitably qualified.

Moment of truth for the Royal Navy's first airship, the ill-fated *Mayfly*

The Eastchurch pilots were, of course, those who had taken advantage of the Aero Club's offer, which was the British answer to the donation of aircraft practised in the Scandinavian countries. At this time, the qualifications of the trained and tested pilot were not those of a government department or agency, but of the aero club of the country concerned, which issued pilots' certificates. By early 1911 the Royal Aero Club had issued a total of fifty-five certificates, compared with 354 issued by the Aero Club de France. Not everyone was happy with the Aero Club de France's tests for the award of certificates, however. Prominent among the dissatisfied was General Rocques,

The Americans also trained pilots, with both the Wrights and Curtiss involved in the work. The latter was of greater significance for naval duties, while Orville Wright tended to concentrate on army pilots. One of the first officially trained USN pilots was Lieutenant T. Ellyson, whose tutors were Eugene Ely and Glenn Curtiss.

It was at this time that air-mindedness began to take root among the authorities in the United States, with the House of Representatives voting $130,000 (£26,000) for the purchase of military aeroplanes. Other countries often left their navies to think about theory and have little opportunity for practice. A good example was Italy, in which, as early as late 1911, Captain Claudio Piomatti produced a paper on the role of the aeroplane in naval warfare.

The use of landplanes for take-off from and landing on platforms constructed on warships was by no means the sole preoccupation of the naval airmen of the period. At that time, and for many years afterwards, as much importance was placed on the hydroaeroplane, as seaplanes and flying-boats were then called, while the airship was also deemed to be very important, not least because of its range and bomb-carrying abilities.

The term 'seaplane' was not used until well into World War I, when it is supposed to have been coined by Winston Churchill, then First Lord of the Admiralty. During the early days such craft were more correctly known as float-planes.

Just as the glider was the immediate ancestor of the aeroplane, the float-glider was the precursor of the float-plane. The first float-gliders had been built in 1905, using a combination of the Wright and Hargrave concepts, by a Frenchman, Gabriel Voisin. They were built to the order of his famous compatriots, Archdeacon and Blériot. The Voisin design actually became airborne while being towed at speed by a motor-boat along the River Seine, near Paris. Surprisingly, neither Archdeacon nor Blériot were to be noted for their work in connection with float-plane development, leaving the design and construction of the first powered float-plane to another Frenchman, Henri Fabre, who made a tentative flight in this machine in 1910.

The real pioneers in this field were the Americans, and in particular Glenn Curtiss. This rival of the Wrights had been a motorcycle manufacturer before devoting his considerable energies to aviation. Caricatured in 1910 by the cartoonist Mich as a lean hungry American with small moustache and big ears, Curtiss was unquestionably a man of great ability and energy, although his actions with regard to the validity of the Wright brothers' patents on lateral control of aeroplanes suggests a less straightforward approach than that of the Wrights.

Curtiss built the first practical floatplane, which he tested on 26 January, 1911, at San Diego, California, drawing the comment from one of his contemporaries that he had made the first significant advance in aviation since the Wright brothers. The following month he made the first flight from land to water, settling down in the water before starting up again, taking off and returning to his starting place. But this machine could not really be considered as the first practical amphibian.

Curtiss then attempted to use his experimental hydroaeroplane design as the basis for the first flying-boat, but it was not until 1912, after further refinement of this basic design, that he could build and fly a practical flying-boat. Even at this stage, the flying-boat held the promise of a sturdier construction than could be achieved with the flimsy float or seaplane. It was also during 1912 that the French designer, Denhout, designed and built his successful Donnet–Leveque flying-boat. This was a single-engined machine with a pusher-propeller and the tailplane mounted on booms, one of its main claims to fame, perhaps, being the introduction of the stepped hull to flying-boat design. Spurred on by this, Curtiss went on to build yet another flying-boat by the end of the year, this time one with a long hull and the tailplane moved aft of the mainplane. He also developed a practical amphibian from his float-plane, although the landing wheels were fixed.

A little later, Curtiss obtained the assistance of a retired Royal Navy officer, Lieutenant-Commander J. C. Porte, in the design of his large twin-engined flying-boat, the *America*, which was sold to the Royal Naval Air Service on the outbreak of war in Europe in 1914. It was to be the forerunner of a number of successful maritime-reconnaissance flying-boats of British and American manufacture, operating from shore bases in protection of Allied shipping.

It fell to a British manufacturer, Sopwith, to build the first amphibian with a retractable undercarriage. This was the oddly and unattractively named *Bat Boat* of 1913, powered by a 90-hp Daimler engine and featuring a flying-boat stepped hull and a tailplane mounted on outriggers aft of the mainplane.

A problem still awaiting solution was to reduce the considerable time it took for a powerful warship to stop, lift a seaplane over the side, and then for the aircraft to become airborne—by no means a certain event a decade or so after the first flights! The obvious answer lay in some form of catapult device, and experiments were conducted by the United States Navy and Curtiss, initially using an overhead wire apparatus for launching Curtiss seaplanes. This suggests that there had been scant progress in launching aircraft since the days of Henson and Stringfellow, the Victorian British pioneers who had launched steam-powered models in the same way.

The real advance came from Captain Chambers, who remained concerned with the development of naval aviation even after Ely's early experiments ended. Chambers designed a compressed-air catapult which, fitted onto a converted barge in the Washington Navy Yard, enabled Lieutenant T. Ellyson, USN, to fly one of Curtiss's new A–1 Hydroaeroplanes from it on 12 November, 1912. At the time, flights onto shipboard platforms and take-offs from such platforms aroused more interest, because of the dangers; later they were still regarded as more interesting, because of their implications for aircraft carrier development. Nevertheless, Chambers' invention of the compressed-air catapult can be soundly described as one of the first significant developments for naval aviation, as well

The first successful torpedo dropping trials, with Longmore flying a Short Folder biplane in late 1914, after the RNAS and RFC had adopted the now familiar roundels

as having an earlier practical use than the take-off and landing platforms.

While undoubtedly lagging behind the Americans, the British were nevertheless still making steady progress. One Royal Navy officer, Lieutenant, later Commander, Oliver Schwann, bought an aeroplane at his own expense and fitted it with floats and gas bags in order to make a water take-off in November, 1911. One of the original batch of graduates from Eastchurch, Lieutenant Arthur Longmore, RN, flew Short biplane No. 38, a Short S.27, fitted with airbags, onto the River Medway on 1 December, 1911, and shortly afterwards took off again.

Longmore was probably the most successful of the early Royal Navy pilots. On 28 July, 1914, flying at Calshot, near Southampton, he had the distinction of making the first drop of a standard naval torpedo from his Short Folder Seaplane, which carried the torpedo on a rack between the floats. By that time Longmore was already a squadron commander. Eventually passing into the new Royal Air

The first flight from a British warship was by Charles Rumney Samson from HMS *Africa* using this Short S.27

Force in 1918, he rose to the rank of Air Chief Marshall, becoming a Knight Commander of the Bath and gaining the Distinguished Service Order on the way.

Almost a year after Ely's historic landing and round-trip flight, and a few months after his death, one of the British pilots, Lieutenant Charles Rumney Samson, was ready to make the first take-off from a British warship, the battleship HMS *Africa*. Unconfirmed reports persist to this day that Samson did in fact make flights from HMS *Africa* in December, 1911, and have never been officially denied, but they are unlikely to have any substance since contemporary reports deal only with the events of January, 1912. One reason for the confusion is the quoting by different official accounts of both dates.

Wednesday, 10 January, 1912, dawned grey and misty at the Royal Aero Club's airfield at Eastchurch, making flying impossible until the mist began to clear towards noon. At midday, Lieutenant Samson climbed into the same Short S.27 biplane which had served Longmore so well the previous December, took off soon afterwards and flew to Cockleshell Hard. When he landed there a well-rehearsed

plan got under way. The aircraft was man-handled onto a lighter, and after being secured was towed by a pinnace to HMS *Africa*, where the ship's derrick lifted the aircraft onto the launching platform—a staging of planks over the forecastle. There were no plans to take off while the ship was under way; instead, at 14.20, while HMS *Africa* was still at her anchor in Sheerness Harbour, the S.27's 50-hp Gnome rotary engine was started up, followed by the run forward along the staging. Then the aircraft was rising steadily. It flew over the destroyer, HMS *Cherwell*, and then back round over HMS *Africa*, before flying along the Medway to the Kentish village of West Minster, and finally arriving back over the airfield at Eastchurch at an altitude of some 800 feet.

The S.27 was fitted with airbags, in case a forced landing on the Medway became necessary, but fortunately the eventuality did not arise. Samson's thoughts about his flight are not on record —in common with many of his contemporary aviators he was not accustomed to making a fuss about his achievements— but authority in the form of his superiors had apparently become concerned about the safety of naval aviators. Admiral Sir E. H. Seymour, RN, went on record at the time as being 'heartened' by the ability of the aircraft to land upon water without sinking.

No doubt concerned at the risk of becoming backward in the new field which was being opened up for aviation by the United States Navy and the Royal Navy, the French decided to devote the then considerable sum of £40,000 ($200,000) to experiments with naval aircraft.

In the meantime, the Royal Navy set out to prove that its aeroplanes were not toys, and also to try and regain some of the ground lost to the Americans. The scene for this effort was the Annual Naval Review, held in 1912 during early May, off Portland. It proved to be the most exciting review for many years.

The Royal Navy took four aircraft to Portland, with a Deperdussin, a Nieuport and two Short biplanes, with one of the latter converted by Samson into a workable hydroaeroplane by the addition of three torpedo-shaped floats. With the sense of flair characteristic of naval aviators, Samson named the hydroaeroplane, in reality Short No. 41, HMS *Amphibian*. The battleship HMS *Hibernia* had a ramp constructed over her forecastle from which to launch landplanes and, even more significant, was officially known as a hydroaeroplane mother vessel—a more cumbersome phrase than aircraft carrier or seaplane carrier.

Flying started with Samson leaving the boat-slip at Portland in HMS *Amphibian*, taking off and flying over the fleet while it lay at anchor. Other flights followed, with the recently-promoted Captain Gerrard, RMLI, carrying a lady passenger, to the delight of the onlookers. Since the onlookers were the crews of the assembled warships, they might have been even more delighted had they known at that instant that the lady in question was none other than the daughter of their commander-in-chief, Admiral Callaghan! Against this, Lieutenant Grey's flights in both the Nieuport and the Deperdussin, and Longmore's flights in the other S.27, were dull stuff indeed.

Later during the review, Samson showed the use of the seaplane for communications duties, carrying a messenger with a letter for King George V and landing alongside the Royal Yacht *Victoria and Albert*, where the messenger was taken off in a dinghy. While this was going on, Lieutenant Grey flew past the royal yacht at 500 feet, and at a safe distance dropped a 300-lb dummy bomb. Remaining airborne, Grey flew past the battleship HMS *Neptune* and caused some alarm amongst his audience by suddenly diving, only to pull out some twenty feet from the sea. Far from there being any fault with his aeroplane, he had merely detected a submarine at periscope depth. This was yet another exciting demonstration of the aeroplane's full potential, although the vessel in question was one of the Royal Navy's then small fleet of submarines taking part in the review.

However, the review's flying activities were most notable for Samson's flight in an S.27 from the ramp over HMS *Hibernia*'s forecastle, while she steamed at $10\frac{1}{2}$ knots into the wind in Weymouth Bay. This event was also witnessed by His Majesty, and Samson was among the officers invited to dine with King George V on board the royal yacht after the review—a fitting end to a review which took its place in aviation history due to Samson's making the first flight from a ship actually under way.

After such a performance, even Samson allowed himself some comment to journalists covering the review, a modest 'Good, good, but we shall do better', which sounded rather like an end of term comment at the bottom of a school report. The comparison may well be appropriate, since the occasion certainly marked the end of the first period for British naval aviation. It had ended in a genuine first with Samson's flight, and, equally important, had meant that the Royal Navy had regained any ground lost while the United States Navy had been forging ahead. There are two advantages to taking off while a ship is moving. First the movement of air over the flight deck assists take-off, and next the time taken for a large vessel to stop (and so become a sitting target for submarines or aircraft) is eliminated. As a result, take-offs from moving vessels are almost obligatory.

At the same time, it is probably true to say that the original American plans for launching aircraft from ships steaming into the wind at 20 knots were over-ambitious given the aircraft speeds of the day. For many years ahead, a strong wind would continue to produce the phenomenon of aircraft flying backwards. The story is told of one Royal Navy pilot who, caught in a bad storm while flying a seaplane, was forced to fly almost on the surface of the sea to minimise the wind's force, but even so took nearly an hour to cover just sixteen miles! To his chagrin, after landing safely his frail machine was picked up by the wind, thrown against a jetty, and damaged beyond repair.

It was to be some time before a landing could be made on a ship under way, this being left to Squadron Commander E. H. Dunning, RN, who landed his Sopwith Pup on the first aircraft carrier, HMS *Furious*, in 1917.

In the meantime, British naval aviation went on to its second term, as the Naval Wing, Royal Flying Corps, following the merger of naval and military aviation in May, 1912, which lasted until the formation of the Royal Naval Air Service in July, 1914. The object of the merger was to provide co-ordination and strengthening of British service aviation. There were also some improved conditions of service. A squadron commander, flight commander or flying officer (equivalent respectively to lieutenant-commander or major, lieutenant or captain, and sub-lieutenant or 1st lieutenant in the Navy or Army) received eight shillings a day flying pay in the RFC! In addition, there was an allowance of £75 ($375) for learning to fly privately, which was indeed generous; and on acceptance of a serving officer for transfer from the other two services into the RFC there was an additional allowance of £40 ($200) for special clothing.

Among the senior RFC posts allocated to naval officers at the beginning was that of Commandant of the Central Flying School at Upavon on Salisbury Plain. The first Commandant was Captain G. M. Paine, MVO, RN. The Central Flying School itself was one of the advantages and innovations of the new organisation.

There was an ominous hint of things to come in October, 1912, when the airship L.1, under the command of Count Ferdinand von Zeppelin, its designer and builder, made a record 1,000 mile flight, leaving its base at Friedrichshafen at 08.35 on Sunday, 13 October, and arriving at Johannisthal, near Berlin, at 15.43 on Monday, 14 October. This was almost a round trip, and a notable achievement. But perhaps its real significance lay in the hue and cry which arose in England as the result of a claim that the L.1 was

Official support for the Royal Navy's aviators came from Winston Churchill, when First Lord of the Admiralty—about to take-off here in a Short S.41 with Samson as pilot

heard over Sheerness during the night of its epic voyage. Questions were asked in Parliament, and they were questions which His Majesty's ministers couldn't answer. Nobody had actually seen the L.1, they only thought they had heard it, but the implications for imperial defence did not need spelling out, even when von Zeppelin himself issued a statement insisting that he had not approached the English coast at any time during the flight.

It was not only the Germans who were interested in the airship. The United States Navy and the Royal Navy were both devoting part of their energies to it, although the British were having some trouble in developing a suitable craft. In an attempt to get a small anti-submarine patrol airship into volume production fairly quickly, the Royal Navy adopted the expedient of putting the fuselage and engine of a Royal Aircraft Factory BE2c under the airship envelope. The First Sea Lord, Lord Fisher, demanded to know how quickly a prototype could be made available, and was told three weeks! Three weeks and one prototype airship later, he demanded forty such airships. By 1915 there were to be sixteen of this particular semi-rigid type in service.

Aviation was just one of Fisher's problems. He had the daunting task of injecting not just new life and efficiency, but also a sense of priorities into a Royal Navy which was not yet fully geared to the demands of modern warfare. By 1913 post-Dreadnought battleships, of which the famous HMS *Warspite* and HMS *Barham* were typical examples, were coming off the slipways, although in still inadequate numbers for the conflict which most believed lay ahead. However, he had made several improvements. One oft-told story of the period before Fisher was that warships on the China Station had had spit and polish carried to such an extreme degree that the water-tight doors on battleships had been worn to a useless state! In spite of his demanding approach, he was a popular Admiral of

the Fleet; but from Nelson onwards, good British admirals have almost always been popular as well as respected.

Fortunately, the political First Lord of the Admiralty was a great believer in the aeroplane, to the extent that his colleagues were in an almost continuous state of anxiety regarding his safety. (The only contemporary statesman to share Winston Churchill's enthusiasm for aviation was Kemal Ataturk, the founder of modern Turkey, who flew as an observer during World War I.) Starting in late 1912 Churchill had a chain of seaplane stations built, with the first on the Isle of Grain, while in 1913 the light cruiser HMS *Hermes* was converted to act as a seaplane carrier for the new Short Folder Seaplane at that year's Naval Review. Although HMS *Hermes* was later reconverted to her original form, a collier was then converted to take her place, and named HMS *Ark Royal*. The Short Folder Seaplane was the first aircraft to have wings which could be folded for hangar stowage aboard ship.

Towards the end of 1912 the French converted the cruiser *La Foudre* into a seaplane carrier. One of the first flights from the converted vessel came at the beginning of December, when Montalent flew a Breguet float-plane from alongside the ship, passing over the fleet with a naval officer as passenger and then flying over Nice before returning to his starting point. Extensive trials followed with *La Foudre* during the spring of 1913.

However, not all the progress in naval aviation had been confined to the British, French and American navies, although technically these were the leaders.

During 1913 the German Naval Air Service was busily acquiring Rumpler–Etrich Taubes, Euler biplanes and licence-built Farmans, towards a total of thirty-six aircraft, mainly float-planes, and two airships at the outbreak of World War I in 1914. The Military Aviation Service, founded in 1912, had seven zeppelins by 1914.

Of course, not everyone had the resources or the need to match these de-

HMS *Ark Royal*, Britain's first seaplane carrier

An early flight from a French warship, a Caudron G.3 leaves the cruiser *La Foudre*

velopments, so progress elsewhere was far more modest. The Royal Danish Navy had acquired two Donnet–Leveque flying-boats in 1913, as had the Royal Swedish Navy, with the addition of two Henri Farman aircraft. It had also achieved the then not inconsiderable feat of having kept its original Blériot flying without accident. Another purchaser of Blériot aircraft was the Japanese Navy, which used the French aircraft to supplement Japan's own Otori and Ushioku biplanes, and in 1913 converted a naval transport, the *Wakamiya*, to act as a seaplane carrier. The Imperial Russian Navy had, by 1914, acquired the staggering total of sixty flying-boats.

Some of the earlier momentum had gone out of the United States effort by this time, with a seaplane station opened at Guantanamo, in Cuba, towards the end of 1912 closed after only a few months. The 1913 aircraft fleet for the United States Navy consisted of just three Curtiss A–1 and two Wright seaplanes, with two Curtiss and a Burgess–Dunne AH–7 flying-boat, and there were thirteen officers qualified as pilots.

In an attempt to maintain the earlier record of success and expansion, a special board was set up to produce recommendations for the future of the United States Navy's air branch. This recommended a comprehensive Naval Aeronautics Service and the purchase of more than fifty aircraft and three dirigibles. Little immediate action followed, although experiments in operating aircraft from battleships and cruisers continued, without, as yet, any fitting of catapults aboard warships. An opportunity for something more realistic than exercises or experiments came with naval operations in 1914 against Mexico, culminating in the so-called Vera Cruz incident during April, when Curtiss aircraft from the battleship USS *Mississippi* and the cruiser USS *Birmingham* undertook reconnaissance duties against the Mexican port.

In contrast with later developments, when a battleship would normally carry three seaplanes and a cruiser two, the USS *Mississippi* then had only a Curtiss seaplane and a Curtiss flying-boat, while the USS *Birmingham* had two flying-boats and a seaplane. At this period of modification and innovation, not to mention improvisation, such a situation was only to be expected, since the more lightly-armed and armoured cruiser offered more scope for alteration than the heavily-armoured battleship, even allowing for the larger size of the latter vessel.

The Vera Cruz incident was not the only one before World War I in which aircraft featured. During 1912 and 1913, Greece and her allies, Serbia, Bulgaria and Montenegro, were pushing Turkey out of practically all her possessions in the Balkans in the appropriately named Balkan War. In the earliest instance of a seaplane being used in war, a Greek seaplane flew a reconnaissance sortie against the Turkish fleet in the Dardanelles on 6 February, 1913.

Full control of British naval aviation returned to the Royal Navy at the beginning of July, 1914, with the formation of the Royal Naval Air Service. At its inception the new service had the not inconsiderable total of fifty-two seaplanes and flying-boats, thirty-nine landplanes, and six (but soon increased to seven) dirigibles, together with 828 officers and men. However, it is worth noting that manpower counts for naval aviation have always been misleading, because of the high number of general service personnel providing support, who cannot be divided, statistically or physically, from those doing actual flying duty.

The new Royal Naval Air Service had a degree of semi-autonomy within the Royal Navy, its organisation being based on the Admiralty Air Department and the Central Air Office, the Royal Naval Flying School and the Royal Naval Air Stations. Ranks included wing captain (as the equivalent of captain), wing commander (for commander), squadron commander (as the equivalent of lieutenant-commander or lieutenant with at least two years' seniority, depending on the number of aircraft in the unit), flight commander (as the equivalent of lieutenant), and flying sub-lieutenant. In some ways, as with the RFC, the shape of the rank structure for the future Royal Air Force was already becoming apparent, and in many ways the RNAS was more akin to the RAF than to the Fleet Air Arm after 1937.

Not the least of the comparisons which can be made between the RNAS and the RAF concerns its duties. In the military use of the aeroplane, the RNAS sometimes led the RFC, having the responsibility for much of the pioneering work with bombs, torpedoes and aircraft-fitted machine guns. As a result, the RNAS was to have the air defence and attack role on the outbreak of World War I, while the RFC was initially employed primarily on duties in support of ground forces. But to place too much emphasis on roles during that fateful summer of 1914 is to forget the sobering fact that at the time the RNAS had the staggering total of two aircraft and one airship fitted with machine guns, while 'bombs' were generally shells, sometimes fitted with guiding fins, sometimes not! It was also soon to be proven true that the seaplane suffered severe disadvantages in the air defence role, being incapable of climbing over the top of an attacking dirigible with anything like enough speed. It was to take World War I to clarify ideas on naval aviation, and indeed on aviation generally.

As war approached, seaplanes were certainly envisaged as being used for aerial attack, and, as with the British Short Folder Seaplane, the French Borel biplane was designed specifically as a seaplane torpedo-bomber, in 1914.

But in keeping with other aviators, the British and French navies spent the last spring of peace in an indulgence of record-breaking, even if the achievements which resulted tended to be rather specialised and even vague. On 7 April Lieutenant Janvier of the French Navy took his Voisin float-plane for a long flight in the dark over the sea near St Raphael, in the south of France—a not insignificant achievement even if, as was likely, the night was clear and there was a full moon. Also important was the seven-and-a-half hour marathon flight of an all-steel DFW Arrow biplane from Gosport to Hull on Wednesday, 12 May, 1914, with Lieutenant C. H. Collett, RNAS, at the controls, flying in heavy rain and against a north-east wind!

Yet despite all the records of early 1914, naval aviation suffered severe limitations, not the least being those of range and load-carrying for shore-based aircraft, and the need to stop the mother ship to get seaplanes or flying-boats airborne. And in spite of all the experiments and the threat from Germany for Britain and France, there was evidence of an attitude of mind in some quarters which saw the aeroplane solely as an instrument of unarmed reconnaissance. Yet limitations exist only to be pushed back—and pushed back they were during the next four years. Indeed, naval aviation as we know it today was to evolve during the war which followed.

2 First Blood

While today the events leading up to the outbreak of World War I—the Great War as it was known at the time and for the following twenty years—may seem less clear cut than those which resulted in World War II, the conflict was by no means unexpected. For some time, commercial and political rivalries throughout Europe had created tensions between the major powers which occasionally resulted in relatively local conflicts such as the Balkan War. The murder on 28 June, 1914, at Sarajevo of the Austrian heir-apparent and his wife was followed by recriminations, increasingly high-handed ultimatums and then by mobilisation in first one country and then another.

To some extent, the opposing sides differed from those in the later conflict. The Central Powers, essentially Germany and the Austro-Hungarian Empire, were later joined by first Turkey and then Bulgaria in 1915. Facing them were the Entente Powers or Allies, initially Britain, France, Russia—still at that time Imperial Russia—and Serbia, but soon joined by Japan and Italy, and later by Romania and the United States and Greece.

Almost from its outbreak, on 3 August, 1914, World War I was to be the first truly modern war, with civilians affected as much as the armed forces in many areas. It was also a war of contrasts. Horse-drawn artillery and infantry charges were still not uncommon, but new weapons such as the aeroplane and the submarine played an increasingly important role. Oddly, in spite of the experiments with bombs, torpedoes and airborne machine guns in the year or two before the outbreak of hostilities, many airmen, including those in the British Royal Flying Corps and the German Military Aviation Service flying over the Western Front in France, found their first aircraft were purely reconnaissance machines; and they would even exchange friendly salutes with their opposite numbers passing in the other direction! Such gentlemanly attitudes were to be short-lived, as they found themselves first greeted by revolver fire, then rifle fire and finally by machine guns fitted to aircraft. The early scout aircraft soon became fighters, and as the war developed, aircraft were fitted first with propeller deflector plates, so that machine guns could fire through the propeller or airscrew, and later with machine guns synchronised to fire through the propeller blades.

The opposing British and German navies, denied all but one major set-piece battle, that at Jutland, contented themselves with a growing interest in obtaining mastery in the air.

On the outbreak of war, only three navies had vessels converted to act as seaplane carriers. Britain had HMS *Ark Royal*, 3,000 tons, converted from a collier; Japan, the *Wakamiya*, an ex-naval transport; and France, the converted cruiser *La Foudre*, which was a useful addition to the 200 men and twenty-four seaplane strength of the Service Aéronautique. In fact, *La Foudre* was dispatched to the Adriatic with two Voisin seaplanes early in the war to reconnoitre the Austro-Hungarian fleet lying in Cattarro Bay, which the ship and her aircraft did with some success.

Other vessels were to follow into both British and French naval service as a growing appreciation of the value of aerial reconnaissance dawned on senior naval officers. The Germans, on the other hand, were slow to adapt the aeroplane for shipboard use or to use ships to carry aircraft. Even so, the commerce raider *Wolf*, operating in the Indian Ocean, later used a reconnaissance seaplane to warn her of approaching Allied warships and also to help track down suitable prey.

While these developments were taking place, the opposing navies had already adjusted from a relatively easy-going peacetime existence of flag-showing, cruises and reviews, to a demanding and arduous wartime routine of patrols, blockades, escort duties and armed reconnaissance, while each side tried, usually in vain, to bring the other to battle.

Shortly after the outbreak of war, the Eastchurch Squadron of the still-new Royal Naval Air Service was posted to Ostend, with Commander Charles Rumney Samson as its commanding officer. The squadron's ten aircraft, of assorted types, were to operate anti-zeppelin patrols for the protection of the British Expeditionary Force which was facing fast-moving German forces sweeping across tiny Belgium. Even before this, British troops had enjoyed the protection of the RNAS, when the airships *Astra-Torres* and *Parseval* had patrolled the English Channel for twelve-hour periods each during the first month of war, keeping a wary eye open for German warships while the British Army moved most of its regular troops from Britain to France, to form the British Expeditionary Force.

Winston Churchill, still First Lord of the Admiralty, volunteered the services of the RNAS to the British Government for fighter protection of the British Isles against intruding German aircraft and, more important, zeppelins. The offer was readily accepted, its main attraction being that it freed the Royal Flying Corps from air defence duties and allowed it to concentrate on offensive and defensive patrols over the front line, as well as providing aerial reconnaissance for ground forces. The RNAS protection of the mother country was accomplished by a force having a total strength of just 128 officers and 700 ratings, who flew in or looked after thirty-nine airships and fifty-two seaplanes, of which only half were operational. The force initially possessed only one seaplane carrier, until other vessels, including channel packets, could be requisitioned and converted.

It was over Ostend that the RNAS recorded its first destruction of a zeppelin in the air. Flight Sub-Lieutenant Reginald Warneford was on patrol in his Short biplane when he spotted the large airship LZ.37 reconnoitring the area. Climbing above the large gas bag, he opened fire with his machine gun, raking the craft along its entire length with machine gun bullets, before seeing it catch fire and start to break-up in mid-air, scattering debris over a wide area of mainly open countryside but including a few farms and a convent. Lacking parachutes, the crew of the zeppelin stood little chance of survival, and were presented with the uninviting alternatives of jumping to their deaths or being burnt

A RNAS coastal airship escorts a North Sea convoy

alive as the airship fell to the ground. The only survivor was the helmsman, who enjoyed a miraculous escape, falling through the roof of the convent onto a—presumably unoccupied—bed! Warneford, the first man to shoot down an airship, braving its defensive armament while his aircraft climbed slowly above it, became the first member of the RNAS to receive the Victoria Cross—Britain's highest award for valour—as a result.

The first forward base for the RNAS detachment in Belgium was at Antwerp, and in November, 1914, four aircraft from Antwerp attacked the zeppelin sheds at Dusseldorf and Cologne, using 20-lb bombs, which were little more than artillery shells fitted with stabilising fins, tossed over the side of the aircraft by the observer/machine-gunner. Another RNAS unit was based on Belfort in the east of France, and in the same month Avro biplanes of this unit flew some 250 miles, mainly over enemy-held territory, to bomb the zeppelin factory at Friedrichshafen.

Yet in spite of their raids on Germany and their success in countering the zep-

pelin threat, the RNAS in Belgium soon found itself fully stretched as the BEF retreated. The RNAS was forced to pull back with the BEF until eventually a new base could be established at Dunkirk.

Both sides established seaplane stations along their coastlines. As the Allies fell back into France, the German Naval Air Service, which had started the war with just two airships and thirty-six seaplanes, established its first operational base for seaplanes at Zeebrugge, captured from the Allies in December, 1914. A second seaplane station was established by the Germans at Ostend as their army advanced. Soon Germany had a string of seaplane bases stretching round the coast from Ostend to the Friesian Islands, Heligoland and Sylt in the Baltic, while the British had bases in Kent (including the Isle of Sheppey, the location of Eastchurch) and in East Anglia, as well as further north along the North Sea coast.

Unfortunately, seaplanes were no adequate counter to the airship. They needed to climb above it, past its machine gun fire, to make a fast strafing run, risking the very real possibility that the great vessel, filled with highly explosive hydrogen, might blow up in their faces. Slow though the airships were, they were fairly well defended, and the seaplanes themselves were not fast. With a maximum speed of less than 100 mph and a rate of climb to match, due to the drag caused by their massive floats, they presented an easy target for the airship's guns.

Early in 1915, on 19 January, two German Navy airships bombed Great Yarmouth, King's Lynn and Cromer on the British east coast. One of these airships, LZ.38, was to crash later, with forty-one casualties. In spite of this excursion by German naval airships, most airships, particularly during the summer of 1914, were in fact operated by the Military Aviation Service, and the German Naval Air Service generally had smaller numbers of zeppelins at its disposal.

The shortcomings of the seaplane, at a time when the modern concept of the fast-climbing fighter-interceptor was so far away as to be beyond visualisation, forced the RNAS to consider alternative ways of defeating the growing airship menace to British towns and shipping. Since the standard RNAS airship, built under Jackie Fisher's crash programme of modernisation, utilised the airframe of a BE2c fighter, it seemed a short step to putting a BE2a biplane under an airship, thus eliminating the initial climb problem and extending the endurance of defensive patrols. The experiment started at the RNAS air station at Kingsnorth in Kent, which provided fighter defence for Chatham Dockyard, and by August, 1915, Flight Commander W. C. Hicks, RN, was able to take a BE2a fighter and an SS airship aloft for trials, as a result of which further modifications were made.

On 21 February, 1916, Lieutenant-Commander de Courcy Ireland and Commander Usborne, RN, tried with another modified BE2a and an SS airship, known as the AP1, with disastrous results. They allowed the airship to rise too high before releasing their aircraft, and a sudden loss of envelope pressure caused the premature release of their aircraft as the front locking device failed and the rear locking device sheared, damaging the BE2a's controls. The sudden jerk as the damaged aircraft fell away from the airship threw Ireland out, while Usborne was killed when the aircraft crashed into Strood railway station sidings.

Yet the airship and aircraft combination was to remain logical to some. A little over two years later, the Royal Naval Air Station at Pulham in East Anglia saw a British-built zeppelin-type airship, R–23, and the naval version of the Sopwith Camel, the 2F–1, matched together, and Lieutenant R. E. Keys RN launched the aircraft from the airship after having first taken the precaution of conducting several unmanned launches. The new launching apparatus worked, yet this invention, known as the Little-Crook system after its inventors, Major I. C. Little and Captain Crook, RFC, never passed the experimental stage. It came so late in the war that the pressing urgency

A Fairey Campania seaplane takes off from HMS *Campania*, of course!

for a reliable anti-zeppelin weapon system had disappeared.

Some idea of the problems facing naval aviators and their seaplanes can be gathered from the performance of one of the more successful types of machine, the Fairey Campania. Designed to operate from the seaplane carrier HMS *Campania*, 18,000 tons, a Cunard liner built in 1893 and requisitioned by the Admiralty after the outbreak of war, the Fairey Campania took off from a 200-foot wooden deck built over the ship's forecastle, a device which made this vessel one of the first to be able to launch an aircraft without first stopping and hoisting it over the side. Take-off was achieved by placing the Fairey Campania seaplane on a wheeled trolley for the take-off run, and once airborne the aircraft was able to fly at just 80 mph, with a 2,000 foot ceiling and a three-hour endurance. The ship also suffered certain shortcomings. After joining the fleet in 1915, her fore-funnel was divided in 1916 to allow a longer take-off platform to be built, but while operating with the battle cruiser HMS *Glorious* in 1918, her 22 knot speed proved inadequate and she was unable to keep station with the rest of the fleet while flying off her aircraft, let alone while stopping to pick up her charges from the sea on their return!

Experiments with HMS *Campania* and other such vessels extended to take-offs with scout landplanes; and as an extension of the experiments with airships, a Porte Baby flying-boat took a Bristol Bullet scout aircraft into the air on 17 May, 1916, for a successful launching. But this system proved to be impractical for regular use, bearing in mind the slow climb of the flying-boat and the high drag of the two biplanes.

The battle against the zeppelins was to continue for almost the entire duration of the war. In 1916, Commander Rankin, RN, experimented with rockets and explosive darts against them and met with some success, but the problem remained one of finding the right kind of defending aircraft rather than using heavier weapons against the intruders.

The Porte Baby flying-boat, ready to take the Bristol Bullet scout aircraft into the air

Some impact was obviously made upon the airships and their crews, however, since in partial defence some airships sought the protection of cloud cover, occasionally lowering their observers through the clouds in a reconnaissance 'egg'. Certainly, the airships did not have everything their own way, and life for their crews was far from easy. During February, 1916 the German military dirigible, L.19, had to ditch in the North Sea, and its helpless crew drowned after the skipper of a British trawler refused to pick them up on the grounds that his ship might be taken over by the enemy!

Nevertheless it is surprising, in view of the intensity of the anti-zeppelin effort, that the second airship to be destroyed in the air by the RNAS did not come until 7 June, 1915, when one was shot down over Ghent in Belgium—almost a year after the first 'kill' by the RNAS.

Generally, the Military Aviation Service operated airships, primarily zeppelin or rigid types, almost as strategic bombers, while most of those in naval hands were used for fleet reconnaissance and were only occasionally involved in bombing raids. The problem of handling these unwieldy aircraft on the ground was solved in part by using revolving sheds, so that zeppelins could be launched and recovered with relative ease and safety, regardless of wind direction. Zeppelins did not normally operate from warships, but wireless telegraphy was used to transmit signals from reconnaissance airships to the fleet, and some warships used balloons or semi-rigid airships to extend their horizons.

The distinction between the semi-rigid airships used by the British forces and the rigid German zeppelins should not be allowed to cloud the major difference in air-mindedness between the two sides. The fact is that the Germans were far more airship-orientated than the Allies, who tended to have a stronger bias toward heavier-than-air aircraft.

Allied forces co-operated closely on occasion. As early as December, 1914, two French Nieuport biplanes were flying reconnaissance missions for British forces in Egypt, against the Turks, aided by two ex-German cargo vessels, *Ann Rickmers* and *Rabenfell*, co-opted by the French as unwilling seaplane tenders. Then, late in 1915, a Service Aéronautique detachment with six pilots and six Schreck FBA flying-boats, went to Venice to help the Italian forces in operations throughout the Adriatic. But as the war progressed the FBA flying-boat became an easy prey for German Brandenburg seaplane fighters.

Not all of the action lay in Europe, although during World War I, in sharp contrast with World War II, the European theatre, if anyone ever thought of it as such, was the only really important one. Activity elsewhere did not have any real effect on the outcome of the war. Even before the start of hostilities, the Japanese Naval Air Force had established a seaplane base and training school at Oppawa and had acquired Curtiss, Maurice Farman and Blériot seaplanes; and shortly afterwards it was experimenting with indigenous designs. Japan declared war on Germany on 23 August, 1914, and almost immediately the Imperial Japanese Navy

laid siege to the German mandate port of Tsingtao on the mainland of China, with the port surrendering to Japanese forces on 7 November.

During the next few years accident of geography was to provide the Japanese with few opportunities to display their allegiance. Their wartime equipment included Monocoque Deperdussin seaplanes, Short reconnaissance and Sopwith fighter seaplanes, and some licence-built Farmans, while the Naval Air Corps, or Yokosuka Naval Air Corps as it later became known, produced the Yokosuka Type 80 biplane in late 1916 as a further step towards building a Japanese aircraft industry. Shortly before the end of the war, some Japanese army pilots were assigned to the French army, but naval pilots were not involved in any such scheme.

Probably the most outstanding combat achievements of the RNAS came with the Dardanelles operation of 1915, the brainchild of Winston Churchill.

In July, 1915, the indefatigable Commander Samson was dispatched with six Nieuport Scouts of No. 3 Wing, RNAS, equipped with Lewis guns, to the Dardanelles, where British and French naval

Samson, in the Dardanelles during 1915

forces had been bombarding Turkish positions since the previous November. On 17 August, a Short 184 seaplane from the seaplane carrier *Ben-my-Chree*, flown by Flight Commander C. H. K. Edmunds, RN, dropped a fourteen-inch torpedo to sink a 5,000-ton Turkish military transport in the Sea of Marmara, Turkey's inland sea between the Dardanelles and the Bosporus. Even though the Turkish transport had already been damaged by submarine attack, this ranks as the first successful aerial torpedo attack.

The RNAS received its second Victoria Cross during the Dardanelles campaign, when Squadron Commander Bell-Davies landed behind enemy lines in November to rescue a fellow naval aviator who had been brought down on occupied territory.

The Germans were to return the doubtful compliment of having a merchant vessel sunk by aerial torpedo attack some two years later, when a German naval seaplane torpedoed a British vessel in the North Sea. Meanwhile, on 15 September, 1916, two Austrian seaplanes sank the French submarine *Foucalt* in the first successful bombing at sea. Later, in 1918, two Turkish vessels with German crews were to be subjected to intensive British aerial attack, particularly after one of them, the battlecruiser *Yavuz Sultan Selim*, formerly the German *Goeben*, ran aground, but little serious damage was done to the heavily armoured vessel.

A convenient ally in the Eastern Mediterranean was Greece, whose navy had enjoyed the help of a British Naval Mission before war broke out, including the setting up of a naval aviation branch. Royal Hellenic Navy officers received training on Farman and Sopwith seaplanes, and British aircraft were ordered, though few were delivered after war broke out and all aircraft were commandeered by the British forces. But by 1916, and with a provisional Greek government in Salonika, the Greeks were able to join in the fighting against Turkish and German forces in the area, and by 1918 the Hellenic Naval Air Service had four squadrons of Sopwith and other aircraft.

The growing strength and confidence of the Royal Flying Corps and the increasing commitments of the Royal Naval Air Service led to the return of the home defence requirement to the RFC in February, 1916. For British towns and cities under threat of zeppelin attack, the first big advantage of the new arrangement was the provision of landplanes, with their far superior rates of climb, instead of seaplanes for fighter defence.

Other changes followed, showing clearly that the future Royal Air Force, which at the outset of the war had seemed so set in the role of the RNAS, was now forming in the roles being acquired by the RFC. RNAS bombing of industrial targets in Germany from the air station at Luxeuil in France came to an end in 1916, but for a time one RNAS squadron was attached to the RFC in France for the support of ground troops, followed by four more which remained until July, 1917. RNAS squadrons were already receiving some landplanes, however, and in fact received their first Sopwith Triplanes in 1916, a year or so before the RFC got its first 'Trikes'. The RNAS Sopwith Triplanes proved more than a match for the German Albatros fighters.

Fleet deployment of seaplanes and their carriers occurred rather less often during World War I than might have been expected, but this has to be set against the relative absence of fleet actions during the war. The one major naval battle was that at Jutland, the first major battle between modern capital ships and also the first major fleet battle involving naval aviation, even though in a small way. The British Grand Fleet, under Admiral Jellicoe in the battleship HMS *Iron Duke*, included the seaplane carrier HMS *Engadine*, an advantage not possessed by the German High Seas Fleet under Admiral Scheer in *Friedrich der Grosse*. On 31 May, 1916, Flight Lieutenant F. J. Rutland, RN, and his observer, Assistant Paymaster Trewin, took off from the seaplane carrier at 15.10, spotted the German battlecruiser squadron and radioed back its position to *Engadine*.

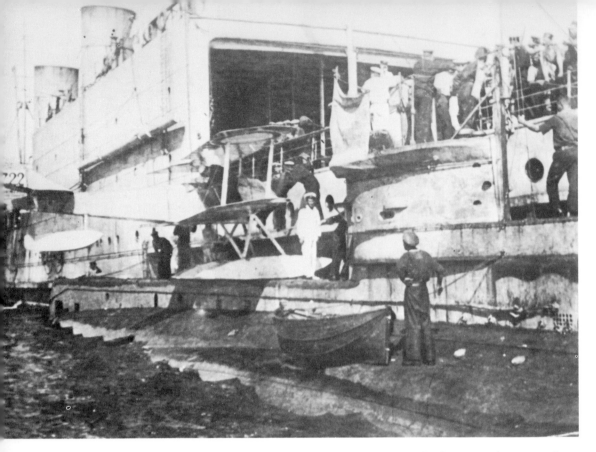

Another early seaplane carrier, HMS *Engadine*, with a Sopwith 'Schneider' seaplane

On their return flight, a broken fuel pump forced Rutland and Trewin down onto the sea, but after repairs they managed to take off and return to their ship. A battlecruiser action between the reconnaissance squadrons of the two fleets followed during the early evening, the inconclusive main battle taking place during the late evening.

Rutland's achievement was not untypical of the man. Shortly afterwards he was awarded the Albert Medal in Gold— an extremely rare decoration—for the rescue of a rating who had fallen between HMS *Engadine* and the crippled HMS *Warrior*, going down into the water between the two vessels at risk of being crushed. Unfortunately the injured rating was found to be dead from exposure when recovered from the water. After the war Rutland was a member of the British Naval Mission to Japan, which taught the

Japanese much about carrier operations. After the entry of Japan into World War II, Rutland, by then a commander with the Royal Navy, committed suicide.

The Battle of Jutland underlined the need for more aircraft-carrying ships for the Royal Navy. The French Navy, meanwhile, received two more flying-boat tenders, the *Nord* and the *Pas de Calais*, before the end of 1916. Both navies intensified their patrols against German submarines—the U-boats—and these patrols were further strengthened as the Service Aéronautique enjoyed an increase in its complement of 360 Schreck FBA flying-boats for both shore and shipboard use. However, in 1917 the Allies were to lose some 2,600 ships due to the action of a German fleet of just 127 U-boats.

For fleet reconnaissance duties, the Royal Navy started to build platforms over the forward gun turrets of major warships, so that aircraft could fly off, starting with the battleship HMS *Repulse* and the cruiser HMS *Yarmouth*.

Events continued to move elsewhere, for even a war cannot stop other changes, and will sometimes even act as a catalyst. The Imperial Russian Navy was the first of Russia's armed forces to be affected by the Russian Revolution, and the Imperial Russian Flying Corps was the last. Even before the revolution of October, 1917, the situation was such that no effective move against Germany came from the Russian fleet, or from its Grigorovich M–5 and M–9 flying-boats.

man F–22s and Spijker trainers, with an assortment of other types. One reason for the assortment was the number of aircraft belonging to the belligerent nations interned after forced landings on Dutch territory, but a number of Swedish Thulins were also obtained.

Neutral Sweden could muster only four aircraft for both its armed forces on the outbreak of war, but the Swedish Navy received a further twenty-five aircraft during the war years. All were of Swedish

Felixstowe F2A flying-boats, the first of a successful series which served with many air arms

Rather more positive was the development of the Brazilian Navy's aviation element. The initial Bossi seaplane for the seaplane school near Rio de Janeiro came in 1913 and was followed by two more within a year; and by 1916 Brazil had a naval air station at Ilha das Enxades in Rio de Janeiro Bay. A number of Brazilian pilots received training in Britain, while their more experienced comrades were seconded to the Italian armed forces. In addition to this contribution to the Italian war effort, Brazil continued to build up both its military and naval air arms during the war years.

In neutral Denmark, the naval aviators survived World War I operating licence-built flying-boats from a base near Copenhagen. In another neutral country, the Netherlands, the Marine Luchtvaartdienst or Naval Air Section was formed on 18 August, 1917. Bases were quickly established at Amsterdam and De Kroog, and later De Moh, with an initial strength of six Martin biplanes, followed by Far-

manufacture and mainly from the Thulins Aeroplanfabrik, but this small country could actually support no less than four aircraft manufacturers at this time! Sweden has had a consistent record of endeavouring to provide the bulk of her armaments from domestic sources.

Portugal supported the Allies, although only Army units saw active service. The Aviação Maritima, founded in 1917 with air stations at Lisbon and Aveiro, sent its pilots to Britain, France and the United States for training, while aircraft supplied included Fairey Campania seaplanes and Felixstowe F.3 flying-boats for anti-submarine patrols.

From the time of war being declared in Europe, the United States made considerable progress in marine flight. Pre-war experiments by Glenn Curtiss and the Royal Navy officer Lieutenant-Commander J. C. Porte, resulted in the

35

Curtiss-Porte flying-boat, which became the basis of the World War I Curtiss H.12, H.16 and HS.1 flying-boats, which were operated by both the United States and Royal Navies. These flying-boats, together with the Curtiss JN–4 Jenny trainer, were the only American-built aircraft in service with the RNAS during the war. In 1914, the United States Navy had just twelve aircraft for training, but even so, by 1915 the establishment of the air units included forty-eight officers and ninety-six enlisted men, while the United States Marine Corps boosted these figures by another 25 per cent exactly. That same year the United States Coast Guard seconded a Lieutenant E. F. Stone to the USN Flying School at Pensacola, as Naval Aviator No. 38. One of his fellow officers studied aviation engineering at the Curtiss factory.

A more consistent and purposeful approach to naval aviation came in 1915, with the formation of a National Advisory Committeee for Aeronautics, on which the USN was represented by two Navy Department members.

Both the USN and the United States Army Air Corps experimented to assess the potential of aerial bombing, although their chances of success were severely limited by the absence of a suitable bomb-sight—something which did not appear until after World War I had ended.

1915 was an eventful year for American naval aviators, with $1 million (£200,000) being allocated by Congress for aircraft procurement, although by the year end only twenty-nine aircraft were available. Two Martin and six Sturtevant seaplanes, with six Burgess Type Q pusher-propeller biplanes, joined the aerial fleet in early 1916, and by November, with United States involvement in the then European war seeming likely, fifty-two seaplanes (thirty of which were Curtiss N.9s), thirty-five landplanes and twenty non-rigid airships were ordered, as well as one rigid. Ten East Coast and twelve West Coast air bases were selected.

Expansion of aircraft output was seriously hampered at first by the lack of suitably high-powered engines, so 450 Hispano–Suiza engines were ordered from France, with a hundred of these allocated to Wright–Martin for USN flying-boats. Fortunately, the rapidly growing American motor industry soon came to the rescue, quickly designing, developing and putting into production the Liberty engine.

Orders were placed for the first of sixteen non-rigid 'A' class airships in February, 1917, followed by early deliveries from the manufacturers, most notably Goodyear, to the training school at Pensacola. The school was by this time also receiving the first of some forty-five new training aircraft, including the Jenny, and a number of kite balloons. Soon the rapid expansion of training was stretching Pensacola beyond its normal complement of sixty student pilots at any one time, so a number of wartime flying schools were established, including those at Key West and Miami in Florida, and also further north at the major naval base of Newport News. In addition, some USN pilots received instruction at Royal Flying Corps schools in Canada.

By the time the United States entered the war on the side of the Allies, on 6 April, 1917, operational aircraft were being obtained from abroad, or built in the United States to British, French and sometimes Italian design. The USN's own factory at the Philadelphia Navy Yard also built some US designs, notably the Curtiss H.16 flying-boats, but even with this support, aircraft had to be ordered from Europe, and there was a shortfall in deliveries of these orders. France, for example, with the demands of her own air arms to consider and part of her territory occupied by German forces, could only deliver a third of the aircraft ordered by the USN before the cessation of hostilities in 1918!

The demand for aircraft and the pressure on European manufacturers, the delay in putting American industry on a war footing, and the shortage of suitable US designs, meant that the first USN pilots arrived in Europe during June, 1917, without any aircraft. They were immediately posted to French air stations. However, by spring, 1918, the United States was able to provide enough men for no less than twenty-eight air stations in the British Isles and France, including one at Killingholme, at the mouth of the Humber, opposite Heligoland Bight. The Killingholme station was eventually to be one of the largest air stations of World War I, with some 2,000 men and fifty aircraft stationed there. To achieve so much in twelve short months must have been noteworthy, and in the meantime many more USN personnel found their way into European squadrons.

As their own aircraft became available, the USN and USMC concentrated on anti-submarine patrols, becoming one of the first air arms to take an active and thorough interest in anti-submarine warfare or ASW, to use the now widely accepted term. On 1 January, 1918, the USMC positioned a squadron of eighteen Curtiss seaplanes of various types on the Azores, giving them a commanding position over a substantial area of the mid-Atlantic. There were also bombing missions from time to time, one of the more important being that by a USN Caproni biplane on the Ostend U-boat pens, on 15 August, 1918, when 1,250 lb of bombs were dropped.

Maritime-reconnaissance became a vitally important part of a conflict which saw submarine warfare progress at least as rapidly as aerial warfare. Allied merchant shipping suffered terribly, with new tonnage not exceeding losses until 1917, and the submarine menace had to be countered by surface vessels and Curtiss and Supermarine flying-boats, including the Supermarine-built version of the Porte, with the then incredible wingspan of 125 feet. The government-sponsored Seaplane Experimental Station at Felixstowe, on Britain's east coast, produced many excellent designs, including the Felixstowe F.5. Built under licence by many manufacturers, including Curtiss and Short, the F.5 eventually underwent

post-war modifications which resulted in its appearance as the first steel-hulled flying-boat.

The flying-boat offered the best means then available for maritime-reconnaissance patrols, but such aircraft could never pretend to be fast. Although many people, including Jacques Schneider, held high, and as events were to prove after the war, by no means altogether unrealistic hopes for the seaplane, it as yet offered a far inferior performance to landplanes. Faced with this problem, the RNAS followed its Sopwith Triplane with the Pup in 1917 and the Camel in 1918. Both the latter aircraft were high performance landplanes of biplane configuration. To get these aircraft where they were wanted, at sea, called for something far better than the seaplane carrier, so naval aviation in its truest and purest sense—operating landplanes from ships underway at sea—made its appearance.

It was left to the Royal Navy to produce the world's first aircraft carriers. HMS *Furious* was originally laid down as a battlecruiser of 22,000 tons displacement and fitted with 18-inch guns. She was one of three ships of a class, the other two being HMS *Glorious* and HMS *Courageous*, of unusual design and known to many as the 'Outrageous class' as a result. During her construction, the design of HMS *Furious* was changed to provide a flight-deck forward and a single 18-inch turret aft, and in this form she joined the fleet in mid-1917.

In spite of the pre-war experiments, no one had yet managed to land an aircraft on a ship underway at sea. On 2 August, 1917, Squadron Commander E. H. Dunning, RN, flew his Sopwith Camel past the funnels of HMS *Furious*, past the superstructure, and then cutting his engine, hovered at stalling speed over the fo'c'sle while his comrades onboard made frantic attempts to grasp the toggles hanging from the trailing edges of his aircraft's wings. They succeeded, and were able to pull the frail machine onto the deck, giving Dunning the very real distinction of making the first landing on a

Above: Dunning's second landing aboard HMS *Furious*, seconds from death

Above right: A landing aboard HMS *Furious* after a landing-on deck had been fitted—note the fore and aft wires to keep the aircraft on the deck

Right: HMS *Furious* with landing-on and take-off platforms

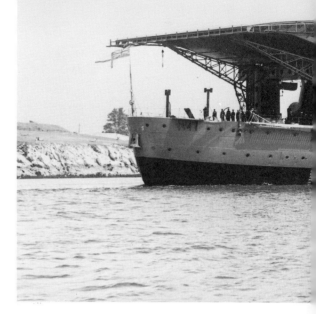

First flat top, HMS *Argus*

ship underway at sea! To modern thinking, the flight deck of the converted battle-cruiser was almost as far from the ideal layout as could be imagined. So it happened that a few days later, when Dunning tried to repeat his success and his engine failed, his aircraft was blown over the side of the ship before the crew could grab it. It crashed into the sea and sank, drowning the gallant and unfortunate Dunning even while frantic efforts were being made to launch the ship's boats.

As a result of this, the after-turret of HMS *Furious* was removed and the flight deck continued aft, dividing round the superstructure and funnels. The after-deck was used for landing, and sometimes for carrying a reconnaissance airship. Now finally worthy of the name of an aircraft carrier, HMS *Furious* could steam at 32·5 knots and carry twenty aircraft. On landing, aircraft would catch arrester wires, at first running fore and aft, with hooks on the undercarriage spreader bar, and as a last resort there would be a high safety net. The vessel rebuilt in this way rejoined the fleet in 1918.

In this form, HMS *Furious* was able to launch the first successful attack from an aircraft carrier when, on 19 July, 1918,

seven Sopwith Camels attacked the airship sheds at Tondern in northern Germany, destroying the airships L.54 and L.60.

After the war, HMS *Furious* was rebuilt twice, following a period of lay-up between 1919 and 1922, rejoining the active fleet in 1925 as a flush-deck aircraft carrier without superstructure. The upper flight deck was used mainly for landing, while a short take-off deck over the bows led directly from the upper hangar deck. A fairly low island on the starboard side was added during a further refit in 1938–39, and the flying-off deck was removed and the upper hangar closed off at the same time.

While HMS *Furious* was completing her first year or so of service, an Italian liner under construction was taken over by the Admiralty and completed as Britain's and the world's second aircraft carrier, HMS *Argus*. Of 15,775 tons and with a speed of 29 knots, the newcomer joined the Fleet in September, 1918. Although the second aircraft carrier, she set the pattern for the post-war rebuilding of HMS *Furious*, having no superstructure at all, although she had only one flight deck. The wheelhouse and

bridge were positioned on a lift, and during flying operations could be recessed completely. Smoke was expelled through large ducts at the stern to keep the flight deck clear, although it must have been as well that aircraft took off with the vessel steaming into the wind! Some twenty aircraft could be accommodated in this ship, which the Royal Navy nicknamed the 'Flat Iron'.

More battleships and cruisers were receiving their own aircraft for operations from short platforms built over gun turrets—normally, but not necessarily, the forward turrets. The RNAS received for this role Sopwith 1½-strutter biplanes, so called because of the short span of the lower wing, and this type of aircraft first operated from the battlecruiser HMAS *Australia*, on 4 April, 1918.

Before World War I ended, the French had also begun to modify ships in this way, with a thirty-foot platform being built over the forward turret on the battleship *Paris*; but these trials, starting on 26 October, within weeks of the Armistice, were somewhat half-hearted, and the platform was removed after the war ended.

One reason why there were so few air-craft carriers by the end of World War I lies in the fact that aircraft carriers have always tended to be slow in building, as are all major warships. This is not only because of their very considerable size, but also because they must be fitted out with more sophisticated equipment than merchantmen. Furthermore, in 1917 and 1918 no one could really be sure that the aircraft carrier would have a future, and the conversion of vessels under construction would normally mean the loss of a new ship to the battle or cruiser fleets. An ingenious way out of the dilemma was not long in coming, with the idea of flying Sopwith Camels off lighters towed at high speed behind destroyers. After experiments on 31 July, 1918, Lieutenant S. D. Culley took off from a lighter in a Camel on 18 August, to destroy the Zeppelin L.53. He then landed alongside his towing destroyer, HMS *Redoubtable*, which salvaged his landplane, picking it up with a specially-designed derrick, the brainchild of Commander Samson, who had made the July experiments.

The lighters could be towed at 30 knots without throwing up spray, but it was vital for men to sit on the bows of the lighters to keep the craft level!

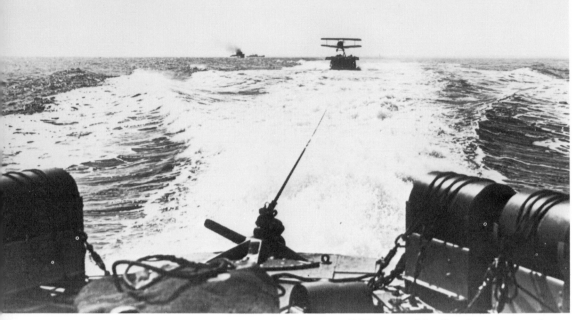

Culley takes off in his Sopwith Camel from a barge

The German airship threat had by now been joined by something rather more formidable, which could have been disastrous had it arrived earlier in the war, since the seaplane would have been completely useless as a defence. The heavy bomber, first introduced by the British with their 0/100, 0/400 and Vimy, and later joined by the French Goliath, eventually appeared in Germany as well, with the Gotha—probably inspired by Igor Sikorsky's large pre-war Russian airliner designs. Gotha bombers raided London on 13 June, 1917, and further raids forced the withdrawal of two RFC fighter squadrons from France to augment the home defences. Fortunately, intense RNAS and RFC fighter defence soon forced the abandonment of daylight raids by the Germans even before summer ended; and effective night raids were prevented by the poor navigational and bombing aids of the day.

While possibly being overtaken by other developments, the zeppelin was a far from spent force, even if the concept suffered from many drawbacks. Its advantages and disadvantages were both well illustrated in October, 1917, when a naval airship, LZ.102(L.57) left its base at Juterborg to make a successful round trip to Daka Oasis in German East Africa, taking just ninety-six hours to travel the 4,200 miles there and back. Unfortunately, on its return, the craft caught fire while entering its shed, and was completely destroyed.

As well as fighters, the Royal Naval Air Service procured bomber and torpedo landplanes, with a landplane version of the Short 184, using Rolls-Royce Eagle engines, and a further development, the 320, with Sunbeam Cossack engines, entering service.

Some idea of the improved performance of the landplane compared with the seaplane can be gathered from the Camel's 120 mph and 19,000 feet compared with the Campania's 80 mph and 2,000 feet— and all this from a mere 130 hp Clerget engine, which also gave an endurance of $2\frac{1}{2}$ hours. Sopwith followed the Camel with the Cuckoo, although this arrived too late for the war, but both Sopwith and Blackburn-built Cuckoos joined HMS *Argus*.

In April, 1918, the RNAS was once again merged with the RFC, but this time to create the world's first truly

The German naval airship, L.53, coming in
to land

One of two Lockheed H2SL flying-boats built
for the United States Navy in 1918

autonomous air service, the Royal Air Force, free of Army or Navy control. At first, old ranks and organisations remained, with RFC ranks predominating, until a new uniform and ranks, with a command structure, could be devised on the return of peace; and in these, RNAS ideas played no small part.

The Armistice of 11 November, 1918, effectively brought an end to the war. By this time, the Service Aéronautique had 1,264 aircraft of FBA, DD and Tellier construction, with thirty-six bases and 11,000 personnel, while the US Naval Flying Corps had 1,412 aircraft, seven-teen airships, 116 kite balloons and 40,383 personnel, of whom a third were based outside the United States; in addition the USMC had 624 aircraft. Neither France nor the United States had any aircraft carriers, although the USN was experimenting with destroyer-towed lighters and with a Curtiss JN-4 Jenny and airship combination. The Royal Navy, on the other hand, had two aircraft carriers, six seaplane carriers, as well as lighters and battleships and cruisers fitted with take-off platforms over their gun turrets; but it had no aircraft that it could genuinely call its own!

3 The Flat Tops Appear

The return of peace saw the aeroplane well established as a weapon of war in its own right. This had already been recognised by the British with their new Royal Air Force, independent of control by the two older traditional services. To some extent, too, the importance of the aeroplane had been accorded international recognition. The Treaty of Versailles, which effectively ended World War I, refused post-war Germany any air arm, even in the purely defensive surface forces. But in a world impoverished by a hard and bitter war, funds for further development of military aviation were in short supply.

In Britain there was another good reason for the contraction of the RAF apart from economic factors, and the new service rapidly underwent a reduction far in excess of anything normally permitted by a cessation of hostilities. Two rival air arms, with fierce traditions and loyalties already forged in the heat of battle, had been decreed to be one by a decision of Parliament. Priority had to be given to ending the old rivalries by starting again as far as possible from scratch, and creating a new air service with a personnel with one commitment only, the defence of Britain in the air. The result was that the Royal Air Force was reduced to a mere twelve squadrons within a year or so of the Treaty of Versailles. The logic of this policy was sound, but it could not contend with the needs of the British Army and Royal Navy for their own organic air power. Still less could it create from scratch an understanding of the importance and value of air power amongst

a new generation of naval and army officers.

However, the benefits of operating landplanes from specially constructed ships had not been lost on the Royal Navy, although it continued to include seaplane carriers in its active fleet for some years to come. While only one of its two World War I aircraft carriers now remained in service, with HMS *Furious* briefly laid up, the Royal Navy added a third vessel, converting the incomplete Chilean battleship *Almirante Cochrane*, originally laid down in 1913 and suspended in 1914, to an aircraft carrier, HMS *Eagle*, 22,600 tons. This vessel was the first with the starboard 'island' superstructure normally associated with aircraft carriers, although—unusually by today's standards —she had two funnels. This new arrangement was not adopted lightly, and trials were conducted in 1920 to see if deck landing would be affected by the new design. Even so, HMS *Eagle* was not finally commissioned until February, 1924. A cambered 'round down' was also provided at the after end of the flight deck to eliminate turbulence which might affect aircraft on their final approach, and the hull was plated up to the flight deck forward, unlike that of HMS *Furious*.

While work and experiments on HMS *Eagle* were well in hand, another aircraft carrier was already building for the Royal Navy, and this ship, HMS *Hermes*, 10,850 tons, was designed and laid down in January, 1918, as the first warship to be conceived as an aircraft carrier from the order stage. After delays while the results

of trials with HMS *Eagle* were evaluated, HMS *Hermes* was commissioned within a few days of HMS *Eagle* in 1924. The single large funnel and the plating of the hull up to flight deck level over much of its length gave this vessel a streamlined and modern appearance.

Important as these developments were, they paled into insignificance compared with those starting to take place on the other side of the world, in Japan; and there the irony of the situation was the fact that from 1919 until 1922 these developments took place with the assistance of a British Naval Mission. Since she was a former ally of the United States and Britain, it seemed perfectly natural that after the war these countries should offer advice and share expertise with Japan, and sell her such equipment as she might require.

Certainly, at the end of the war, the Japanese Naval Air Force was largely dependent on aircraft bought from her wartime allies, notably Britain and France, and early orders reflected this. Nevertheless, Sparrowhawk Mars IV shipboard fighters and the indigenous Mitsubishi Type 10 featured in early trials from the battleship *Hamishiro* in 1922, operating from a platform built over the vessel's forward turret, in the first trials of their kind in the otherwise progressive Imperial Japanese Navy.

The JNAF's aircraft inventory did not lack variety at this time. It included Short F.5 America, Schreck FBA. 17 and Tellier flying-boats, Avro 504 trainers and an almost bewildering variety of aircraft obtained in small numbers for evaluation, including Martinsyde F.4s, Parnall Panthers, Sopwith Cuckoos, Airco (de Havilland-designed) D.H.9s, Vickers Vikings, Blackburn Swifts, and Supermarine Seals and Channels—an incredible mixture of the famous and the obscure.

Some idea of the pressure of develop-

HMS *Hermes*, the first aircraft carrier to be laid down as such

ment building up on the JNAF at such an early stage can be gathered from the 1920 decision to convert a new oiler building for the Imperial Japanese Navy's fleet train, to an aircraft carrier, within months of the vessel having been laid down in late 1919. Completed in late 1922, *Hosho* was ready for flying trials in February, 1923. At first she had a small starboard side island, with three funnels some way aft of it, but this was removed before she joined the fleet, since it proved extremely unpopular with the aircrew participating in the trials. Throughout the rest of her life, the navigating position was immediately below the forward end of the flight deck at hangar level. In defence of the decision to move the starboard island, it must be remembered that *Hosho* was one of the smallest fleet carriers ever built, at just 7,470 tons!

Forceful and determined the early Japanese aircraft industry might have been, but successful designs at first eluded it. Aichi built the Short F.5 and Nakajima the Avro 504 under licence, while Mitsubishi actually recruited British designers in an attempt to get a generation of Japanese aircraft onto the drawing board. These were the Type 10s used for the battleship trials, which also included a range of fighter, torpedo-bomber, scout and training aircraft. When other Japanese manufacturers also attempted to build aircraft for the JNAF, they only added to a growing list of disappointments, so that by the late 1920s, foreign aircraft were still being ordered, although normally licences were acquired for their manufacture in Japan. Nakajima built the Gloster Gambett as the A1N1 Type 3 fighter, while a Blackburn design was adapted by Mitsubishi as its B2M1 Type 89 naval bomber and C1M2 reconnaissance aircraft. The Heinkel HD25 seaplane emerged as Aichi's Type 2. Amongst the few Japanese designs suitable for service were the Yokosuka E1Y1 seaplane and the Hiro H1H1, H1H2 and H2H1 series of flying-boats.

However, Japan was not the only country to be giving naval aviation its due consideration. Although the United States Navy and United States Marine Corps both saw a slimming down of their air arms after the Armistice, it was not as serious as that suffered by their British opposite numbers. After the war, the USN and USMC introduced a number of new designs to service, and the aircraft operated included the following formidable list: licence-built Airco D.H.4Bs, Curtiss JN–4 Jenny, Martin MBY and Thomas-Morse M.1 aircraft; Curtiss N.9 and R–6, and Boeing CL–4 seaplanes; and Curtiss NC.1, licence-built Felixstowe F.5, Aeromarine 40L and HS.2L flying-boats. Sopwith Scout biplanes were obtained for flights from platforms constructed over gun turrets aboard battleships, and the first such take-off in one of these aircraft was made by Lieutenant-Commander Edward O. McDonald, flying from the USS *Texas*, on 9 March, 1919, while the warship cruised off Cuba. Before long, eight battleships were converted in this way.

At first, there were some additions to the USN's air stations, including one at Pearl Harbor and another at Hilo in Hawaii. But soon the inevitable reduction in peacetime defence expenditure resulted in several bases being closed, until at one stage just six seaplane stations remained. Unlike the Royal Navy, the United States Navy still did not include aircraft carriers or seaplane tenders, so the decision was taken to convert the fleet auxiliary collier *Jupiter*, into the USN's first aircraft carrier, the USS *Langley*, 11,500 tons. The new ship entered service in March, 1922, by which time the USN had also gained a seaplane tender, the USS *Wright*.

Unlike most other conversions from merchantmen or fleet auxiliaries, including that of the *Hosho*, the USS *Langley* retained her collier's machinery, and so had the unimpressive service speed of just 14 knots! Nevertheless the new designa-

tion introduced for this vessel and all subsequent US carriers, CV.1 (cruiser, heavier-than-air, no. 1), indicated that she was a combat vessel, while the seaplane tender USS *Wright* was designated as an auxiliary, AV.1. In common with some of the earlier carriers, including HMS *Argus* and HMS *Furious*, the USS *Langley* could also handle seaplanes, and the catapaults or accelerators, operated pneumatically, could launch seaplanes mounted on a trolley. Landings were assisted by a combination of longitudinal and transverse wires.

It was not until October, 1922, that Lieutenant-Commander G. Chevalier, USN, made the first landing on and take off from the USS *Langley*, but the arrival of the new ship marked some of the first big orders for new aircraft for the United States Navy in the immediate post-war period. These included some British and French types obtained for trials from the ship, along with a number of Naval Aircraft Factory PT, Douglas DT, sixty Vought UO–1 and sixty Martin MO–1 aircraft.

Other developments were pressing ahead. The new Curtiss flying-boat, the NC.1, was proving its worth. A modified version lifted a record fifty-one passengers for a brief flight, while other aircraft were modified to produce the NC.2, 3 and 4 adaptations. On 8 May, 1919, Commander J. H. Towers, USN, took off from Rockaway Beach to lead a flight consisting of an NC.1, an NC.3 and an NC.4, across the Atlantic, stopping at Newfoundland and the Azores. In the end, the NC.4, piloted by Lieutenant-Commander Read, USN, was the only aircraft to reach the other side at Lisbon, and from there it flew on to Britain. This achievement was bettered shortly afterwards when two British officers flew a Vickers Vimy non-stop from Newfoundland to Ireland.

The United States Navy had also ordered an American-designed airship, ZR–1, named the *Shenandoah*, which entered service in 1919. After the British R–34's epic return trans-Atlantic crossing

48

The USN Curtiss NC.4 flying-boat on arrival
at Calshot, near Southampton, after its epic
Atlantic flight

Wreckage of the ill-fated USN airship, ZR–2,
in the River Humber

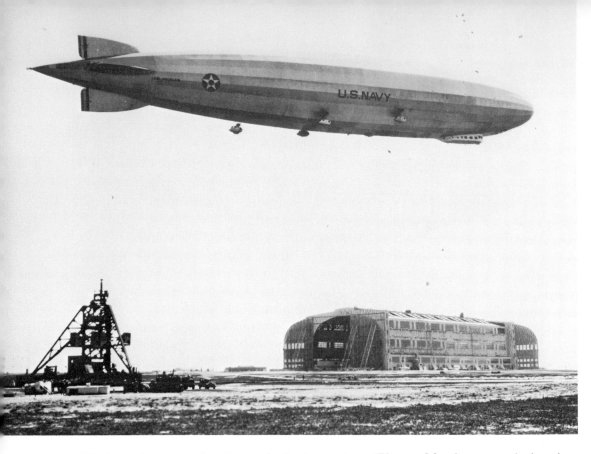

ZR–2's replacement, the German-built *Los Angeles*

in July, another order followed—for the British-built R–38, to be designated ZR–2. But the R–38 failed to justify the USN's confidence, crashing into the River Humber during her acceptance trials on 24 August, 1921. Not to be cheated of an airship, the ZR–3, *Los Angeles*, was ordered from the German zeppelin factory at Friedrichshafen under the reparation programme outlined by the Versailles Treaty, and this craft was delivered safely in 1924.

An increasingly confident United States Navy was also ready to formalise its aircraft procurement and development policies. In June, 1921, the Navy Bureau of Aeronautics, or BuAer, was formed under Rear-Admiral William A. Moffett, USN, sometimes known as the architect of US naval aviation, to advise the Chief of Naval Operations on aeronautical affairs and developments. New aircraft continued to arrive meanwhile, including

ten Glenn Martin torpedo-bombers while the USMC received Curtiss JN–6H landplanes.

Inter-service rivalry soon reared its ugly head during the early years of peace. Such rivalries, which can sometimes be beneficial in maintaining morale, *esprit de corps* and efficiency if kept within reasonable bounds, tend to become over-intensified by peacetime restrictions on procurement and manpower.

The USN and USMC took part with the USAAC in a bombing experiment on captured German and obsolete United States warships anchored in Chesapeake Bay. The event became famous after General Mitchell of the United States Army Air Corps ignored the rules covering inspection of targets between bombing raids and on the maximum size of bombs permitted, using 2,000 lb bombs to sink the 'unsinkable' German battleship *Ostfriesland*. Mitchell was to be court-martialled and dismissed from the USAAC in later years, mainly for the manner in which he conducted a vigorous campaign to have US military aviation organised on British lines; but in this particular instance, his breaking of the rules made the trials worthless to the USN, even though Navy flying-boats sank the U-boat, U–117.

The USN undoubtedly had a point. The object of the exercise was not simply to destroy or sink warships at anchor. If it had been, Mitchell would have been right to use the largest bomb he could find. One of the main objectives was to test the effect of different types and weights of bomb and torpedo on a variety of warships, and thus learn the relative value of different types of bombing technique, as well as something of the values of different armoured plating and variations in ship design in resisting the effects of aerial bombing—a vital factor for the Navy! In any case, in a carrier-borne aerial attack, few of the aircraft of the day could have hoped to lift bombs as large as those available to the USAAC.

Aircraft design was not stagnating, and the early 1920s saw the USN receive its first all-metal monoplane, the ugly Martin MO–2. This aircraft was intended for operation from the twenty US battleships and ten cruisers fitted from 1921 onwards with power-operated turntable catapults (for three seaplanes on the capital ships and for two seaplanes on the cruisers). The need for greater speed and warloads, and also the stresses of operating to and from ships, prompted BuAer to issue a requirement for new aircraft carriers to be capable of operating the new all-metal aircraft, which even at this early date seemed to be no longer in the future. Indeed, the next deliveries of aircraft to the USN had an increasing use of metal in their construction, notably the seventy-five Martin SC–1 torpedo-bomber biplanes, which accompanied a large number of Curtiss F4C–1 fleet fighters, Vought O2U observation biplanes and Douglas T2D torpedo-bomber biplanes into service.

BuAer also introduced a standard system of aircraft and squadron designation, in June, 1922. Under this system, F prefixed a fighter aircraft, PB a patrol

A battered *Ostfriesland* slides below the waves, leaving the United States Navy and Army to argue over the results of the bombing trials

bomber, and so on, with the manufacturer's initial letter following the type number, and this in turn followed by a variation of the type. Thus F4C–1 would mean Fighter Type 4, built by Curtiss, variant no. 1, although Vought O2U meant Observation Type 2, built by Vought! The squadron designations included the VF prefix for fighter squadrons, VO for observation, VS for scout, VT for torpedo and bombing, ZK for kite balloons, and V for airships, followed by the squadron number. Squadron strengths were fixed at eighteen aircraft, in two flights.

Unusually, the next major step by the United States Navy, the Royal Navy and the Imperial Japanese Navy was to be largely decided by something which had nothing to do with either the planned development of their respective air arms or with technical innovation. In an attempt to avoid a fresh arms race and to minimise the chance of hostilities being provoked by major naval expansion, Britain, the United States, Japan, France and Italy agreed by the Washington Naval Treaty of 1922, on a series of limitations on the size of their fleets and on the maximum sizes of individual warship classes. This was to have a profound effect on the next generation of aircraft carriers, and induce a strange coincidence.

The treaty restricted the British and American fleets to a total tonnage of 525,000 tons each, while Japan was limited to 315,000 tons, and France and Italy to 175,000 tons each. The maximum tonnage for a capital ship was fixed at 35,000 tons, for cruisers at 10,000 tons, and for aircraft carriers at 27,000 tons (with certain exceptions that concerned only the United States and Britain). Furthermore, Britain and the United States had to limit their total aircraft carrier tonnage to 135,000 tons, while Japan was limited to 81,000 tons of aircraft carriers, and France and Italy to 60,000 tons each. Both Britain and the United States were permitted to build two carriers only of 33,000 tons each, but the USS *Langley* was accepted as an experi-

mental ship and not deducted from the US aircraft carrier allocation. The maximum calibre gun which could be mounted on an aircraft carrier was limited to 8 inches.

Strangely, the three largest treaty navies all had battlecruisers surplus to their allocation, and immediately set in hand their conversion to aircraft carriers! The coincidence went even further, in that each navy had just two battlecruisers to convert!

Two battlecruisers, USS *Saratoga* and *Lexington*, were still uncompleted during the drafting of the Washington Naval Treaty, and the decision was taken to convert these two powerful warships to aircraft carriers before the treaty was signed. Not only did these two vessels take full advantage of a clause permitting two vessels of up to 33,000 tons each; they took further advantage of a clause permitting up to 3,000 tons of armour plating as protection against bombs. In this way, two aircraft carriers of almost 36,000 tons standard displacement, 40,000 tons full load, slipped into the USN during the late 1920s! The irony of the situation was quite simply that these warships were intended to be American counterparts of the British HMS *Hood*, already completed at the time of the Treaty. But the objective of the treaty was also to prevent any escalation in warship sizes, which would have resulted had the *Hood*'s tonnage become accepted as a standard battlecruiser size. Yet in the event, both the two new American carriers were far in excess of the desired maximum for this type of warship.

Unusually for American carriers before World War II, both ships had an armoured flight deck. Extremely large single funnels were mounted on the starboard side, aft and clear of the island, while the hulls were plated up to flight deck level. No less than ninety aircraft of twenties' size could be carried, and all could be ranged on the 888-foot long flight deck at any one time! Equally impressive was the vessels' maximum speed of 34 knots. Single electrically-operated catapults were incorporated in the flight deck, but seldom used because of the vast size of the flight deck, and—a step forward—only transverse arrester-wires were fitted.

The USS *Saratoga* joined the Fleet in November, 1927, and was followed by her sister ship just a month later.

The decision to convert the two British battlecruisers, HMS *Courageous* and HMS *Glorious*, into aircraft carriers was also taken in advance of signing the Treaty, at a time when these two late World War I vessels were laid up and, because of certain design limitations, would probably have been scrapped. Sister ships of HMS *Furious*, their conversion reflected development of the aircraft carrier since the war had ended, and both the 'Treaty' carriers had starboard side islands incorporating single large funnels. Two obvious similarities with their World War I sister were the large torpedo bulges intended to broaden their beam and enhance stability—they were not really torpedo proof—and the lack of a full length flight deck, due to their having take-off decks leading out from the forward end of the upper hangar deck. The take-off decks had a relatively short life, in line with their uselessness as aircraft speed and size increased. Unlike the USS *Saratoga* and USS *Lexington*, they were not at first fitted with catapults, but these, still known to the Admiralty as accelerators, were added to the 22,500 tons vessels during the late 1930s.

Both vessels offered a fair, if not exactly startling, turn of speed at around 30 knots, and were useful additions to the fleet when they joined, with HMS *Courageous* commissioning in May, 1928, and HMS *Glorious* almost two years later, in March, 1930.

Japan opposed many of the conditions of the treaty at first, and in particular wanted a far larger total tonnage allocation, which was refused. This clue to Japanese ambitions led to a marked cooling of relations between Britain and Japan, bringing an end to British naval assistance. In an attempt to make the best of a bad job, the Japanese started to convert two uncompleted battlecruisers, the *Amagi* and *Akagi*, into aircraft carriers. An earthquake caused severe damage to *Amagi* before she could be launched, so the battleship *Kaga*, launched and fitting out at the time of the treaty but barred from entering service under its provisions and thus due to be scrapped, was converted instead.

As completed in March, 1927, *Akagi* was a freak. While the lack of an island was not in itself so unconventional, its flight deck was. It was used purely for landing on, while there were two flying-off decks, an upper one some sixty feet in length leading from the upper hangar and used to launch fighter and reconnaissance aircraft, and a lower one, some hundred or so feet longer, leading from the lower hangar and used by torpedo-bombers and other heavier aircraft.

Kaga was far more conventional, and although lacking an island, she had only one flying-off deck, leading forward from the upper hangar, when she joined the Japanese Fleet belatedly in 1930 after two years of trials.

Both these Japanese vessels exceeded the Washington Treaty limits, with *Akagi* at some 30,000 tons and *Kaga* only slightly smaller. The former battleship lacked some of the speed of a battlecruiser, with some 27 knots as against *Akagi's* 31 knots. The shortcomings of the designs were soon apparent, but it was not until 1934 that reconstruction work was put in hand for *Kaga* This included extending her flight deck for the full length of the hull, building a starboard side navigational island and removing the stern funnel ducts, which were replaced by a starboard side funnel, protruding from the hull and pointing downward! The rebuilt *Kaga* rejoined the fleet in 1935, and two years later a similar reconstruction followed on *Akagi*, with the main difference that the island was placed on the port side, even though the single downward-pointing funnel was positioned to starboard!

The French battleship *Bearn* was

The first, and for many years only, French aircraft carrier, the *Bearn*

converted after the Washington Naval Treaty, but not directly as a result of it. Although she was originally laid down in 1914, work was suspended on her during the war, so it was not until 1920 that she was completed. Throughout the rest of that year and in 1921 she was used for flying trials with a short wooden platform built on the quarterdeck. Full conversion to aircraft carrier standard did not start until 1923, and the *Bearn* joined the Marine Nationale in 1925. British experience with HMS *Eagle* was incorporated in the *Bearn*, which had a starboard island and large single funnel, but the new vessel must have been something of a disappointment, with her maximum speed of just 21 knots and an aircraft complement of only twenty-five in her 22,146 tons.

Bearn's joining the fleet came in the year that the French Service Aéronautique became the Aéronautique Maritime. Three squadrons of aircraft were obtained for the aircraft carrier, including Levasseur PL.7B fighters and PL.10R three-seat reconnaissance aircraft and Dewoitine D.1 fighters, while the *Commandant Teste* seaplane carrier operated Latécoère 29 torpedo-carrying seaplanes and Gordou-Leseurre GL–80 reconnaissance seaplanes. This was a marked improvement over the immediate post-war strength of the French naval aviators, when they had just a fleet co-operation squadron, or Aviation d'Escadre, at St Raphael and a long-range squadron, or Escadrille de Grands Raids, although the latter lacked long-range bomber aircraft! In the 1925 re-organisation, six Districts Maritimes had been formed, but these were reduced to four in 1929, by which time some elderly Farman Goliath bombers were being phased out and replaced by C.A.M.S.37 and 55s.

The United States Naval Air Force, as it had become known, was by this time organised into Atlantic and Pacific Fleet Air Forces, based respectively on Hampton Roads, Virginia, and San Diego, California, with six squadrons each, while eight naval air stations remained open in the continental United States and Hawaii. The United States Marine Corps had just four squadrons. Possibly as some consolation for the problems caused by inter-service rivalries during the Chesapeake Bay exercise, USN and USMC aircraft were allowed to take part in further experiments, with the aircraft of Torpedo and Bombing Squadron No. 1 of the Atlantic Fleet launching their weapons at battleship targets anchored off Virginia.

Reorganisation also took place in the Royal Navy, as a result of recommendations made by the Balfour Committee of 1923, which had examined Royal Navy and Royal Air Force co-operation. In 1924, the Fleet Air Arm of the Royal Air Force was formed, with five squadrons, as part of the then Royal Air Force Coastal Area. Naval aircraft of the time included Fairey Flycatchers, IIIDs and IIIFs, Blackburn Fleet Spotters and Darts, Avro Bisons and Supermarine Seagull amphibians. RAF aircrew and groundcrew looked after shore-based aircraft and those attached to aircraft carriers or seaplane tenders, and the squadrons were under Admiralty control while afloat and Air Ministry control while ashore. Royal Navy officers received flying training so that they could operate the aircraft carried by battleships and cruisers. RAF units based in the Mediterranean and the Middle East included flights earmarked for operation from aircraft carriers visiting those areas.

Shore-based, if not entirely landbound, aircraft were becoming progressively more important as the need for long-range maritime-reconnaissance in a future war became more apparent, and as the flying-boat in particular developed, aircraft suitable for these duties became available. RAF Coastal Area included three squadrons of Blackburn Iris and Supermarine Southampton flying-boats.

Dornier Wal flying-boats, designed in Germany but built elsewhere because of the Treaty of Versailles restrictions on aircraft manufacture in Germany, became popular in a number of countries. These included Argentina, where they operated alongside Supermarine Southamptons, and Spain, where the Aeronautica Navale operated these aircraft as well as Macchi and Savoia flying-boats, including the Macchi M.18, and a few Blackburn Darts and Supermarine Scarab amphibians. Some of the Wals were actually built in Spain.

Argentina was one of many Latin American countries to establish naval air arms after the war in Europe ended, receiving help from an Italian Air Mission in 1919. As so often happened, such help resulted in orders for the aircraft industry of the country concerned— which was part of the exercise. So early aircraft preceding the Wals and Southamptons in Argentina included Italian

A Levasseur PL.7 is readied for flight aboard the *Bearn*

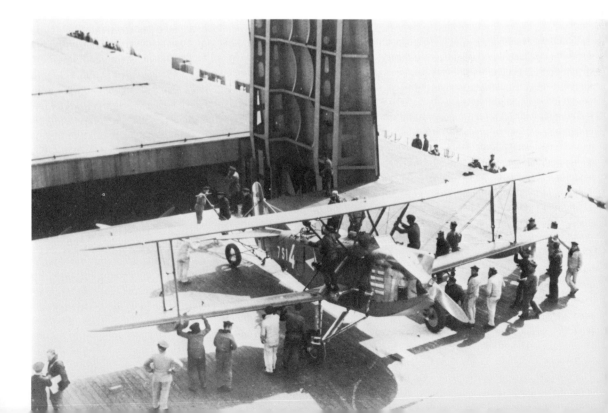

Macchi M.7, M.9 and Lōhner L–3 flying-boats, although Curtiss HS.2Ls were also acquired. Chile received British assistance, but its air arm was relatively short-lived, becoming the Fuerza Aérea de Chile—Chilean Air Force—in 1930.

Among other Latin American countries eagerly establishing small naval air arms was Colombia, which formed a flying-boat flight in 1922 as part of the Colombian Navy, later replacing these with Seversky SEV–3MWW amphibians. In 1920 Peru formed the Peruvian Naval Air Service with American assistance, and at first flew Curtiss Seagull flying-boats, but a merger with Army aviation units resulted in the Cuerpo de Aeronáutica del Perú being formed in 1929, when Douglas M–4 seaplanes were retained specifically for naval co-operation duties. Uruguay's Aviación Naval dated from 1920, and the Venezualan Navy established an aviation section in 1922.

The post-war break-up of the old European empires resulted in independence for a number of nations in Europe, and in these countries considerable priority was accorded to developing naval and military aviation often with good reason.

Finland had seized its chance during World War I to take its independence of Russia, torn by revolution. The new Finnish Air Force, the Ilmavoimat, was founded in 1920, and soon introduced Georges-Levy flying-boats, later building Hansa-Brandenburg seaplanes under licence. The new Union of Soviet Socialist Republics itself operated Tupolev TB-1P seaplane-bombers and MDR–2 long-range flying-boats during the 1920s. The new Yugoslavia acquired Hanriot H.41 seaplanes for its infant navy.

During the 1920s, Britain helped the countries of her empire to establish small air forces or air arms, particularly those countries which had achieved dominion status—semi-independence under the Crown. This was known as the 'Imperial Gift' of war surplus aircraft, with the choice of aircraft largely on a first-come-first-served basis within a rough allocation of types and number of aircraft. The Royal Canadian Air Force, Royal Australian Air Force, Royal New Zealand Air Force and the then Union of South Africa Air Force all owed their origins to the 'Imperial Gift'.

The first country to take advantage of

Byrd's Fokker F.VII trimotor before the first of its polar flights

this bounty was Canada, which had had a Royal Canadian Naval Air Service formed in 1918 and disbanded in 1919! The new Royal Canadian Air Force was formed in 1923. It was under Army control, but almost from the start maritime-reconnaissance and search and rescue aircraft were included, with Curtiss H.16 flying-boats and Vickers Vimy flying-boats, supplemented in 1925 by Canadian-built Vickers Vedette seaplanes. The Royal Australian Air Force came next, and in 1925 established a Fleet Co-operation Flight with six Supermarine Seagull Mk.III amphibians, later joined by Supermarine Southampton flying-boats.

Some of the established air arms had been able to re-equip when the return of peace made aircraft available from the main manufacturing nations. The Royal Danish Navy acquired ex-German aircraft and also some Avro 504 trainers in 1920, and its air unit achieved the status of a Naval Flying Corps in 1923, with a strength of two squadrons, or Luftflotille, by 1926. During the late 1920s, the Danish Naval Flying Corps had Heinkel He8 seaplanes and licence-built Hawker Woodcocks.

Greece, too, with British assistance and ex-British aircraft, expanded its air arm, the Royal Hellenic Naval Air Service, dropping the 'Royal' prefix once a republic was declared following a referendum in 1924. The immediate post-war expansion, however, was very short-lived. Severe economic difficulties prevented further acquisition of new aircraft until a Greek Air Force Fund was devised to raise money through public subscription for the purchase of aircraft by the navy and army. Salonika provided funds for the purchase of twenty-five aircraft; and the Hellenic Naval Air Service eventually received its share, including Avro 504 trainers, Hawker Horsley torpedo-bombers, licence-built Blackburn Darts, known appropriately in Greece as the Velos, and Armstrong–Whitworth Atlas general purpose biplanes.

Some of the older air arms maintained steady and unspectacular progress. At the end of the war, the Dutch Marine Luchtvaardienst introduced Martin seaplanes and Farman F–22s, which were mostly deployed in the Netherlands East Indies. These were later supplemented, and eventually replaced, by forty Hansa-

Brandenburg W–12 seaplanes. Hansa-Brandenburg fighters, the W–33, entered service with Norway's Marinens Flyvevaeson, while Portugal's Aviaçâo Maritima introduced three Fokker T.IV reconnaissance seaplanes, a small number of Curtiss HS.21 and C.A.M.S.37 flying-boats and some Hanriot H.41 seaplanes.

Chile and Peru were not the only countries to amalgamate their naval and military air arms into air forces, and amongst others following Britain's example were Italy, with its Regia Aeronautica, and Sweden with the Flygvapnet.

Yet interest in marine aircraft could flourish even in an autonomous air arm. In 1926 the Regia Aeronautica won the Schneider Trophy for Italy, with a Macchi M.39 flown by Major Mario de Bernardi at 246 mph; and in 1927, 1929 and 1931 the Royal Air Force won the same trophy for Britain, with Supermarine S.5, S.6 and then S.6B seaplanes, eventually establishing a world air speed record with a seaplane—the most unlikely of aeroplanes to a World War I fighter pilot! The RAF and Supermarine combination meant that the trophy was won outright for Britain, but success in the final contest was only possible due to the generosity of a private benefactor after official support for the RAF's entry was withdrawn.

The United States was also involved in the Schneider Trophy contests, often entering USAAC teams as well as USN teams for this event, which was very much one for hydroaeroplanes, and inter-service rivalry was much in evidence. In 1925 the USAAC won the Trophy against the USN's identical Curtiss R3C–1 seaplanes, leaving the naval team behind while their military colleagues represented the United States. But in 1926, the USN actually took part in the contest while the USAAC dropped out, leaving Italy to win! In the United States, USN and USAAC teams competed against each other in the Pulitzer Trophy contests for landplanes, and in 1923 the USN won with a Curtiss R2C–1. At the same time the USN actually held no less than twenty-one out of thirty-four world records with this aircraft!

Against this rather fast image, the USN still included fifteen airships in its inventory during the mid-1920s, with some three hundred heavier-than-air aircraft.

It was a time for exploration as well as for routine naval duties. In 1925, three Loening amphibians and a Vought UO–1 accompanied a polar expedition by the Norwegian Antarctic explorer Amundsen and USN officers, including Lieutenant-Commander Richard Evelyn Byrd. The following year, Lieutenant-Commander Byrd flew a Fokker F.VII/3M trimotor airliner over the North Pole, following this with a flight over the South Pole in 1929, using the same aircraft.

Another adventurer was Commander John Rodgers, USN, who set out from California with two Naval Aircraft Factory flying-boats and one Boeing PB–1 metal-hulled flying-boat to cross the Pacific to Honolulu. Only Rodgers' aircraft reached Honolulu, after covering 1,841 miles in the air and the remainder on the sea. After force landing Rodgers and his crew sailed the aircraft, using the fabric from the lower wings as sails!

In June, 1926, the Morrow Board on American military aviation recommended that there should be a five-year naval procurement programme which would include 1,000 aircraft and three airships, with two-thirds of the aircraft going to operational units and one-third being placed in reserve. Meanwhile, the USN made a considerable effort to ensure that the two new aircraft carriers, USS *Saratoga* and USS *Lexington*, would be operating with suitable aircraft on joining the fleet. During 1925 and 1926, landplane and seaplane versions of the Boeing PW–9 USAAC fighter started to appear as the FB series for the USN. Starting with the FB–5, a whole series of fighters was produced with 'beefed-up' undercarriages and arrester hooks. FB–6 fighters were ready for trials aboard the USS *Saratoga* on New Year's Day, 1928, so that the production F3B–1, with some

Boeing F3B-1's aboard the USS *Saratoga*, one of two squadrons aboard this ship

sweepback to the leading edge of the upper wing, could join the two big new carriers in 1929, along with Martin T4M torpedo-bombers. The original Vought Corsairs also arrived in 1929 for operation from battleships.

The F4B series which followed the F3B included retractable undercarriages, and joined the carriers during the early 1930s, leading the way into the inter-war USN fashion for 'tubby' fighters.

Exercises near the Panama Canal Zone during 1929 gave the USN an early demonstration of the value of the carrier group as a naval task force, but a possibly more interesting illustration of the power of the new carriers came later in the year, when Tacoma's power station broke down and the USS *Lexington* supplied the city with electrical power from her generators.

Throughout the 1920s, the British and American navies were both helped by the continued development of the aeroplane. Most aircraft, for shore or for carrier operation, were still biplanes, and would be for a few more years yet, but flaps were helping to reduce landing and take-off speeds, although variable pitch propellers and retractable undercarriages were still some four or five years away from widespread use. Folding wings, originally introduced for the Short Folder Seaplane and the Fairey Campania, were also returning for carrier operations.

While so much attention was being paid to the development of the aircraft carrier, the airship had not been altogether abandoned as a means of carrying aircraft for offensive or defensive purposes. In July, 1929, a Vought UO-1 biplane landed under the airship *Los Angeles*,

The airship USS *Akron* at her moorings

ZR–3, and this led to experiments in 1931 with the *Los Angeles* and another airship, *Akron*.

True novelty came with a more unusual aircraft carrier, the submarine. The idea itself was not new, and a number of pre-World War I aircraft designs had been intended for submarine operation, but the first true attempt came with a modified British 'M' class submarine. Built at the end of World War I, the 'M' class consisted of just three submarines, each of which was completed with a 12-inch gun, salvaged from a Majestic class battleship, intended to be fired as the submarine surfaced briefly near a suitable target and then submerged again—a principle favoured by some navies, including the French, who described such vessels as corsair submarines. The idea had novelty, but little else to commend it to the Admiralty, who took the understandable view that any target worth a 12-inch shell would be worth a torpedo, which could be fired accurately at far less risk to the submarine and its crew.

The first of the class, M1, sank in a collision in 1925, and M3 was converted to a minelaying submarine, but M2 was converted to become an aircraft-carrying submarine and in this form was recommissioned in 1927.

An aircraft, the Parnall Peto biplane, was specially designed by one of the smaller British manufacturers to operate from the submarine. A hangar was provided forward of the conning tower or fin, and on surfacing, the hangar door would fold flat, allowing a catapult launcher to be quickly assembled over the door and the deck while the aircraft was brought out of its small hangar and its wings unfolded. The whole operation took but a few minutes. On landing after a flight, the Peto could be picked up by a derrick fitted to the conning tower and placed on its catapult. Then, with wings folded, it could be pushed back into its hangar, after which the catapult would be folded away.

Much was made of safety and precautions were taken to minimise the risk of

Opposite above: An airship crewman's view of the Vought UO–1 observation biplane hooking on to the airship *Akron*

Opposite below: The ill-fated submarine *M–2*, with the Parnall Peto on the catapult

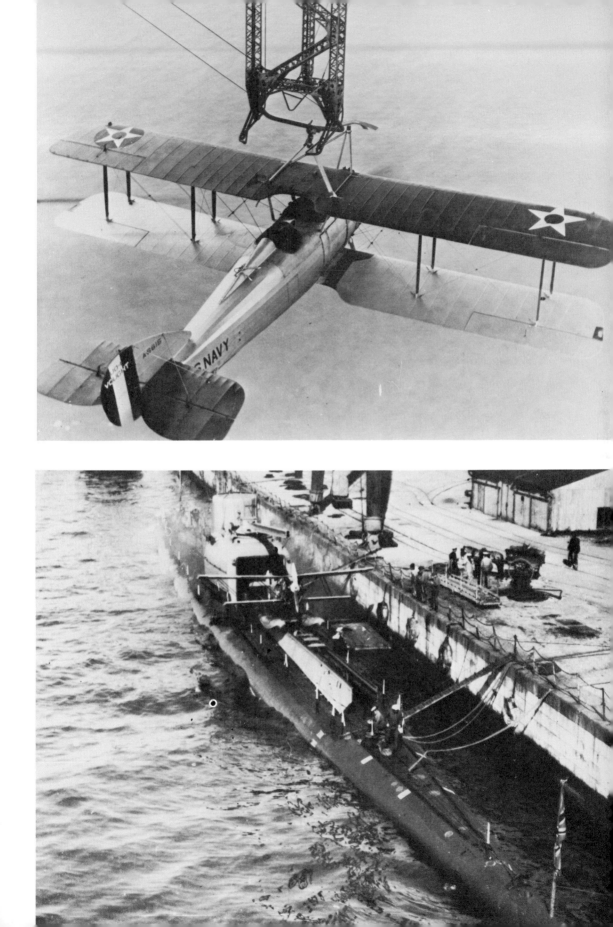

Another unsuccessful aircraft-carrying submarine of later years, the French corsair submarine, *Surcouf*

the hangar door being open at the same time as the internal hatch between the hangar and the conning tower. Nevertheless, there was no actual mechanism built in to the system to prevent this happening.

The very small, underpowered, two-seat Peto was fitted with a radio for reconnaissance duties, but was unarmed. True or false, the story current at the time was that the observer had to leave his heavy flying boots behind and wear plimsolls if the pilot wished to take any extra equipment! The aircraft had the reputation of handling badly on landing in a seaway.

Trials started in 1927, with a flight by Lieutenants C. W. Byron and C. Keighley, RN, who received double danger money as aviators and submariners. Several years of successful trials followed, hindered only by the limitations of the aircraft, until tragedy struck. On 26 January, 1932, the M2 dived off Portland, in the English Channel, never to surface again. Divers located the vessel, but some sixty officers and men had died, and efforts to raise the wreck to discover the cause of the accident failed in spite of the efforts of experienced Royal Navy salvage teams, who during the summer of that year very nearly brought the vessel to the surface

until defeated on several occasions by bad weather. It is generally accepted that M2 probably shipped a heavy sea through the hangar door and into the conning tower hatch, swamping the submarine.

The idea of aircraft-carrying submarines did not die, and one of the largest conventional submarines ever built, the French *Surcouf*, commissioned in 1934, was also intended to carry a small aircraft. In common with the 'M' class, *Surcouf*, 3,304 tons on the surface, was fitted with a heavy calibre gun and was a corsair submarine. In this vessel, designed from the start to carry an aircraft, the hangar was behind the conning tower and the object of the aeroplane was to reconnoitre enemy vessels so that *Surcouf* could act as a convoy or merchant raider. Refitted at Brest in 1940, the submarine escaped to Devonport on the fall of France, where she was forcibly taken over by the Royal Navy and in 1941 transferred to the Free French. Assigned to the Pacific, she was on passage to the Panama Canal on 18 February 1942 when she was in collision with an American cargo vessel, and sank in the Gulf of Mexico.

Peace in 1918 had not meant peace in the literal sense, but, as usual, simply the absence of major wars, so that the vast majority of the world's population could ignore the conflicts which occur from time to time. Almost immediately, the

Royal Navy became involved in rescuing refugees from the Russian Revolution, and on 18 August, 1919, aircraft from the seaplane tender HMS *Vindictive* bombed the Red Fleet in Kronstadt harbour.

Further action was required a year later, when extreme Turkish nationalists seized power and attacked Greek forces occupying part of European Turkey before facing British occupation forces in Istanbul—then known as Constantinople —and Chanak. This was in spite of the fact that the Dardanelles, the Bosporus and the Sea of Marmara in between, with the surrounding inland areas, had been declared a neutral zone by the Versailles Treaty.

Immediate action was required, and the seaplane carrier HMS *Ark Royal*, later re-named HMS *Pegasus*, was dispatched in haste from Egypt with five Fairey IIID seaplanes aboard, all manned by RAF personnel. After evacuating army units in Chanak, the ship's aircraft flew spotter patrols until joined by reinforcements, including HMS *Argus* with Nieuport Nightjars and additional Fairey IIIDs; but the next batch of reinforcements had to be delivered by merchant vessel! After that, the seaplane carrier acted as aircraft transport, transferring aircraft, including RAF Bristol F.2B 'Brisfit' fighters, to HMS *Argus* for reassembly and flying off. As well as flying patrols (so successfully that British negotiators in the conference which followed were often better informed about Turkish troop movements than their own generals), the RAF aircraft continued their training exercises, and on one occasion a Fairey IIID successfully bombed a torpedo!

Some problems also faced the American forces. In 1927, USMC units were forced to take action against Nicaraguan bandits, with the assistance of Naval Aircraft Factory and Boeing versions of the DH–4B.

However, by the end of the 1920s, the aircraft carrier was firmly established in four of the world's major naval fleets, with the Royal Navy actually having six vessels of this type, against three in the United States Navy and the Imperial Japanese Navy, and one in the Marine Nationale. All was not well with naval aviation in Britain, however, for a hard-pressed RAF, struggling to maintain sufficient aircraft for its own needs, was neglecting the needs of the Royal Navy, even though the number of squadrons was rising from just twelve in 1919 towards the more realistic 1933 figure of seventy-four, plus thirteen auxiliary or reserve squadrons. Just a small part of this strength could be devoted to the needs of the fleet, with its few Hawker Horsleys and Blackburn Darts serving aboard six ships, against the hundreds of USN and USMC aircraft, with just three ships to operate from.

4 Arms Race

In spite of the good intentions of the Washington Naval Treaty, the overall impression of the 1930s tends to be one of an arms race, an impression borne out in some part by the unsuccessful bid by Japan at the London Naval Conference of 1930 to obtain parity in permitted warship tonnages with Britain and the United States. And if the preceding ten years had seen a number of minor conflicts, the ten years after 1930 were to see an increasing number of serious, if still fairly localised, wars.

Certainly, the decade was also one of increasing ability in naval and maritime aviation, with every air force or air arm of any importance having a plausible maritime-reconnaissance capability, often centred on the flying-boat, by now rapidly reaching the zenith of its development. It was also a decade of experiment, sometimes leading to developments with a great future, and sometimes concerned with projects for which the need had long since passed. Among the latter were the continuing trials with the airships *Los Angeles* and *Akron* in the United States, to which the new Curtiss XF9C1 Sparrowhawk prototype and the production F9C1 were to attach themselves successfully in October, 1931 and June, 1932 respectively, long after the need for aircraft and airship combinations had passed.

One of the more spectacular achievements of the decade was mounted by the

Two Savoia-Marchetti S.M.55X flying-boats of the Regia Aeronautica

Italian Regia Aeronautica, which between 1 July and 12 August, 1933, sent a flight of no less than twenty-four Savoia–Marchetti S.M.55X flying-boats on the long return flight from Orbetello near Rome to New York, flying 11,500 miles to enhance the prestige of Italy and its dictator, Benito Mussolini. The man who could run Italy's trains on time could with equal confidence initiate mass flights capable of giving the world's cities a fore-taste of the unnerving effect of lying below a throbbing formation of heavy air-craft. Indeed, in making the Orbetello to New York flight the Regia Aeronautica was not making any extraordinary effort by its own standards, for by 1933 it could proudly boast of no less than thirty-seven squadrons of reconnaissance aircraft of all types.

In contrast, the Royal Danish Naval Air Service could only just manage to purchase sufficient Hawker Danetorps, modified Hawker Horsleys, to re-equip one squadron in 1932. Yet the Royal Danish Navy was responsible during the 1930s for one of the most significant scientific achievements of the aeroplane at that time, and one which was to be invaluable to the Allies in World War II. It was the first major photogrammetric survey—that of the vast wastes of Denmark's colossal overseas possession, Greenland. Starting on 10 July, 1932, with three Heinkel He8 three-seat recon-naissance seaplanes, the survey lasted until 1938, by which time a Dornier Wal flying-boat—which also accompanied an expedition to the north of Greenland—had been purchased to assist in the task. Taking seven summers, the only time of year when weather conditions and hours of daylight were sufficiently good for the work, the survey was a major achievement for aircraft with few navigational aids and flying without the benefit of ground-based navigational equipment. The experience of sustained arctic flying and the thorough knowledge of Greenland that was gained was to help the Allies during World War II in finding suitable locations for air bases, from which to protect convoys, and

through which they could also stage air-craft being delivered from the factories of North America to the British Isles.

Throughout the thirties, the Royal Danish Naval Air Service was neverthe-less short of aircraft, and it was not until 1935 that Hawker Nimrods were pur-chased to replace the earlier Danecocks.

However, developments in Europe pale into insignificance compared to those taking place in far away Japan. The Japanese Naval Air Force was not only to develop both technically and in strength during the decade, but also to flex its impressive muscle and gain con-siderable operational experience when Japan became involved in an intermittent and not insignificant conflict on mainland China.

The League of Nations had allowed Japan to base troops, known as the Kwantung Army, in China to guard the Southern Manchurian Railway. On 18 September, 1931, an explosion on the railway gave Japan the excuse for allow-ing the Kwantung Army to occupy the province of Mukden, followed by Man-churia. In 1932 the Army created a new state, Manchukuo, which was refused League of Nations recognition. By this time, the Imperial Japanese Navy had also become involved as unrest around the major Chinese city of Shanghai—the appropriately-named Shanghai disturb-ances—resulted in Japanese troops being sent to the area, ostensibly to protect Japanese interests and nationals. The *Kaga* was dispatched from Japan, arriving off Shanghai on 30 January with twenty-four Nakajima A1N Type 3 fighters and thirty-six Mitsubishi B1M Type 13 attack aircraft, giving Japan control of the area in the face of minimal Chinese resistance in the air. The *Hosho* followed shortly after with reinforcements.

The immediate overwhelming superi-ority of the Japanese forces was soon challenged on the ground, and the Japanese Army then realised that it had grossly under-estimated the potential of the Chinese 19th Route Army. In retalia-tion, aircraft from the *Kaga* destroyed the Chinese-held areas of Shanghai, and maintained complete aerial superiority in spite of Chinese aircraft being sent to the area. The conflict lasted through February, but by mid-March Shanghai was firmly under Japanese control. By early May the Japanese were able to force the Chinese to accept a demilitarised zone.

The Japanese Naval Air Force was still finding the domestic product disappointing and European aircraft preferable, even though the policies being adopted were hardly likely to improve relations with Britain or France. Japanese-designed aircraft in service with the JNAF in 1930 included the Type 90 series, the Nakajima A2N1 shipboard fighter and its twin-seat trainer variant, the A3N1, and the E4N1 Type 90–2 reconnaissance-seaplane—together with the Kawanishi E5K1 Type 90–3 reconnaissance-seaplane and the Hiro H3H1 Type 90–1 flying-boat.

The year 1932, during which the Japanese Naval and Army Air Forces started annual air defence exercises, also saw the first of the 7–Shi (7th year of the Showa reign) series of aircraft, including fighters, dive-bombers and reconnaissance seaplanes, coming from the Japanese aircraft industry. Of these, only two, the Kawanishi E7K1 Type 91 reconnaissance-seaplane and the Hiro G2H1 Type 95 twin-engined maritime-reconnaissance landplane, actually entered full production and JNAF service. A fighter design, the Mitsubishi 7–Shi failed, and the Nakajima A4N1 Type 95 was put into production as a stop-gap measure, although it was really only an up-rated Type 90. To obtain a dive-bomber for carrier squadrons, the Heinkel He50 was put into production as the Aichi D1A1 Type 94.

While development of the 9–Shi series pressed ahead, a number of foreign aircraft were obtained for evaluation, including the French Dewoitine D.510 fighter monoplane, considered to be one of the outstanding fighter aircraft of its day, for which an order was envisaged.

However, to the JNAF's surprise, the 9–Shi fighter aircraft, the Mitsubishi A5M1 Type 96–1, proved to be superior to the D.510, and a provisional order for the French aircraft was cancelled. Indeed, the 9–Shi series as a whole made up for the disappointment of the 7–Shi series. By 1936, the A5M1 and its improved production variants, the A5M2 Type 96–2 and A5M2b, were all in service, and being joined by the G3M1 Type 96–1 shore-based long-range attack bomber from the same factory. Other aircraft entering JNAF service during the mid-1930s included the Hiro G2H1 in modernised form with the first retractable undercarriages in JNAF service, and the Aichi D1A2 Type 96 shipboard bomber, developed from the D1A1, while Nakajima provided the B4Y1 Type 96 carrier-borne attack bomber. There were also some hydroaeroplanes, notably the Waternabe E9W1 Type 96 reconnaissance seaplane, at first intended to be operated from submarines, and the Aichi E10A1 Type 96 night reconnaissance-seaplane, while Kawanishi built the H6K1 Type 97–1, the JNAF's first four-engined flying-boat.

This was an impressive performance from an aircraft industry which had not been renowned for its past brilliance, and more was to follow, in an attempt to satisfy the insatiable appetite for new aircraft of Japan's increasingly confident and aggressive armed forces. In marked contrast to their British counterparts, the carrier-borne squadrons were not being neglected, being equipped with Nakajima B5N1 Type 97–1 and Mitsubishi B5M1 Type 97–3 attack aircraft, while for the squadrons ashore Mitsubishi built the C5M1 and C5M2 Type 98 reconnaissance aircraft, Aichi the E11A1 Type 98 night reconnaissance aircraft and D3A1 Type 99 dive-bomber, with Hiro building the H5Y1 Type 99 twin-engined reconnaissance flying-boat.

Development of the first 12–Shi prototypes, which were to be the aircraft forming the backbone of the JNAF during World War II, started in 1937.

Japan's first purpose-built aircraft carrier, the *Ryujo*

Naturally, the ambitions of the Imperial Japanese Navy meant that attention was given to the state of the carrier fleet, and as the number and quality of aircraft increased, so too did the ships. The first Japanese aircraft carrier to be designed as such, the *Ryujo*, 10,600 tons, was laid down in 1929 and delivered in May, 1933. In an attempt to make the most of their permitted aircraft carrier tonnage under the Washington Naval Treaty, the Japanese deliberately designed this vessel to operate as many aircraft as possible consistent with a low displacement and a reasonable speed. In fact her initial displacement was lower than the 10,600 ton figure, but problems with stability and sea keeping required the fitting of enlarged torpedo bulges and modifications to the fo'c'sle after her first year of service.

A genuine flat-top, *Ryujo* lacked an island although two funnels were mounted on the starboard side, ducting downwards. While it could stow forty-eight aircraft, this figure dropped by a quarter if operations were envisaged. Two problems were the small size of the forward lift, which meant that most JNAF World War II aircraft could only be handled through the after-hanger lift, and the short flight deck, which limited the number of aircraft that could be ranged for take-off under combat condi-

tions. The six twin five-inch gun turrets with which the vessel was originally fitted had to be removed to improve stability.

The shortcomings of *Ryujo* were such that the next carriers to be built for the Japanese Navy were designed to a more substantial tonnage, although only one of these could be completed without infringing the Washington total. Two more aircraft carriers were approved during the early 1930s. The first, *Soryu*, was laid down in 1934 and the second followed in 1935. In common with *Ryujo*, *Soryu* lacked adequate defensive armour, but the tonnage was increased to 15,900 tons and a starboard island was fitted, while two funnels ducting downwards were also positioned on this side. The oddities of the vessel were the provision of three lifts to the single hangar, and the relatively narrow beam, which contributed to the high speed of 34·5 knots. Although the flight deck ran virtually the entire length of the ship, the hangar did not, and the fo'c'sle and quarterdeck were open. Intended to operate more than sixty aircraft, *Soryu* entered service in December, 1937.

The second new carrier, *Hiryu*, followed in July, 1939. Although of 17,300 tons standard displacement, she had the same aircraft accommodation and turn of speed as the earlier and smaller vessel, but with a rather better radius of action and a broader beam, which improved stability. *Hiryu*'s most marked characteristic, however, was the port side island, even though funnels remained on the starboard side!

In 1934, Japan formally notified the other Washington Naval Treaty signatories that she no longer considered herself bound by the restrictions of the treaty, and during the late 1930s several more aircraft carriers were laid down or started to be converted from other naval vessels.

Tension between China and Japan did not abate at all as the decade progressed, and it became evident that Japanese ambitions in the area could not be reconciled with the natural desire of the Chinese to recover their lost territory. The expected clash came on 7 July, 1937, when Japanese and Chinese troops started fighting near Peking, and full scale war followed. The main opposition to the Japanese came from the forces of General Chiang Kai-shek, who was largely supported by the West although he also had a non-aggression pact with the Soviet Union. But by 28 July the Japanese forces had occupied Peking and in August besieged Shanghai, following these operations with an amphibious landing in the region south of Shanghai, at Hangchow Bay, in November. Tientsin had fallen the day after Peking, while Nanking was taken on 13 December.

The Japanese ground forces enjoyed strong air support from carrier and shore-based aircraft of the JNAF, which could put rather more than two hundred aircraft in the air over China, against a Chinese defending force of about a hundred aircraft. The fast-moving Japanese carriers could also launch their bombers against Chinese cities without fear of location, let alone retaliation. Typical of the campaign were the Hangchow landings, with strong air support including bombers with fighter cover from Nakajima A2N and A4N1 fighters.

When the Chinese did have aircraft available, the Japanese found themselves facing fierce and skilful resistance, often from American-supplied aircraft with volunteer pilots also from the United States. In August, the Nakajima fighters had shown themselves to be out-dated in battles with Chinese fighters, and more than fifty aircraft were lost to Nanking's fighter defences. The *Kaga* was returned to Japan in haste to collect Mitsubishi A5M2 Type 96–2 fighters, nicknamed 'Claude' by the World War II Allies, while modifications to the Mitsubishi G3M1 bomber and extra gun positions on the G3M2 helped these aircraft in defending themselves. Many of the A5M2 fighters, however, were modified to lift extra fuel and also used drop tanks so that long-range fighter escort could be provided. The net result was the withdrawal of Nanking's fighter defences some little time before the Chinese Government abandoned the city to Japanese ground forces.

While the JNAF mounted such notable operations as sending Mitsubishi G3M1 Type 96 bombers from bases in Taipeh and Kaohsiung in Formosa to raid Kwangteh Province, a round trip of 1,250 miles, it also attempted to put pressure on the Chinese by bombing cities to scare the civilian population.

Japanese forces continued their advance, spreading rapidly over the Chinese mainland as 1938 progressed, and forcing the government to move to Chungkin. It became difficult for aircraft to keep pace with the changing position on the ground, and soon most of the JNAF units involved were based ashore. As longer range bombing missions were required once again, the loss rate rose, and one attack on the Chinese Air Force headquarters at Hankow lost the Japanese thirty-six out of forty bombers assigned to the raid. Concerned at the level of losses, the JNAF ordered Heinkel He112 fighters from Germany and Seversky 2PA–B3 fighters from the United States, but the combined effects of increased aircraft production in Japan and more forward bases close to the frontline rendered both aircraft types unnecessary, so that the JNAF found itself flying more of the now well tried A5M2s. After so many years of dependence on foreign aircraft designs, this was a particularly fortunate development, since both the German and the American aircraft were far from notable successes. The JNAF did not deploy the few He112s delivered in China, but by coincidence the Chinese Air Force obtained 2PA-B3s and found the aircraft to be disappointing. After the capture of Hankow on 25 October, 1938, the JNAF was free to conduct long-range bombing missions at will.

Most of the effort in the war had fallen to the JNAF, due to the poor performance of the Japanese Army Air Force, which was confined to the border with the Soviet Union, along which the situation remained tense before finally breaking out in a brief but severe conflict on 11 July, 1938.

In Germany, a continental rather than a maritime power, the prospect for naval aviation had been less bright, although the first heady days of the Hitler regime seemed to promise much for German service aviators; but in the end that promise was kept only for the Luftwaffe.

German plans for a small group of experienced military pilots had been laid as early as 1920, but in secret. It was not until 1926 that the Paris Air Agreement removed the restrictions placed on German civil aviation and aircraft production by the Versailles Treaty, but by that time Germany already had an incredible 50,000 members of gliding schools. In addition, subsidiary factories of German aircraft firms had been established in Sweden and Russia, as well as elsewhere on a smaller scale. Hitler finally came to power in 1933, and Herman Goering was soon appointed Air Minister, while military and quasi-military aircraft started to be produced by the aircraft industry, already capable of producing successful flying-boat and seaplane designs for civil and other uses. In March, 1935, the Luftwaffe was officially established by proclamation and had almost two thousand aircraft of all types available

for its immediate use—a flying start indeed! Aircraft output was soon to mount to three hundred airframes a month, giving German manufacturers one of the highest peacetime production rates of any aircraft industry.

The London Naval Treaty of 1935 eased the Versailles Treaty restrictions on the post-World War I German Navy, which had effectively reduced it to the status of a coastal defence force, but still limited the total tonnage of new vessels to 35 per cent of the tonnage for the Royal Navy. Within this figure, the Germans were allowed parity with the Royal Navy in submarine strength!

The new German aircraft industry applied considerable imagination and ingenuity to the future development of the aeroplane. Dr Hans von Ohain in Germany worked on the jet engine, paralleling the work in Britain of Sir Frank Whittle, while at least as important for the future of naval aviation, the first practical helicopter, the Fa61, was also developed. A twin-rotor design with laterally offset rotors, the Focke–Achgelis Fa61 first flew during 1936, and although it only appeared in prototype form, it did lead to the Fa223 which was built in limited numbers during World War II.

The Luftwaffe, like the JNAF in the Far East, was not long in obtaining its first valuable taste of battle. In November, 1936, the Legion Condor, a mercenary force, was sent to Spain to counter strong Soviet involvement in the Spanish Civil War, initially operating a Heinkel He59 and He60 seaplane squadron for reconnaissance operations. The force, small at first, soon had to be expanded to balance the Soviet and French forces, which at the time also had superior equipment.

The Luftwaffe devoted a considerable effort towards providing a strong maritime-reconnaissance force, and by the time of the Munich Agreement—a vain attempt by Britain to stave off the threat of war with Germany—in September, 1938, the Luftwaffe had some 185 maritime-reconnaissance and naval co-operation aircraft.

An opponent's view of the sleek Focke-Wulf Fw200 Condor maritime-reconnaissance aircraft

In spite of the enthusiasm for aviation, the development of German naval aviation was hampered by an inter-service dispute, with Goering demanding control of all German service aviation, and getting his way. The small naval air arm which had been developing from the start of rearmament was promptly absorbed by the Luftwaffe on the outbreak of war, by which time it was already the navy's poor relation anyway, operating obsolescent Heinkel He59 and He60 seaplanes, Dornier Do18 flying-boats and Heinkel He115 amphibians, although Arado Ar196 seaplanes were starting to replace the He59 and He60 types. An aircraft carrier, the *Graf Zeppelin*, was under construction on the outbreak of war, and was towed to Gdynia in Poland out of reach of Allied bombers, but completion was delayed while the Luftwaffe and the German Navy restarted their quarrel over who should fly the carrier's Messerschmidt Bf109 fighters and Junkers Ju87 Stuka dive-bombers once she entered service!

Any speculation as to the outcome of the war at sea had the *Graf Zeppelin* joined the German Fleet is pointless, since factors other than technical merit enter into the picture. However, the Ju87 was itself an out-moded form of aircraft by the late 1930s, although doubtless still fairly effective, while the Bf109 design sacrificed strength for speed, and might not have stood up to carrier deck landings too well. The design of the *Graf Zeppelin*, built to a standard displacement of 23,450 tons, was dated in certain respects, indicating a lack of experience in carrier design among German naval architects. At first, a separate flying-off deck was planned, but this was abandoned as the design progressed; otherwise the design was fairly sleek, with a low island and large funnel on the starboard side. The rather broad beam required extremely powerful machinery to give a design speed of more than 33 knots. Aircraft stowage was planned for forty-two machines, which some commentators have considered unduly conservative or misleading, but the truth may simply have been that folding-wing aircraft were not envisaged. A sister ship was laid down at the start of World War II, but never launched.

In one respect, however, the Germans were doing very well for themselves, developing a new generation of maritime-reconnaissance aircraft during the last years of peace. Most important of these were the two strikingly attractive land-planes, the Junkers Ju290 and Focke-Wulf Fw200 Condor. In common with many of the German bomber aircraft of their day, these two four-engined aircraft were developed as civil airliners for Deutsches Lufthansa, and unlike many of their contemporaries could carry up to forty passengers in considerable comfort, being at least as worthy in this respect as their more innocent British and American rivals. Both types, the civil version of the Ju290 being designated the Ju90, entered service in 1938 with DLH.

Before war broke out, the Fw200 helped to boost German prestige, establishing a number of long-distance speed records. On 13 and 14 August, 1938, Flugkapitan A. Henke flew his Fw200 from New York to Berlin in twenty hours, at the then magnificent average speed of 199·7 mph. This was followed by a Berlin–Hanoi–Tokyo flight, which started on 28 November, reaching Hanoi on 30 November in $34\frac{1}{4}$ hours, at an average speed of 151·25 mph, and continuing to Tokyo in a total time of $46\frac{1}{3}$ hours from Berlin at an average speed of 119 mph.

During the late 1930s, grants helped German companies outside the aircraft industry to enter it, so that activity was no longer confined to the well-established and famous firms of the industry. One new entrant was the shipbuilder, Blohm und Voss, who built Bv138 and Bv222 flying-boats for the Luftwaffe during the late 1930s and during World War II, when these played a part in Germany's anti-shipping effort.

The close relationship between civil and military design was not something unique to the Germans, although else-where the military had to be content with modified civil designs, whereas in Germany military aircraft were deliberately given a civilian guise to avoid frightening the neighbours too much while peace lasted. The American Lockheed Electra led eventually to the Lodestar of 1939, with a military transport derivative, the C–56, and a maritime-reconnaissance development, the Hudson, which entered service with the Royal Air Force at the outbreak of World War II in Europe. Another RAF aircraft of the day with a civilian pedigree, also intended for maritime-reconnaissance, was the Short Sunderland flying-boat, developed from the Short Empire 'C' class flying-boat built for Imperial Airways and Qantas, while the Avro Anson light bomber was developed from the Avro 19 airliner.

Far-reaching changes had been taking place in the British services meanwhile, with the relationship between the services being changed once again.

The changes had the right aim in mind, being intended to correct the errors of the earlier inter-war years. Disturbed at events elsewhere, although still not really prepared to re-arm, the then Prime Minister, Stanley Baldwin, vowed in March, 1934, that British air power would not be allowed to become inferior to that of any country within striking distance of its shores. Fine words, and indeed at the time the Fleet Air Arm was receiving some fine new aircraft for a change, in the form of Hawker Osprey seaplanes, developed from the RAF's series of beautiful Hawker biplanes, the first of which had been the Hart light bomber. More important, in 1936, RAF Coastal Area was elevated to full command status, as RAF Coastal Command, an important change for a service on the verge of a modernisation and expansion programme. Further, the Royal Navy's aviation requirement, which had suffered some neglect as the RAF diverted scant resources to its own needs as a strategic bomber and fighter force, soon received the attention it deserved when, in 1937, the Fleet Air Arm reverted to full Admiralty control,

becoming once again an integral part of the Royal Navy. At first, many RAF air and groundcrew remained while sufficient naval personnel were trained, but eventually all personnel, ashore and afloat, were members of the Royal Navy.

A hasty expansion of the Fleet Air Arm then followed, with a backlog of equipment renewal receiving attention as the few specialised naval aircraft available from British manufacturers were ordered and placed in service, including the Blackburn Skua dive-bomber and Roc fighter, and the Fairey Swordfish torpedo-bomber, known affectionately as the 'Stringbag'.

Preparations for war started in earnest as Admiralty control was resumed, although the RAF retained within Coastal Command full responsibility for search and rescue and maritime-reconnaissance. New aircraft carriers were already on order, with one actually delivered during the late 1930s while the remaining six, of

a new class, did not enter service until after war had broken out in Europe.

The old seaplane carrier, HMS *Ark Royal*, had been renamed HMS *Pegasus* in 1934, and the new aircraft carrier bore the discarded name when she entered service in November, 1938. Designed from the keel up as an aircraft carrier, HMS *Ark Royal* had been delayed due to the general shortage of money for defence during the inter-war period, and had not in fact been ordered until 1935. Her design reflected the then British desire to reduce the Washington Naval Treaty limits further, with a maximum tonnage for aircraft carriers of just 22,000 tons. To offset this slightly, considerable use was made of welding in the construction, and relatively little armour plating was used; although some armouring of the hangar deck existed, unusually for a British carrier, the flight-deck was not armoured. Also unusual for a British carrier, the ship had three lifts, and the flight deck ex-

HMS *Ark Royal* at Gibraltar

tended beyond the hull at both ends in order to fit the maximum length of deck onto the limited size of the vessel. Two catapults, still known to the Royal Navy as accelerators until the early years of World War II, were positioned at the forward end of the flight deck, largely to enable floatplanes to be launched on trolleys. The accelerators for HMS *Courageous* and HMS *Glorious* had been fitted slightly earlier, during the mid-1930s.

These differences apart, HMS *Ark Royal* conformed to the British standard carrier pattern in many respects, with a starboard side island and funnel, while at 32 knots the ship also had a reasonable turn of speed. Up to seventy-two aircraft could be accommodated, although a true operational figure tended to be closer to sixty.

The next six aircraft carriers were ordered after 1935—the first four in 1936 and the remainder in 1937. Then in 1938

a fleet maintenance carrier was also ordered, to provide support for aircraft operating from the standard aircraft carriers whenever the fleet might be away from shore bases for extended periods.

In 1938 the Admiralty was given Parliamentary authority for a three hundred per cent increase in Fleet Air Arm personnel. While the first four of the new class of aircraft carrier building had originally been intended as replacements for the *Argus*, *Furious*, *Eagle* and *Hermes*, it was realised that the new ships would in fact be an expansion of a fleet which was to be sorely tried in the years of conflict ahead.

On the outbreak of war in September, 1939, the RAF could muster 171 aircraft in Coastal Command. There were ten general reconnaissance squadrons with the Avro Anson twin-engined light bomber, one squadron of Lockheed Hudsons and two of Short Sunderlands—both new aircraft—while another four

Australia's first seaplane carrier, HMS *Albatross*

flying-boat squadrons operated obsolescent Saunders-Roe (Saro) London and Supermarine Stranraer aircraft, and two torpedo-bomber squadrons operated Vickers Vildebeest biplanes, which were long past their prime. This strength was soon supplemented by four Bristol Blenheim FI fighter squadrons for patrols over the North Sea, and by the first Royal Australian Air Force Sunderland squadron, which was working up in Britain on the outbreak of war, and promptly transferred with aircrew and aircraft to the RAF!

During the 1930s, the Royal Australian Air Force had been less well off than the RAF for equipment to meet its naval co-operation and maritime-reconnaissance duties, which included operations from the Royal Australian Navy's first seaplane carrier, HMAS *Albatross*, a vessel that had been transferred from the Royal Navy in 1929 but withdrawn from active service in 1933. Before war broke out, the marine element consisted of a few Hawker Demon fighters for naval co-operation duties, Avro Cadet training biplanes, and Supermarine Walrus amphibians, known in Australia as the Supermarine Seagull V, and this assortment of aircraft—operating from cruisers—accounted for the bulk of the Australian naval and maritime-reconnaissance effort, having replaced Westland Wapiti general-purpose biplanes delivered to coincide with the arrival of HMAS *Albatross* in Australia. However, on the outbreak of war in Europe, Japan was still a non-belligerent so that the threat to Australia was still remote, and many Australians served with the RAF and the Royal Navy.

Canada, which had also been able to view international developments from the security of distance rather than with strong defences, replaced Vickers Vedette amphibians with licence-built Fairchild 71–C amphibians during the early 1930s.

At the outset of the 1930s, the French Aéronautique Maritime had Levasseur P.L.7B and P.R.10R biplanes aboard the *Bearn*, although these were later replaced by Dewoitine D.373 fighters. The force's shore-based elements operated Breguet Bizerta—licence-built Short Calcutta—and Liore 70 flying-boats, while the *Commandant Teste* operated Liore 210 fighter and Latécoère 298 torpedo-bomber seaplanes. Further expansion of this small force was planned as war approached, including the laying down of

A Royal Canadian Air Force Supermarine Stranraer flying-boat on a visit to the US Naval Air Station at Pensacola

two 18,000 ton aircraft carriers, the *Joffre* and the *Painleve*. But plans to modernise the *Bearn*'s aircraft were seriously affected by the disorganised state of the newly nationalised French aircraft industry during the late 1930s, and eventually Vought–Sikorsky VS–156–B1 dive-bombers had to be ordered from the United States.

This situation—the general lack of preparation—was not untypical of the condition of the European democracies as the international situation deteriorated during the late 1930s. Greece, for example, could raise only one squadron of Avro Ansons, one of Dornier Do22 and one of Fairey IIIF seaplanes.

The Netherlands bothered little with defence between the wars, relying for their safety in the policy of neutrality which had in fact served the country reasonably well during World War I. Belatedly, in 1937, the Navy received a dozen Fokker T.VII–W torpedo-bomber seaplanes, fourteen Fokker C.XI–W and twenty-four C.XIV–W reconnaissance seaplanes, while the elderly Dornier Wal flying-boats in the Netherlands East Indies were replaced by Dornier Do24K–1 and F–2 flying-boats, of which almost forty were built under licence in the Netherlands. Some training types were also ordered.

Norway had formed a Naval Air Service under the Defence Act of 1933, with an initial planned strength of sixty-four aircraft. These were to consist of twenty fighters, the same number of torpedo-bombers and twenty-four reconnaissance aircraft, and each type of aircraft was to be equally apportioned between the main bases of Horten, Kristiansand, Bergen and Tromso. In spite of an order for six Heinkel He115 seaplanes and twenty-four Northrop N–3PB reconnaissance seaplanes during the late 1930s, only the Heinkels were delivered, and the strength of the Naval Air Service in 1939 amounted to twenty-one M.F.11 reconnaissance seaplanes, six Heinkel He115s, six Douglas DT–2B and six DT–2C torpedo-bomber biplanes, and a solitary Junkers Ju52/3M transport.

In fact, the severe economic problems that had struck at rich and poor nations alike during the period between the two wars had worked against the development of strong armed forces in all but a few countries. Needless to say, these exceptions were the very countries that in fact posed the threat which was recognised so

An Aeronautique Maritime Dewoitine D.373
fighter from the *Bearn*

An Aeronautique Maritime Breguet Bizerta
flying-boat, a licence-built Short Calcutta

belatedly by Britain and France, and for that matter, the United States.

Outside of Europe and North America, two of the more active naval air arms were in Argentina and in Brazil. By 1934, the Armada Argentina had three air stations, including one far south in Tierra del Fuego, and during the late 1930s operated a variety of British and American aircraft types, particularly the latter, including Vought V.65F and V.142 Corsair reconnaissance aircraft, Grumman JF–3 and Douglas Dolphin amphibians, Consolidated P2Y–3 flying-boats and Douglas DB–8A–2 attack bombers. Grumman J2F–2 amphibians replaced Fairey IIIF seaplanes aboard the cruisers *Almirante Brown* and *Veinticino de Mayo*, while the British-built cruiser, *La Argentina*, delivered in January, 1939, arrived equipped with two Supermarine Walrus amphibians.

In Brazil, the Naval Aviation Workshops at Rio were expanded and re-named the Fabrica de Gateao, building forty Focke–Wulf Fw44J Stieglitz basic trainers and twenty-five Fw58B Weihe advanced twin-engined trainers. Some Brazilian-designed Monig trainers also entered service, along with Boeing fighters, Curtiss–Wright Osprey general-purpose aircraft and Fairey Gordon reconnaissance aircraft, all in what had to be something of a twilight for Brazilian Naval Aviation, which was merged into the Forca Aérea Brasileira on 20 January, 1940.

Shortly before this, one air force that was autonomous by name but not in strict actuality finally achieved its ambition when, on 19 November, 1938, the Royal Canadian Air Force became no longer answerable to the Canadian General Staff. A modest expansion plan started in 1935 began to gain momentum after this, and with the help of the Canadian subsidiaries of British and American aircraft manufacturers an increasing number of different types soon began to appear in service. These included Canadian Vickers-built Supermarine Stranraer flying-boats as well as Vickers Vancouver flying-boats, while Boeing built Blackburn Shark torpedo-bombers and Fairchild, in Montreal, built the Bristol Blenheim under licence as the Bolingbroke, modified for Canadian conditions in such a way that the aircraft could operate with skis or floats as well as with a wheeled undercarriage. Once war broke out, Canadian industry was also to help supply aircraft for Europe.

While many countries were preoccupied with Japanese, German or Italian expansion and territorial ambitions, Russia was presenting no small problem for Finland. Anxious to preserve its comparatively new independence, Finland re-equipped the Ilmavoimat during the late 1930s before finally having to face a Russian attack during the so-called Winter War of 1939. Finland faced overwhelming odds with small numbers of obsolescent aircraft, including Blackburn Ripon II reconnaissance and torpedo-bombing biplanes.

Meanwhile, the period had seen mixed fortunes for the United States Navy and the United States Marine Corps. It had started well enough, with the first permanently deployed USMC carrier squadrons—VS–14M aboard the USS *Saratoga* and VS–15M aboard the USS *Lexington*—on 2 November, 1931.

However, the decade was a difficult one for equipment procurement, as the effects of the depression kept the armed forces starved of adequate funds. If this alone were not bad enough, tragedy struck when the USN's airship *Akron*, delivered in 1931 and the veteran of seventy-three flights by March, 1933, crashed with the loss of all seventy-three USN personnel on board, including Rear-Admiral Moffatt, the father of US Naval aviation.

Rear-Admiral Ernest King succeeded Moffatt as Director of the Bureau of Aeronautics, and in this, at least, a serious misfortune was turned to some advantage. The new chief was held in high esteem by President Roosevelt, who was in any case a staunch supporter of a strong USN. A Thousand Aircraft Programme allowed the USN and USMC 125 dive-

bombers, 32 torpedo-bombers, 179 fighters, 173 reconnaissance-bombers, 147 patrol bombers, 208 observation and scouting aircraft, 42 utility aircraft, 19 transports and 75 trainers during the mid-1930s. These numbers were increased to a total of 1,650 aircraft under the Vinson-Trammell Naval Bill of 1934, which also authorised two further aircraft carriers, while the USN had in fact received its first purpose-built carrier that year.

The 1934 aircraft carrier, the USS *Ranger*, had been laid down in 1931, and represented an attempt by the USN to see just how many small vessels could be fitted into the remaining tonnage permitted under the Washington Naval Treaty. Ideally, they hoped for five 13,800 ton carriers, although the first and only ship to be built under this tentative programme, the USS *Ranger*, displaced 14,500 tons. The design seemed out-dated even by the standards of the early thirties. The vessel was originally intended as a pure flat-top, although before completion a starboard island was added; but this still left no less than three funnels on each side of the flight deck, aft of the island position! The funnels could fold down to

the horizontal position, but normally would be upright, unlike those of the Japanese carriers. In spite of the ship's low tonnage, achieved partly through sacrificing armour plating and having a minimal anti-aircraft armament, more than seventy aircraft could be operated from it. A reasonable 30 knots could be attained, due largely to the low drag of the ship's narrow beam, but in fact the design proved to have severe limitations fully justifying the reservations of a 1930 Congressional Committee.

Commonsense prevailed with the next aircraft carrier to be ordered, the *Yorktown*, first of the Yorktown class. Both the USS *Yorktown* and her sister ship USS *Enterprise* were laid down in 1934 and paid for under the Public Works Programme, to stimulate employment in the depressed shipbuilding industry. By this time the USN had firmly decided on the shape of its carrier fleet, and both vessels were built to a reasonable standard displacement of 19,800 tons. Each incorporated one large funnel in the starboard island, and could attain a good 33 knots. Both vessels could carry almost eighty aircraft, and were equipped with three lifts plus two catapults forward. Two un-

The first US aircraft carrier to be designed as such, the USS *Ranger*, with funnels in the down position

The first USS *Yorktown*

usual features were the placing of arrester wires forward, so that in a strong wind aircraft could land over the bows while the carrier steamed downwind, and an angled catapult positioned to launch aircraft through either port or starboard side apertures on the hangar deck. Neither feature proved to be of great worth and were seldom used, even though the forward arrester wires were copied by some later carriers, including certain British types. However, the hangar catapult illustrates one feature of American carrier design at this time—the apertures for ventilation in the hangar walls, which were also the sides of the hull—which was in marked contrast to British practice. British carriers then had a fully enclosed hangar with stores at the sides. The US concept certainly provided a greater aircraft capacity, but it had several disadvantages. Not only was it not watertight, but it also caused difficulties when attempting to darken ship before night operations. Furthermore, the risk of the hangar walls being penetrated and shells detonating amongst fuelled and armed aircraft was obviously increased.

The new carriers entered service in September, 1937 and May, 1938, by which time a further carrier, the USS *Wasp*, had been laid down to an improved design based on the USS *Ranger* tonnage. When the war in Europe started, by which time, of course, the Washington Naval Treaty was a dead letter, another Yorktown class vessel, the USS *Hornet*, was laid down.

Almost unnoticed, the forerunner of the successful Catalina flying-boat, the Consolidated P2Y–1, had entered service in 1934 with USN Squadron VP–10F.

A successor to *Akron*, the *Macon*, had joined the USN on 23 June, 1933, but its life was short-lived, with a structural defect leading to a failure in early 1935, although mercifully with only two casualties resulting. Following this, the USN operated non-rigid airships only, including the Goodyear types, during the remainder of the 1930s and 1940s.

By the late 1930s, just before war broke out in Europe, the USN already had Consolidated Catalina flying-boats on order, with Chance–Vought SB2U–1s, Curtiss SOC–1 Scout and BF–23C–1 Hawk fighters, and 135 Curtiss O3C–1 observation aircraft. In May, 1938, growing tension in Europe and concern over the rapidly deteriorating situation in the Far East led Congress to authorise a total aircraft strength for the USN and USMC of three thousand, with the creation of new naval air stations and the enlargement of sixteen existing stations. But even while this plan was being implemented, further increases were to be authorised.

The stage was being set for another major war, though not one as bloody as the 'Great War'—a name to be dropped as soon as the world realised that a second world war was underway. While World War II was to be one for all three services, it was to be above all the war of the aeroplane, and at the same time a naval war as well!

5 War in Europe

Even those nations wishing desperately to avoid war found the last few years of the 1930s to be a period of preparation for the conflict ahead; and the Munich Agreement of 1938, which saw Britain and France attempting to guarantee the territorial integrity of Czechoslovakia and has often been derided for its seeming naïvety, provided a further merciful twelve months of peace in which to rectify the ravages that economic depression and pacifism had wrought on the armed forces of the democracies. For other nations, of course, the decade had been one of opportunity and of covert and overt preparation for war, although it can be argued that they, too, had hoped to avoid it, having been encouraged by the weakness of the others to believe that no hand would or could be raised against them.

In spite of the Munich Agreement, Germany invaded first Czechoslovakia and then, on 1 September, 1939, Poland, and on 3 September, after the expiry of an Anglo–French ultimatum, Britain and France declared war on her. Soon almost the whole of Europe was involved in the war, exceptions being Sweden, the Iberian states, Switzerland and Finland, although the latter was at war with the Soviet Union from November, 1939 to March 1940, and remained at war with that country at intervals throughout the duration of the war.

The first few months of World War II amounted to what the British aptly described as 'the phoney war', with little

A Luftwaffe Blohm und Voss Bv138 flying-boat, at sea but aboard ship!

action at sea, in the air or on land, other than the movement of the British Expeditionary Force to France. The main conflict was to await the following spring, while in the meantime the opposing forces weighed up the situation and attempted to predict exactly where and when the first positive moves would be made. Germany and the Soviet Union (which had soon followed the German invasion of Poland by an invasion of its own, although it was still not at war with any of the major powers) consolidated their gains in Poland, and in March, 1940 the USSR also forced an uneasy and unwelcome peace upon Finland, although the peace was not a dishonourable one; following fierce fighting between Finnish forces and the stronger forces of Russia.

However, in spite of the relative inaction, the first weeks of war saw the first action by carrier-borne aircraft, with a Luftwaffe Dornier Do18 flying-boat shot down by a Blackburn Skua, flown by Lieutenant B. S. McEwen, RN, from Britain's most modern aircraft carrier, HMS *Ark Royal*, on 26 September. Rather more dramatic was the destruction before this, on 17 September, of the British carrier, HMS *Courageous*, torpedoed by U-29 in the Western Approaches—south-west of Ireland. Such actions were warlike enough to be convincing to both sides!

Heavy fighting broke out on 9 April, 1940, when German forces attacked Norway and Denmark at the same time, attempting to subdue the defending forces quickly. The speed of the attack, coupled with the weak state of Denmark's defences, meant that resistance was pointless for the Danish, and with most of their military aircraft destroyed on the ground the government soon surrendered. Just a few aircraft managed to escape with their aircrews to Britain.

Norway, slightly farther away and an inhospitable country, cruel to defender and invader alike, was a rather more difficult proposition. Determined resistance came from the Norwegian armed forces, with the support of a British Expeditionary Force, and strong opposition from the British Home Fleet.

The rugged and deeply indented Norwegian coastline dictated the importance of naval units to the Norwegian campaign, and the Luftwaffe was quick to appreciate this, deploying anti-shipping aircraft, including some forty Dornier Do17 and thirty Heinkel He115 seaplanes, with a few Do24 flying-boats, amongst a force of more than four hundred aircraft, grouped together in Fliegerkorps X. Against this strong force, Norway's own defences were weak, and the Naval Air Service's paper strength of sixty-four aircraft proved in reality to amount to twenty-one M.F.11 reconnaissance seaplanes, four operational Heinkel He115 seaplanes, a handful of Douglas DT-2B and DT-2C torpedo-bombers and the solitary Junkers Ju52/3M transport. This force was driven northward as the Germans advanced, although two He115s and an Arado Ar196A seaplane from the cruiser *Hipper* were captured and pressed into service.

Unfortunately, the distance of the Norwegian coast from Britain and the shortage of suitable airfields in Norway, as well as the lack of long-range fighter aircraft in the Royal Air Force at the outset of the war, meant that air cover for British and Norwegian forces had to be provided almost entirely by the Fleet Air Arm, which operated Blackburn Skua, Gloster Sea Gladiator and Fairey Swordfish aircraft from the three aircraft carriers, HMS *Ark Royal*, HMS *Furious* and HMS *Glorious*. A succession of mainly destroyer actions resulted in heavy German losses, while on 10 April, Royal Navy Blackburn Skua dive-bombers, flying from a base in the Orkneys, sank the German cruiser *Königsberg* in Bergen Fjord. However, the Norwegian campaign proved to be a severe drain on the limited resources of the British Army, and troops soon had to be withdrawn as German units began their advance through France and Belgium. Final evacuation from Norway came in early June.

As the last British troops were being evacuated from Norway, the German fleet mounted a major offensive against the British fleet, with the battlecruisers *Scharnhorst* and *Gneisenau*, the heavy cruiser *Hipper* and escorts anxious to press home their attack. On 8 June, they succeeded, finding and sinking the aircraft carrier HMS *Glorious*, and two escorting destroyers. The Royal Navy was not slow to seek an opportunity to destroy the German fleet however, and on 13 June, fifteen aircraft from HMS *Ark Royal* attacked the *Scharnhorst* at Trondheim, losing eight aircraft in the attack, and scoring only one direct hit on the battlecruiser, and this with a bomb which failed to explode!

Meanwhile, as the German forces completed their advance through Norway, many Norwegian airmen managed to escape, initially to Scotland. From there they were sent to Canada, where aircrew from both Army and Navy units formed a flying school, preparing their countrymen for new aircraft destined to form a Norwegian squadron. The new aircraft, twenty-four Northrop N–3PB seaplanes, had in fact been ordered by the Norwegian Government before the fall of Norway, and using these machines, the Norwegian squadron became fully operational by August, 1941, when it was dispatched to Iceland as No. 330 Squadron, Royal Air Force Coastal Command. The squadron spent twenty months in Iceland, with its aircraft spread between three bases, and achieved a high standard of operational readiness in spite of the harsh environment.

The countries of the British Empire were quick to enter World War II on the side of Britain and France, ensuring that the war was indeed a world war from the start. The only hesitation had come from the South Africans—not unnaturally in view of the relatively high number of Germans living in that country, mainly as the result of German South-West Africa having been incorporated in the Union of South Africa following the German defeat in World War I. Canada, Australia, New Zealand, South Africa and the then Southern Rhodesia, now

A pre-delivery shot of one of the Aeronautique Maritime's Vought–Sikorsky VS–156–B1 dive-bombers

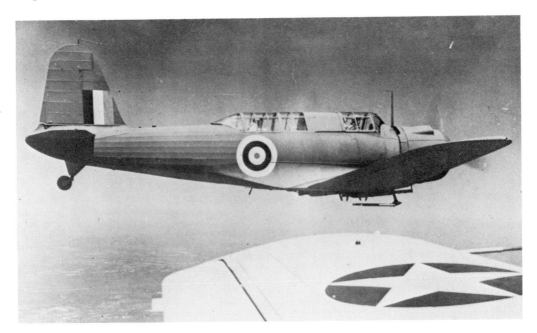

Rhodesia, were the main contributors to the Empire Air Training Scheme, which officially came into existence on 17 December, 1939. This scheme owed its origin to a British suggestion that pilots from Britain and the Empire should be trained in the better climates of those countries, where they would not provide sitting-duck targets for marauding enemy aircraft in the hostile skies over the British Isles. During the years which followed, naval aircrew were to take their fair share of training places in the scheme.

Meanwhile, as Norway had fallen, so had France. German forces attacked Belgium, the Netherlands and Luxemburg on 10 May, 1940 and within three days were on French territory. Aéronautique Maritime aircraft, which had been conducting intensified coastal anti-submarine and anti-shipping patrols from the outbreak of war, were hastily redeployed onto the front with German forces, operating in support of British and French ground forces. Some of the naval air squadrons received Potez 631 twin-engined fighters, and others began to receive Liore–Nieuport LN–40 attack aircraft, while the *Bearn* started a delivery shuttle service across the North Atlantic, bringing American-built aircraft to Europe, including Vought–Sikorsky VS–156–B1 dive-bombers. At all times, the Aéronautique Maritime squadrons were in continuous operation against German forces, even though heavy losses were suffered, including many aircraft destroyed on the ground during a German raid on Boulogne.

On 10 June, 1940, Italy entered the war on the side of Germany, causing some of the Aéronautique Maritime aircraft to be transferred to the Mediterranean to keep watch on the Italian Fleet, and some of the VS–156–B1s actually raided Genoa. However, Italian participation did not begin until less than a fortnight before the final surrender of France, for with the Netherlands and Belgium already overrun by Germany, along with much of France, particularly in the north, the French accepted an armistice on 22 June.

With the fall of France, Britain effectively stood alone with her Empire, and although many of the French troops who had escaped to Britain along with the remnants of Armée de l'Air and Marine Nationale units intended to continue the fight against the Axis Powers—Germany and Italy—others had naturally headed for French territories in North Africa. The bulk of the French fleet had in fact headed for its base at Mers El Kebir near Oran, with a few vessels arriving at the British naval base at Devonport. With the Vichy French Government coming to terms with the all-conquering Germans, this situation held the very real risk of a powerful and generally modern fleet falling into enemy hands. In short, some form of pre-emptive action seemed necessary.

Commando raids were the answer to gaining control of those vessels in British ports, but the rest, lying in heavily defended ports in North Africa, presented a far more difficult problem.

British warships in the Mediterranean had been grouped into a powerful force under Vice-Admiral Somerville, who on 3 July, 1940, presented Admiral Gensoul, the senior French naval officer, with the stark choice of surrender or destruction of his entire fleet. The British ultimatum was rejected, and Vice-Admiral Somerville's Force H attacked, mainly using shellfire, although Fairey Swordfish aircraft from HMS *Ark Royal* sank the battleship *Strasbourg*, whose Liore 130 reconnaissance aircraft had also attempted to attack the aircraft carrier.

A few days later, on 8 July, the aircraft carrier HMS *Hermes* used her aircraft to attack other French warships in port at Dakar, damaging the battleship *Richelieu*. Then in September, the British with their Free French allies attempted an invasion of the Vichy stronghold at Dakar, with support from HMS *Ark Royal* and other Royal Navy vessels, but this campaign was unsuccessful.

In contrast, however, two years later a Royal Navy officer, Commander B. Nation, flew over the Vichy airfield at

Blida near Algiers, and wrongly assuming that the lack of activity in the area meant that the French had surrendered, he landed. He was promptly surrounded. Drawing his revolver, he demanded to be taken to the Commanding Officer, and threatened him with the bombing of the airfield unless surrender came within fifteen minutes. After several frantic telephone calls, the French Commanding Officer surrendered the airfield, with sixty aircraft and some 500 troops!

However, after the attack on Mers El Kebir, only the occasional action resulted between British and Vichy French forces. In one such action two Bizerta flying-boats were lost to Blackburn Skuas of the Fleet Air Arm, which caught the French aircraft shadowing the British Fleet, and in another Gibraltar was attacked by French Martin 167Fs, while in yet another some Aéronautique Maritime aircraft attacked British forces in Syria. After the British invaded North Africa in 1942, many Vichy French airmen joined the Free French, with Aéronautique Maritime units normally coming under the Armée de l'Air, due to the absence of suitable warships from which the Free French could mount any kind of sea-going air operations. Generally, the Vichy French lacked the heart to fight a war with the British, and their actions were prompted by bitterness over the British attacks on Mers El Kebir and Dakar. Nevertheless, the power of the forces available to the Vichy French could not be discounted, and it would have been a complete disaster had such forces, including several battleships and battlecruisers and some 800 aircraft, fallen into German or Italian hands intact.

During this period, the *Commandant Teste* had been at Mers El Kebir, while the *Bearn* had been in the West Indies, at Martinique, where it remained for three years until the Vichy French allowed the Free French to take control of the island.

Britain's position had become much more dangerous as Italy entered the war and French resistance to the Axis collapsed, although neither eventuality had been entirely unexpected. British possessions in the Mediterranean—Gibraltar, Malta and Cyprus—immediately came to the forefront of the conflict, with Malta in particular soon under heavy aerial attack, along with the major British supply routes through the Mediterranean. Malta was left with just three veteran Gloster Gladiator biplane fighters for defence.

The Italian Regia Aeronautica could provide two groups of C.R.D.A. Cont. 2.506B torpedo-bomber seaplanes—a total of twelve squadrons—plus another fifteen squadrons of C.R.D.A. Cont. 2.501 maritime-reconnaissance flying-boats, and another twenty units with naval co-operation aircraft, so that some 15 per cent of the 2,600 aircraft front-line strength was devoted to maritime-reconnaissance in a relatively small and confined sea area. Anti-shipping operations started as soon as Italy entered the war, and even the successful Savoia-Marchetti S.M.79 trimotor bomber was soon diverted into torpedo-bombing operations, accounting for many of the merchant vessels lost in the ill-fated Malta convoys. Malta was eventually reinforced, receiving Supermarine Spitfire fighters transported to the island aboard the aircraft carrier HMS *Eagle*, which made no less than nine such delivery voyages during the first half of 1942, on one of which she was accompanied by the American aircraft carrier USS *Wasp*.

As the war progressed, the Royal Navy started to recoup its earlier losses as new and more modern aircraft carriers entered service. In the mid-1930s an aircraft carrier programme had been initiated with the intention of replacing the four older aircraft carriers with four new ones, and when war in Europe became almost certain the number was increased to six vessels. The Illustrious class consisted of HMS *Illustrious, Victorious, Formidable, Indomitable, Implacable* and *Indefatigable*. These ships were intended to be an improved version of HMS *Ark Royal*, with the same waterline beam, but shorter length overall and improved armour protection; and with an increase in tonnage to just 23,000 tons, the aircraft complement was increased by 40 per cent. Only two lifts were fitted, but the flight deck, hangar deck and the sides of these vessels were all armoured. Just one catapult was fitted, on the port side of the flight deck, but on all except HMS *Illustrious*, forward arrester wires were fitted for landings over the bows, even though, as on the American carriers, this system was seldom used. A reasonable speed of just over 30 knots was attained in these ships, among the few Royal Navy vessels to have three, rather than two or four, screws.

clipped as a result! To increase aircraft capacity as the war progressed, or rather to accommodate the planned fifty or more aircraft as aircraft sizes increased, the first three vessels were fitted with outriggers to take the tailwheels of aircraft on the deck park, thus allowing the mainplane and main undercarriage wheels only onto the flight deck while the tailplane hung over the side!

The first vessel of the class, HMS *Illustrious*, was completed on 25 May, 1940, and was followed on 24 November by HMS *Formidable*, while the planned second ship of the class, HMS *Victorious*,

HMS *Victorious*, with Fairey Albacores and Grumman Martlets (Wildcats) ranged on her flight deck

Generally the design was most effective, and these were among the few aircraft carriers of pre-World War II design not to be lost to enemy action during the war. The one big failing was that the ships were designed with pre-war aircraft in mind, and had to face a war in which aircraft size mounted rapidly. This presented problems of capacity and of space in the hangars, which had rather less headroom than might have been wished. Some aircraft operating from Illustrious class carriers had to have their wings

had fallen back in the programme and did not join the Fleet until 15 May, 1941, followed by the fourth ship, HMS *Indomitable* in October. It was to be some time before the two last ships, which had been added to the original four-ship programme, could join the Royal Navy. Of the four ships due to be replaced by the Illustrious class vessels, not one had been touched by enemy attack at this stage in the war, but obviously there could be no question of retiring older vessels, particularly with the loss so early in the conflict of HMS *Courageous* and HMS *Glorious*.

In fact, the demand for more air cover for ships at sea, balanced against the high cost and lengthy time of aircraft carrier construction, even if not damaged by air attack while in the shipyard or delayed by a shortage of materials or equipment, was soon to lead to some major innovations, which appeared during 1941.

Placing just one aircraft at the disposal of ships at sea, the first of these innovations was to some extent a reminder of the barge-based aircraft of World War I, but in World War II the aircraft were catapulted from the decks of merchant vessels and fleet auxiliaries. Anti-shipping patrols by the Luftwaffe, mainly using Focke-Wulf Fw200 and Junkers Ju290

aircraft, forced this development. The first occasion when an aircraft flew from a ship equipped with a catapult in this way was in August, 1941, when Lieutenant Everett, RN, flew a Hawker Sea Hurricane from HMS *Maplin*, a British supply vessel. Before long a large number of vessels were fitted with catapults to launch fighter aircraft, becoming CAMs, or catapult-armed merchant ships, with most such vessels entering service in 1942. Both Fleet Air Arm and Royal Air Force pilots were used, although their operational unit, the Merchant Service Fighter Unit, was officially a part of the Royal Air Force.

Since a CAM had no landing facilities, the obvious drawback was the fact that only one aircraft could be carried, and this was inevitably lost on the first and only occasion that it was used; furthermore, the vessel was put at risk while stopping to pick up the pilot, who would have parachuted into a cold North Atlantic! So, early in 1942, appeared the first of the so-called Merchant Aircraft Carriers, cargo vessels or tankers fitted with a wooden flight deck over the cargo holds, but with a hangar below the flight deck for three or four Fairey Swordfish to protect the convoy from submarine attack. Naval airmen joined the merchant service crew of such vessels, which continued to carry cargo.

The next stage, which also appeared in 1941, was the escort carrier, designated CVE in the United States but more usually known as the 'Woolworth Carrier'. At first these vessels were built in the United States and in Britain, normally from converted cargo vessels although occasionally from scratch, using a cargo vessel design. Operationally, they were entirely Royal Navy or United States Navy manned, and carried a mixture of anti-submarine and fighter aircraft to protect the precious and vital convoys. A typical vessel was HMS *Audacity*, with a speed of just seventeen knots and a complement of eighteen aircraft. Once the American Lend-Lease programme started, the availability of CVEs from the United States encouraged the British Admiralty to use these vessels rather than incur the cost of buying similar ones from British yards.

Some innovations were more concerned with improving the effectiveness of the aeroplane. One such was the fitting of radar to aircraft on a wider scale than previously—even to the veteran Fairey Swordfish biplanes—to improve their anti-submarine capabilities. Some Royal Air Force Wellington bombers were also fitted with special equipment to explode magnetic mines.

One unusual event was the surrender of a German U-boat to an RAF Coastal

A Hawker Sea Hurricane being positioned on the catapult of HMS *Maplin*

Precursor of the escort carrier, the merchant aircraft carrier continued to carry cargo and was manned by the merchant navy; one of the first, the *Empire Mackay*

Command Lockheed Hudson in mid-1941!

Traditionally, naval aviation had been seen from the outset as an extension of the guns of the Fleet, as having a reconnaissance role, and even as being of value on convoy escort duties, guarding against attack from the air or by submarine. This general attitude still prevailed. Only during the attack on the French vessels at Mers El Kebir had there been any indication of a possible strategic role for the naval aviator, and even then, the operation against the French had been primarily one for the guns of the British Mediterranean Fleet.

The traditional view of naval aviation changed completely on 11 November, 1940. The British Mediterranean Fleet had left Alexandria, on 6 November, under its commander, Admiral A.B. Cunningham, RN, with just one aircraft carrier, the brand new HMS *Illustrious*. Originally, the intention had been that there should be two aircraft carriers, but HMS *Eagle* was forced to remain in Alexandria for repairs to damage incurred during an Italian aerial attack, although the ship had also been in several operations against units of the Italian Fleet and also against Italian merchantmen, and had attacked Benghazi. The target for Cunningham's force was the Italian naval base at Taranto, in the south of Italy. At 21.00, on 11 November, HMS *Illustrious* flew off the first of two waves of Fairey Swordfish torpedo-bombers for the 170 mile flight to Taranto. These slow and frail aircraft then braved heavy anti-aircraft fire to sink the Italian battleships *Littorio* and *Caio Duilo*, and to damage the *Conte di Cavour* so severely that she could not be repaired before the end of the war, as well as damaging other vessels and shore installations. No less than eleven torpedoes from a total striking force of just twenty aircraft found a home in an Italian warship, and only two aircraft were lost. Afterwards, even though the *Littorio* was later refloated, the Italian Fleet which had half of its battleships put out of action by the attack, moved to a safer anchorage, farther away from Malta and British supply routes.

For some inexplicable reason, the operation received scant recognition in Britain, since relatively few details were released to the British public at first, but the lesson was not lost on the Japanese naval planners!

That winter and the following spring saw the Royal Navy's aircraft carriers hard worked indeed. Just a couple of weeks after the attack on Taranto, the Royal Navy's Force H, with HMS *Ark Royal*, was protecting fast merchantmen in the Mediterranean when they were discovered by the Italian Fleet under Admiral Campioni, whose force in turn was discovered by aircraft from HMS *Ark Royal*. The Battle of Cape Teulada, Sardinia, resulted, and although inconclusive it did involve an unsuccessful attack by aircraft from the carrier against the Italian battleships *Vittorio Veneto* and *Guilio Cesare*. On 10–11 January, 1941, another convoy of fast merchantmen was being escorted through the Mediterranean by Force H when it came under heavy attack by Luftwaffe aircraft based in Sicily. HMS *Illustrious* was hit by six bombs and had to limp to Malta for repairs after suffering severe damage.

Far more successful from the British point of view was the action off Cape Matapan, Crete, on 28 March, 1941, when Admiral Cunningham faced Admiral Iachino. At the start of the action, the Italians attempted to trap the British ships between the *Vittorio Veneto* and the Italian cruiser force, but attacks by aircraft from Britain's newest carrier, HMS *Formidable*, forced the Italians to withdraw. In the chase that followed, the Italian vessels started to outrun those of the British force. A fresh attack by Fairey Albacores from HMS *Formidable* slowed the Italian retreat, with an attack on the *Vittorio Veneto* causing damage which stopped the battleship for fifteen minutes and reduced her speed afterwards, while the cruiser *Pola* was also hit. A gun battle ensued, with the sinking of the *Pola* and two destroyers. Soon after this, in April,

1941, aircraft from HMS *Formidable* attacked Italian shipping at Tripoli.

Not all of the Royal Navy's successes were confined to the Mediterranean or to encounters with the Italian Navy, for engagements with the German Navy had been far from one-sided. The first opportunity to deploy naval air power effectively in an attempt to hunt down a major German warship came in May, 1941, in the North Atlantic. On 18 May, the German battleship *Bismarck* and her escorting heavy cruiser *Prinz Eugen* left Germany to raid North Atlantic commerce, but both ships were spotted three days later by a Royal Air Force reconnaissance aircraft while in the Korsfjord, near Bergen, and the following day detachments of the British Home Fleet were deployed in an attempt to bring the German ships to battle. After an encounter with two British capital ships, resulting in the loss of the British battle-cruiser, HMS *Hood* and all but three of her ship's company, on 24 May aircraft from HMS *Victorious* launched a torpedo attack on the *Bismarck*, although the torpedo hits did little apparent damage. The following day, Force H, under Vice-Admiral Somerville, RN, left Gibraltar in an attempt to deny the German vessels a safe retreat to a French port. Meanwhile, *Bismarck*'s location had been lost in bad weather. The ship was not rediscovered until spotted by an RAF Catalina flying-boat on 26 May, and that night aircraft from Force H's aircraft carrier, HMS *Ark Royal*, pressed home a torpedo attack at dusk, scoring two hits and causing severe damage to *Bismarck*'s steering gear. The ship was finally destroyed by gunfire from British battleships the following day, the *coup de grace* being delivered in a cruiser torpedo attack.

The Germans eventually had their revenge on HMS *Ark Royal*, which was sunk on 14 November east of Gibraltar after a torpedo attack the previous day by U-81. The loss of the ship—following slow flooding, with the boilers eventually being extinguished—was due more to poor design than to severe damage. If either the funnel trunking had been better designed or an auxiliary diesel generator had been fitted, the ship might have been saved. Only one member of her crew died in the incident.

The British successes at sea had not been matched on land, here the powerful German and Italian forces seemed to sweep everything aside in their steady advance across Europe and, for a while, North Africa. Although at the end of 1940 the Greeks had, with British help, fought off an attempted invasion by Italy, a more determined German attack on 6 April, 1941, succeeded, destroying the Royal Hellenic Air Force, and by 23 April, all Greek forces were faced with the alternative of surrender or leaving the country. In fact, many Greek combat units had been withdrawn to Crete with the retreating British forces, and the Germans invaded the island less than a month afterwards in one of the first major airborne assaults. Nevertheless, part of the RHAF survived to escape to British-held territory. The RAF formed them into a light bomber squadron, initially using Avro Ansons and then Bristol Blenheim IVs, and being deployed on reconnaissance duties.

The end of the German–Russian alliance came in June, 1941, with Operation Barbarossa carrying massive German forces across eastern Europe and into the Soviet Union, towards Moscow and Leningrad. The Red Fleet was attacked by German aircraft and warships, and pulled back as the German Army occupied increasing areas of Russian territory. In an attempt to help the Russian defence, the Royal Navy was soon involved in escorting many large convoys to Russia, facing heavy attack from German aircraft, surface vessels and submarines, and battling against severe weather in Arctic winter conditions. Not all of these operations were without success, however, and in particular Convoy HG76 under Commander J. F. ('Johnny') Walker, RN, one of the Royal Navy's greatest convoy experts, gave a good account of itself. Charged with the responsibility of looking after thirty-two merchantmen, with nine escort vessels, three destroyers and HMS *Audacity*, the Royal Navy's first escort carrier or CVE, between 14 and 23 December, 1941 Walker's force fought against twelve U-boats, sinking five for the loss of three merchant vessels, HMS *Audacity* and a destroyer. The price was certainly a high one to pay, but it must be remembered that the poor weather and few hours of daylight favoured the German submarines and presented the defending Royal Navy warships with no advantages at all!

Not every action could be presented as a success, and typical of the less successful ones was the attack by aircraft from HMS *Furious* and HMS *Victorious* on Petsamo and Kirkenes to the north of Finland and Norway in July, 1941, in which fifteen aircraft were lost to anti-aircraft fire for no great gain.

From the summer of 1940 onwards, the Germans had complete possession of the Atlantic and North Sea coasts of Europe, excluding only Iberia; and while the Luftwaffe attempted to destroy the Royal Air Force in the Battle of Britain and then British industrial bases in the blitzkrieg on major cities and ports, Marine Gruppe West of the Luftwaffe, based at Lorient in France, attempted to complement the efforts of the U-boat packs in blockading Britain. A small but effective force of Heinkel He115 seaplanes and Focke-Wulf Fw200 Condor maritime-reconnaissance landplanes was employed on this task, so that before long it became very unsafe for British coastal shipping to pass through the English Channel.

Clearly, it was to be some time before the tide could be turned, since the Royal Air Force and Royal Navy—some of whose pilots had been seconded to the RAF for the Battle of Britain—were simultaneously attempting to retain control of British airspace, maintain effective ASW patrols, keeping a watch for German surface raiders and also counter German anti-shipping aircraft. Even at best, the last-mentioned operation could only be partially successful, particularly once convoys were well beyond the reach of air cover from shore-based aircraft, and without the protection of the still-inadequate number of escort carriers. (These escort carriers, incidentally, carried Fairey Swordfish aircraft, which had been replaced aboard the attack carriers by the Fairey Albacore, although this aircraft was itself to be replaced by the Fairey Barracuda while the Swordfish soldiered steadily on to the end of the war!)

Royal Australian Air Force, Royal New Zealand Air Force and Royal Canadian Air Force personnel, aircraft, and sometimes whole squadrons, helped the RAF and the Fleet Air Arm in their struggle. And as well as its British-based operations with the Royal Air Force, the Royal Canadian Air Force in Canada operated Douglas DB–280 Digby and Lockheed Hudson landplanes, Boeing and Vickers-built Consolidated PBY–5 Catalina flying-boats, and PBY–5A Canso amphibians along Canada's Atlantic coast. The RCAF also maintained a relatively small anti-submarine presence on the Pacific Coast, and a Pacific Coast-based Bristol Bolingbroke was later to sink a Japanese submarine; but in general little activity came the way of Canadian forces in the Pacific during the war.

From its small strength of just 1,160 regular officers and men in September, 1939, the Royal New Zealand Air Force quickly expanded, with many personnel either acting as instructors for the Empire Air Training Scheme or joining RAF squadrons in Europe. However, because of the uncertainty already apparent in the Pacific at that time, a strong RNZAF presence was established in Fiji, including No. 4 Squadron with Vickers Vincents for ASW. These were later joined by additional Vincents and Short Singapore flying-boats, as well as the inevitable Hudsons, with no less than thirty-five aircraft of this type in RNZAF squadrons by late 1941.

The Royal Australian Air Force had allowed its first Sunderland flying-boat

squadron to be transferred to the Royal Air Force at the outbreak of war, and eventually there were nineteen Australian squadrons in the Royal Air Force, the first being No. 10 Squadron, RAF Coastal Command. RAAF squadrons also found themselves with Hudsons before long.

Not surprisingly, the South African Air Force entered World War II against Germany with equipment completely out of step with that of the other British Empire air forces. Initially its aircraft included Junkers Ju86 bombers, but by 1940 these were being replaced by Avro Ansons.

Following the collapse of the Netherlands, nine Fokker T. VIII–W seaplanes of the Netherlands Naval Air Service arrived in the British Isles to become No. 320 Squadron, Royal Air Force Coastal Command. This squadron was re-equipped with Avro Ansons as an interim step before Lockheed Hudsons were delivered in February, 1941.

The Americans had not been content simply to act as a large aircraft factory supplying crippled and blitzed Europe— or more correctly as the war progressed, a beleagured British Empire and expatriate European 'free' air arms. The generous Lend-Lease Programme to help Europe meant that the USA was far more than just another arms supplier. But while this scheme was well in line with their national temperament, the Americans were quick to realise the strong probability of becoming actively involved in the conflict themselves, and to foresee the possibility that war would not be confined to Europe, nor even to the North Atlantic and Mediterranean.

Wisely, once war was declared in Europe, the United States Navy was given full authority to hasten the expansion put in hand during the late 1930s. Of the 3,000 aircraft on order in 1939, only 1,800 were actually in service by mid-1940, bur during the second half of the year the strength of the USN's air element was raised by Congress first to 4,500 aircraft, then to 10,000, and finally, as German forces stormed across Europe,

to 15,000. In addition, the USN was authorised to buy forty-eight non-rigid airships or 'blimps' for ASW operations. The new aircraft introduced during this period included Brewster F2A Buffalo and Grumman F4F Wildcat fighters—the latter also having started to enter Fleet Air Arm service, where it was known at first as the Martlet, although later the USN nomenclature was adopted. There were also Douglas SBD Dauntless dive-bombers and TBD Devastator torpedo-bombers; Consolidated PBY-5 Catalina, PB2Y Coronado and Martin PBM Mariner flying-boats; and Vought–Sikorsky OS2U Kingfisher observation and reconnaissance seaplanes for operations from battleships and cruisers.

Even while these aircraft were joining their squadrons, the pace of development was such that other aircraft were already at the prototype stage, or even ready to enter production, including some of the most famous American-built aircraft of World War II, such as the Chance–Vought F4U Corsair and Grumman F6F

Hellcat fighters, the Curtiss–Wright SB2C Helldiver (to replace the Dauntless), and the Grumman TBF Avenger. The first US single-engined aircraft to offer a power-operated rear-gun turret and to be able to carry a 22-inch torpedo, the Avenger replaced the Devastator after the Battle of Midway as well as entering service with many non-American air arms, including, of course, the Fleet Air Arm, which received its first Avengers for anti-shipping and anti-submarine warfare duties in 1942.

Even before the United States entered the war, the USS *Wasp* was operating anti-submarine patrols and ferrying aircraft to Iceland for the United States Army Air Corps, which became the United States Army Air Force shortly before war broke out in the Pacific. The aircraft were flown off the ship while she steamed off the Icelandic coast. Meanwhile, the Atlantic Fleet of the USN operated air and surface patrols as far south as Trinidad, ensuring the safety not only of US shipping, but also of British

93

A Douglas Dauntless dive-bomber

A trials shot of the USS *Wasp*

and other Allied shipping while inside American territorial waters—and this at a time when almost all of the USN carriers were in the Pacific, with the exception of the newest vessel, the USS *Wasp*. In return for equipment, Britain was already allowing the United States the use of British bases on Caribbean and Pacific islands. In certain other instances, too, Lend-Lease was far from one-way. Certain items of British equipment and some British escort and frigate-sized vessels were transferred to the USN under 'Reverse Lend-Lease', so that British expertise in anti-submarine equipment could be shared by her ally.

The United States Navy had re-organised its Atlantic Fleet in February, 1941, under Admiral Ernest King, USN. This was a month before Congress finally passed the Lend-Lease Act and two months before US forces were garrisoned in Iceland to ensure that in the event of US involvement in the war a substantial area of the North Atlantic would be under American and British control. Aircraft supply started to build up rapidly as the manufacturers adjusted to a wartime level of demand, but even so, the number of aircraft in USN and USMC service by the end of the year amounted to just 5,260.

The USS *Wasp* entered service with the USN before America was drawn into World War II, commissioning in April, 1940. By that time the Washington Naval Treaty had been abandoned, even though it had in fact dictated the size of the ship, which was fundamentally an improved *Ranger*. An attractive vessel, she had a single funnel incorporated in the starboard island, and the arrangement of lifts, catapults and arrester wires was identical to that for the Yorktown vessels, even including the hangar catapult. Within a standard displacement of just 14,700 tons, she could carry some seventy aircraft, and her design speed was just under 30 knots. Obviously some sacrifices had to be made

American aircraft manufacturers maintained a preference for single-float seaplanes, with one of the finest examples being the Vought–Sikorsky OS2U observation seaplane

to achieve this remarkable specification, and these included minimal armour protection and relatively little anti-aircraft armament, even though internal subdivision for damage control was far superior to that of the *Ranger*.

Apart from delivering aircraft to Iceland, the USS *Wasp* performed the same role in the Mediterranean, delivering aircraft for the RAF to Malta twice, and then operating during the early days of US involvement in World War II as part of the Royal Navy's Home Fleet. Her work in the Mediterranean elicited the congratulations of the British wartime Prime Minister, Winston Churchill, in his famous message to the ship: "Who said a Wasp couldn't sting twice?"

The third ship of the Yorktown class, the USS *Hornet*, was still building as war broke out in the Pacific, but in 1940 Congress approved the first ships of a new class of large carriers, named after the lead ship, USS *Essex*, which were intended to be vastly improved versions of the *York-*

town. In contrast, the first escort carrier, or CVE, the USS *Long Island*, entered service with the USN in May, 1941, and was the first of a hundred such vessels for the USN and RN.

The normal wartime practice of incorporating the United States Coast Guard service within the United States Navy took place in November, 1941, by Presidential Decree, transferring valuable reinforcements for the USN's maritime-reconnaissance operations to Navy control. These included Hall PH–2 and PH–3, Consolidated PBY–5 Catalina, Viking OO–1 and General PJ–1 flying-boats; Douglas RD–4, Grumman JF–2, JRF–2 and J4F–1 amphibians; Curtiss SOC–4, Lockheed R30–1 and R50–1, and Waco JRW–1, Fairchild JK–1 and JK–2 landplanes. Also included were many ships suitable for escort and coastal patrol duties.

The Japanese had certainly not been idle during the period between the outbreak of war in Europe and the spread of war to the Pacific. Most of their energies had been directed towards completing the conquest of China, although this could never be wholly achieved, due to China's vast area and large population. However,

Japanese aircraft about to take off from a carrier, with a Mitsubishi A6M Zero nearest the camera

after the closure of the Burma Road into China in July, 1940, the country was largely subjugated, due mainly to the Japanese Naval Air Force obtaining and maintaining aerial superiority.

New ships and aircraft continued to enter Imperial Japanese Navy service at the same time. The aircraft were increasingly those which would fight World War II, of which the most famous was undoubtedly the Mitsubishi A6M2 Type O Model 11 fighter, the Zero-Sen, or to the Allies 'Zeke'. This was the aircraft that provided fighter cover for the Mitsubishi G3M2 bombers which continued to raid Changking and other Chinese cities. Other new types included the Aichi D3A1 Type 99 dive-bomber; Nakajima B5N1 Type 97–1 and Mitsubishi B5M1 Type 97–3 attack aircraft; Aichi E13A1 Type O three-seat reconnaissance seaplanes for operation from battleships, cruisers and seaplane carriers; Kawanishi H6K2 Type 97 flying-boats and Mitsubishi C5M2 Type 98 reconnaissance aircraft. These were followed in May, 1941 by the Mitsubishi G4M1 Type 1 land-based bomber.

The Japanese carrier fleet also developed, and, surprisingly in view of the lack of attention paid to such vessels by the British and Americans by this time, so did their small fleet of seaplane carriers. In fact two identical seaplane carriers, *Chitose* and *Chiyoda*, had entered service during 1938, in July and December respectively. Since Japan had still been observing the Washington Naval Treaty restrictions at the time these vessels were laid down, they were intended to provide reconnaissance support for the fleet, while the aircraft carriers were used on attack duties. These two vessels were undoubtedly among the finest seaplane carriers ever built, with a speed of just below 30 knots, an endurance far in excess of any other Japanese warship, and accommodation for the high figure of twenty-four seaplanes, which could be launched by four catapults and picked up by one stern and six amidships cranes. Tonnage was just 11,000 tons standard displacement, which seemed to be enough, possibly because the use of combined diesel and steam turbine machinery helped to reduce weight and

One of the finest seaplane carriers ever, the Japanese *Chitose* before conversion to an aircraft carrier

extend range at the same time. Seaplane accommodation on *Chitose* and *Chiyoda* was reduced by half in 1941, when both vessels were modified to carry midget submarines. Whether or not this was a good idea, they were converted into true aircraft carriers after Japan entered the war.

By coincidence, the other pre-war aircraft carrier classes included one of three vessels originally laid down as fast submarine tenders! The first ship, *Taigei*, was completed as a submarine tender in 1935, but proved to be such a disappointment that work was all but halted on the next two vessels, with the second vessel, *Tsurugisaki*, not entering service until 1939, while meanwhile the last vessel, *Takasaki*, was being converted as an aircraft carrier, and re-named *Zuiho*. The *Zuiho* was completed in December, 1940, after extensive modifications and the fitting of new engines. The result was a ship of 11,262 tons, of relatively narrow beam, which probably accounted in some part for its single hangar deck and lack of any island to maintain stability, and she was generally similar to the earlier *Ryujo*, with a navigating bridge forward below the flight deck. Although little armour-plating was incorporated, the anti-aircraft armament was fairly heavy. Speed was a nondescript 28 knots. *Tsurugisaki* was then converted, and reappeared as an air-

The Imperial Japanese Navy's aircraft carrier, *Shoho*, converted from a submarine depot ship

craft carrier, the *Shoho*, in January, 1942. The remaining vessel, *Taigei*, was also modified, in rather different form to give a displacement of 13,360 tons, and re-appeared as the aircraft carrier *Ryuho* in November, 1942. Her conversion was far less successful than that for her two sisters and she was only used operationally in desperation and then only for short periods in between lay-up—in the middle of a major conflict!

The Japanese completed just one other class of aircraft carrier in time for the out-break of war, the two sister ships *Zuikaku* and *Shokaku*. These broke away from Japanese carrier tradition in being large, fast and well-armoured vessels, for which the true British counterpart would have been the Illustrious class, although relatively little deck armour was fitted. In common with the earlier *Soryu*, they were fitted with a starboard island, but the twin funnels curved downwards rather than sloped. Three lifts were fitted, while arrester wires were placed fore and aft, but there has never been any indication that the Japanese found this kind of layout more satisfactory than did the British or the Americans. More than seventy aircraft could be accommodated on these two ships, which were probably the first air-craft carriers anywhere to have bulbous bows. This feature enhanced speed and stability with reduced drag, and contri-buted in no small measure to the impres-sive maximum speed of 35 knots.

Like the United States, Japan did not confine herself to equipment alone in the preparation for war, but also sought to consolidate her position by making more strategically-located bases available to her forces. After the fall of France, pressure was applied to the Vichy French to permit Japanese forces to use bases, particularly airfields, in French Indo-China (now Vietnam, Cambodia and Laos), and this was eventually conceded, although before long the Japanese found themselves able to use the whole territory much as they pleased.

The Tripartite Pact between Japan, Germany and Italy, signed on 27 Septem-ber, 1940, was followed on 13 April, 1941 by a Russo–Japanese Neutrality Pact, and the latter created some stability in relations between the two antagonists of the late 1930s.

These moves by the Japanese did nothing to lessen tension, and with grow-ing knowledge of Japanese atrocities in China, the United States retaliated by blocking Japanese assets in the United States. This meant that the Japanese could not afford to purchase crude oil or iron ore, and left them with the stark choice of either withdrawing from China or invading Dutch territories in the Pacific area to secure adequate supplies of crude oil, even though Japan held an eighteen month war emergency fuel stock. The Japanese were hardly likely to withdraw from China, and the one major problem in the way of any plan to seize the Dutch East Indies was the size and power of the United States Navy's Pacific Fleet. With unquestionable logic the Japanese de-cided that a major pre-emptive blow was required to reduce the US forces in the Pacific to a manageable size!

The main United States Naval base in the Pacific was that at Pearl Harbor, on the island of Oahu in Hawaii. On the night of 6–7 December, 1941, Vice-Admiral Nagumo approached the base through a bad weather zone, so escaping detection, with a powerful naval force, including the aircraft carriers *Akagi*, *Kaga*, *Hiryu* and *Soryu*, and the new *Shokaku* and *Zuikaku*, which had entered service the previous August and Septem-ber respectively. This force was protected by two battleships, three cruisers and a sizeable force of destroyers, although its real teeth were the 423 aircraft carried on the six aircraft carriers. (The Japanese and American forces in the Pacific were really even, but the Japanese envisaged the possibility that the United States might also be able to redeploy its Atlantic forces in the Pacific, and because of its superior industrial capacity could replace any losses quickly, and it was this possi-bility that made the elimination of the Pacific Fleet a temptation to Japan.) The

Pearl Harbor—an aerial view after the Japanese surprise attack on the US naval base

time of the attack had been well chosen, with eight out of the nine US Pacific Fleet battleships anchored in Pearl Harbor on the morning of 7 December, although unfortunately for the Japanese, the three aircraft carriers, USS *Lexington*, *Saratoga* and *Enterprise*, were at sea on exercises. Inadequate security precautions and defensive measures on the Americans' part also aided the Japanese, whose declaration of war could not be delivered in Washington until several hours after the attack.

So it happened that 350 of the Japanese aircraft took off from the carrier force and flew to Pearl Harbor, virtually unnoticed —a radar operator mistook their formation for a flock of birds—where they succeeded in blowing up the USS *Arizona*, sinking the USS *Oklahoma*, and also sinking the other battleships, USS *Virginia*, *Nevada* and *California*, although these sunk on an even keel and could later be refloated. Many other vessels were also exploded or sunk, and aircraft at the USN and USAAF air station were either destroyed on the ground or while attempting take-off to intercept the Japanese aircraft. All this was done for the loss of just twenty-three Japanese aircraft.

Defence analysts have since judged the operation to have been a partial failure, since the Japanese might have produced a better result if they had attacked harbour installations instead of warships. There is obviously considerable truth in this, because many of the ships were refloated and the base itself was never untenable. The ideal result for the Japanese would have been to destroy both ships and shore facilities, thus gaining both the temporary and the long-term advantages. However, the Japanese opted for the temporary advantage, while the analysts would presumably have opted for the long term.

It is perhaps worth recalling that the Royal Navy attempted both objectives in its attack on Taranto in November, 1940. In fact that operation was in many respects more devastating and successful than Japan's attack on Pearl Harbor, since it forced the Italians virtually to abandon the base for operations; and in proportion to the number of aircraft it employed it also caused far greater damage than the Japanese managed to inflict.

Three days after Pearl Harbor, the British battleship HMS *Prince of Wales*, and battle-cruiser HMS *Repulse*, under Rear-Admiral Phillips, were both attacked by Japanese aircraft flying from Saigon in Indo-China. After fighting off the first attack they were finally sunk by the second wave of Japanese aircraft. In part, this defeat was due to the decision to leave HMS *Hermes*, the small aircraft carrier attached to the force, behind in Singapore, while the two capital ships steamed along the Malayan coast.

By this time, the Japanese armies and amphibious forces were forging ahead in an attempt to gain every possible strategic advantage before the United States could attempt retribution, and before the end of December they had already added Wake Island in the Pacific to the list of their conquests. Yet, by tackling the United States and bringing her into the war, the Japanese had unleashed a whirlwind which would play a fundamental role in destroying both them and their allies in Europe.

The traumatic events of December, 1941, tend to overshadow other developments. One of the most important of them was the expansion of US naval aviation, which during that year had been all-embracing. In the very month of the attack on Pearl Harbor, a Naval Air Transport Service was founded, ready for operations to begin the following February, using Consolidated PBY Catalina and Martin PBM–3 transport flying-boats, with Douglas R4D and R5D, and Lockhead R50 aircraft. Indeed, in the war ahead, flying-boats were to prove highly effective for operations in areas without air stations or where runways were heavily damaged or too short for heavy aircraft—criteria which applied to much of the Pacific and most of its numerous islands.

The airship, too, was to play an important role, and while aircraft deliveries tended to fall behind the total authorised strength of the USN and USMC, all forty-eight of the pre-Pearl Harbor order for airships had entered service by late 1941, while others of the G, K and M classes were on order. One, K–74, was to be shot down by a U-boat operating on the surface during July, 1942, but although submarines were to be a major threat to the airship, these craft could generally operate safely in areas free from enemy aircraft, and no ship was ever lost from an airship-escorted convoy.

The active involvement of the United States in World War II meant that late 1941 was the end of the beginning, and although a long struggle lay ahead, it was also the beginning of the end for the Axis Powers!

6 The Carrier Fleets Clash

The dawn of 1942 saw the fortunes of the Allies at their lowest, with Germany and Italy in control of most of Europe and a substantial part of North Africa, and the Japanese, fresh from their victories over the British and American fleets, advancing across the Pacific and South-East Asia almost without a pause. Indeed, the speed of the Japanese advance was far ahead of anything experienced in Europe. Malaya and Singapore fell by mid-February and Burma in early March, while Sumatra was invaded on 14 February, followed shortly afterwards by Java. Meanwhile, the Japanese Naval Air Force's 11th Air Fleet, under Vice-Admiral Nishiyo Tsukahara, was already attacking the Philippines, using Mitsubishi G3M2 'Nell' and G4M1 'Betty' long-range bombers, supported by Zero fighters, operating from bases in Formosa. This was a softening up raid, making way for the main attack, and although the United States Army defending the Philippines fought heroically, it was eventually forced to retreat to the fortress island of Corregidor, close to Manila, where it endured some three hundred heavy bombing raids before finally surrendering.

The Imperial Japanese Navy's carrier force was kept busy during these first few months of war in the Pacific, with cover from the *Ryujo* for the landings at Palembang in Sumatra, and from the *Akagi*, *Soryu*, *Hiryu*, *Shokaku* and *Zuikaku* for the landings in Java. Dutch, British and American warships in the area assembled under the Dutch Admiral Karel Doorman in an attempt to stem the Japanese advance, but on March 1 suffered defeat in the Battle of the Java Sea. They had had to fight without any air cover, while the Japanese had the support of aircraft from the *Ryujo*, which helped to sink the British cruiser HMS *Exeter* and two destroyers.

Japanese confidence ran high at this time, and on 19 February Vice-Admiral Nagumo took a carrier force comprising the *Akagi*, *Kaga*, *Hiryu* and *Soryu* to mount a heavy aerial attack on Darwin, in the Australian Northern Territory. His fleet sank eleven merchant vessels and an American destroyer. Afterwards, the Japanese Fleet moved into the Indian Ocean, with the aircraft carriers *Akagi*, *Hiryu*, *Soryu*, *Shokaku* and *Zuikaku* raiding Ceylon during early March, while on 5 April, fifty aircraft from the Japanese carrier force sank the cruisers HMS *Cornwall* and HMS *Dorsetshire*. Then on 9 April, the veteran British aircraft carrier HMS *Hermes* was sunk by eighty Japanese bombers as she attempted to escape south from Japanese raids on Ceylon.

At first there was relatively little that the badly disorganised Allies could do. The American aircraft carriers USS *Enterprise* and USS *Yorktown* attacked Japanese bases in the Marshall Islands with little tangible result, while in May, British forces landed in Diego Suarez, in Madagascar, with strong naval support, including air cover from the carriers HMS *Indomitable* and HMS *Illustrious*, under the command of Rear-Admiral Syfret.

Somewhat earlier than this the rapid

An early victim of the war in the East was HMS *Hermes*

Japanese advance set a virtually insoluble problem to HMS *Illustrious* when she attempted to ferry aircraft to Singapore for the defending British forces. The *Illustrious* had to be diverted to Sumatra, since Singapore fell while she was still on passage; but even so, most of the aircraft she succeeded in taking there fell into Japanese hands when Sumatra fell in turn.

The Dutch had declared war on Japan on learning of the raid on Pearl Harbor, and they had not been kept waiting long before they too were attacked. But fortunately, many of the new Consolidated Catalina flying-boats, which had been delivered to the Netherlands East Indies Naval Air Service after the fall of the Netherlands, escaped to Australia, and then to Ceylon. Their Dutch aircrew were later to rejoin their comrades from Europe at the Dutch Flying School in the United States.

This was certainly a dark period for the Allies, with few signs of hope. On 12 February, three German capital ships, the *Scharnhorst*, *Gneisenau* and *Prinz Eugen*, were able to steam through the English Channel in poor weather, flaunting German strength in front of the British, who had always prided themselves on their ability to control this vital stretch of water during wartime. The three warships were not spotted until after they had passed through the Straits of Dover. However, in late afternoon in the poor light of a dull winter's day, Lieutenant-Commander Eugene Esmond, RN, took a formation of just six Fairey Swordfish into the air, in a desperate torpedo attack on the fast-moving and well armed Germans. But his slow-moving and obsolete aircraft fell a prey to the intensive

The Soviet war effort depended largely on British and American equipment and supplies, but amongst the Russian aircraft used were the Beriev Be–2 flying-boat

anti-aircraft fire of the warships, and all six of them were shot down, with only five aircrew being rescued from the total of eighteen in the flight. Lieutenant-Commander Esmond, among those lost, was awarded the Victoria Cross, post-humously.

The Allies were tightly stretched indeed, and even though the Soviet Union was by this time heavily engaged in the war against Germany, the new-found and unsolicited ally was in very many ways just another burden for the Western Allies to carry. Russian industry, in-efficient even before the German attack, could not provide for the needs of the Soviet armed forces, and the Royal Navy in particular had to devote much of its thinly spread resources towards protect-ing the convoys sailing north to Russia, and, somewhat ironically these convoys were carrying armaments which could have been used elsewhere in the battle to free Europe or Asia.

Even at this time, with frantic attempts being made to provide as many small escort carriers as possible, not every con-voy could enjoy the protection of carrier-borne aircraft. One such unlucky convoy was the PQ 17, although the Home Fleet with one aircraft carrier was not too far away from it. Unfortunately, both the ships in the convoy and the Home Fleet believed, wrongly, that the powerful German North Sea Combat Group was in the area, which suggested that the best chance of survival was to scatter the convoy, while the Home Fleet concen-trated on being ready for the expected battle. The convoy was duly scattered, and fell an easy victim to German sub-marines and aircraft. Twenty-three out of thirty-four merchantmen were lost, together with one of the three rescue ships, while the Germans lost only five of their aircraft. This mischance occurred between 2 and 13 July, 1942.

Between 12 and 18 September, a very different story was to emerge from convoy PQ 18, which consisted of forty-one merchantmen escorted by twenty-one vessels, including an aircraft carrier. This time three U-boats were sunk and forty aircraft destroyed. Even so, and with an incredibly heavy proportion of escorts to cargo vessels, this was achieved only at the cost of ten merchant vessels.

Life for those aboard convoys was no quieter in the Mediterranean, in spite of exceptional protective measures. Possibly no convoy ever enjoyed better protection than the Malta-bound convoy coded 'Operation Pedestal', between 10 and 15 August, 1942. Its fourteen cargo vessels and tankers were under the protection of the aircraft carriers HMS *Indomitable*, *Eagle* and *Victorious*, and the elderly HMS *Furious* (which was acting as an aircraft transport, with fighters to fly off to Malta), as well as the battleships HMS *Rodney* and *Nelson* and no less than seven cruisers and twenty-seven destroyers! Although the Italian Fleet was confined to harbour due to severe fuel shortages, and possibly still-vivid memories of earlier encounters with the Royal Navy and its Fleet Air Arm, determined Axis air, motor-torpedo boat and submarine

attack took a heavy toll of the ships in the convoy, striking escort and escorted alike. The submarine U–73 sank HMS *Eagle* with four torpedoes early in the afternoon of 11 August, while the cruisers HMS *Manchester* and *Cairo* and a destroyer were also sunk, along with no less than nine of the merchantmen. Severe damage was also done to HMS *Indomitable* and *Victorious* and two cruisers, as well as to almost all of the surviving cargo vessels and the solitary surviving tanker, *Ohio*.

The older carriers were generally being used as transports by this time. HMS *Argus* also took her share of this unglamorous duty, delivering twenty-four RAF Hawker Hurricane fighters to Murmansk in Russia, to help defend Soviet forces against heavy German air attack. Eight Royal Air Force Catalina flying-boats were also stationed at Archangel, to provide extra air cover for the vital convoys. Yet in spite of the effort devoted to aiding Russia, it was the vastness of the country and the severity of its winters—for which the Germans were

HMS *Eagle*, sinking after being torpedoed in a convoy bound for Malta

unprepared—that provided the ultimate defence and give the Russians eventual victory.

But as 1942 progressed, more positive victories were to come to the Allies, and in achieving these the aircraft carrier in all its forms came to play a vital role.

The heavy losses which the Allies had suffered in the Mediterranean, especially in keeping open the supply routes to the beleagured island of Malta, had not been in vain, for on 8 November, 1942, Allied Forces were able to land simultaneously at Algiers and Oran in Algeria and in French Morocco. Air cover for the landing at Oran came from the veteran HMS *Argus* and from an escort carrier, while Force H, with the aircraft carriers HMS *Furious*, *Victorious* and *Formidable*, patrolled the western Mediterranean to guard against any possibility of the Italian Fleet attempting to intervene to disrupt the landings. From HMS *Furious*, Supermarine Seafire fighters, carrier-borne developments of the famous Spitfire, flew long patrols to defend the British warships from air attack by Luftwaffe or Regia Aeronautica units. After the invasions, a number of Fleet Air Arm squadrons, with Fairey Swordfish and Albacores, were shore-based to provide support for the Allied ground forces rapidly advancing across North Africa.

By May of the following year the war in North Africa was over.

In early July, 1943, less than a year after the successful landings in North Africa, the Allies were poised to invade Sicily, landing on 10 July. Again Force H protected the invading forces from Axis counter-attack at sea, with the aircraft carriers HMS *Indomitable* and HMS *Formidable* providing air cover. In a little more than a month, the Axis Forces evacuated the island.

On 3 September, Italy concluded an armistice with the Allies, just six days before Allied forces landed at Salerno, in southern mainland Italy, with the support of one of the new American light fleet aircraft carriers, or CVLs, and four escort carriers. Yet again Force H, this time with HMS *Illustrious*, *Formidable* and *Unicorn*, providing air cover. Later Allied landings further north in Italy, at Anzio, were conducted without carrier-borne air cover.

Before the main assault on Italy at Salerno, other Allied units had already crossed the Straits of Messina from Sicily. Soon, the southern part of Italy was under the control of the Badoglio Government, which had negotiated Italy's surrender with the Allies, while in the north the German-occupied part of the country became the Republica Sociale Italiana, or RSI, and the remnants of the Regia Aeronautica became the Aviazione della RSI. Most of the Regia's aircraft, however, had been flown south on Italy's surrender to join the Allies as the Italian Co-Belligerent Air Force. While the Aviazione della RSI contributed its Savoia-Marchetti S.M.79 tri-motor bombers to the Axis anti-shipping forces in the Mediterranean, the changed overall situation in Italy meant that Axis forces were stretched even further.

One casualty of the surrender was the first and only Italian aircraft carrier, *Aquila*. Originally conceived in 1932, but later abandoned, the plan to build a carrier for the Italian Navy was revived after the start of war in Europe, when it was decided to convert the liner *Roma* into an escort carrier. However, a further change of mind lead to a fullscale and thorough conversion at Genoa, with the almost complete rebuilding of the vessel, including the fitting of new engines. Unusually, the flight deck of the new carrier overhung the stern but stopped short of the bows; but otherwise she conformed to accepted ideas, with a starboard island and the funnel incorporated into the superstructure. Two Heinkel catapults were positioned forward on the flight deck, with two lifts to the hangar, which had the unusual feature of accommodating part of the aircraft complement hanging from the deckhead! The planned aircraft capacity of just over fifty Reggiane Re.2001 fighter-bombers was artificially low, due to the lack of wing folding. The

23,500 ton vessel was intended to have a service speed of some 30 knots, and possessed the fine lines normally associated with Italian warship design.

Aquila was almost complete by 8 September, 1943, and on the following day— the day of the Salerno landings— was sabotaged by her crew to prevent her from falling into German hands.

Indeed, of the three Axis Powers, only Japan was able to send aircraft carriers to sea, this aspect of naval operations eluding the German and Italian navies. The 1919 Treaty of Versailles had originally forbidden Germany to have any air arm at all, but the London Naval Treaty of 1935 allowed her to build a total of 47,000 tons of aircraft carriers, with a maximum individual tonnage of 23,000 tons. She decided to build two such carriers, with the first, the *Graf Zeppelin*, being laid down in 1937 and the second in 1938. *Graf Zeppelin* was almost complete in 1940, when work was suspended, later to be restarted and then abandoned completely in 1943. Originally intended to be similar in appearance to the British *Glorious*, the *Graf Zeppelin* was designed to include a flight deck of almost full length, two Heinkel-designed catapults and three lifts to two hangars, while her long but rather low starboard island incorporated the funnel. Armour was intended to be light, and the vessel would have been extremely short on range, although possibly this would not have been a problem for operations in the Baltic, the North Sea and the North Atlantic. Some experts consider the vessel's planned aircraft capacity—about fifty aircraft—to have been low for the space provided, but the Messerschmitt Bf109 fighters and Junkers Ju87 Stuka dive-bombers would not have had wing-folding.

Although the *Graf Zeppelin* was scuttled at Stettin on 25 April, 1945, she was raised by the Russians, loaded with equipment and valuables looted from Germany, and towed to Leningrad. Some reports claim that she struck a mine on the way and was sunk, others that she

was refloated and later scrapped after being towed to Leningrad, while a third version allows an uneventful voyage to Leningrad and a trip to the breakers in 1948.

The second proposed German aircraft carrier, *Peter Strasser*, was abandoned in 1940 and scrapped on the slipway. Inter-service rivalry and the refusal of the Luftwaffe to allow the Navy to have its own integral air power, or to allocate squadrons for service at sea, sealed the fate of what would undoubtedly have been a useful and menacing, if limited, naval air arm.

Although actions between German and British surface vessels were far more numerous during World War II than in the earlier conflict, they were still relatively few and far between, with Hitler insisting that his prized battleships in the German High Seas Fleet should not be endangered. To sink vessels such as the *Graf Spee* or the *Bismarck* was very much a task of locating them and attempting to bring them to battle before they could seek the shelter of a friendly or at least neutral, port. While the Japanese would be at sea spoiling for a fight, the Germans only ever used their submarines in this way.

The battleship *Tirpitz* was sheltering in the Kaafjord in spring, 1944, and the only means of attack available to the Royal Navy, which had already attempted to attack the ship using X-craft (midget submarines), was the Fleet Air Arm, which had tried to attack the ship while she was at sea two years earlier. On 3 April, in appalling weather, Fairey Barracuda torpedo-bombers from HMS *Furious*, *Victorious*, *Searcher*, *Fencer*, *Pursuer* and *Emperor* flew in two strikes of twenty-one aircraft each, with an escort of eighty fighters—mainly Supermarine Seafires and Gruman Hellcats—to press home an attack which succeeded in damaging their quarry. However, the *Tirpitz* was not finally sunk until Avro Lancaster heavy bombers of the Royal Air Force's famous 617 'Dam Busters' squadron were able to attack her on 12 November, using 12,000 lb bombs. Even then, one senior naval officer suggested that she had not been sunk because the hull was not under water—she had in fact capsized!

Increasingly from this time on, the Fleet Air Arm and the Royal Navy generally became more heavily committed to operations in the Pacific. However, British maritime aviation still had some work left to do in Europe, following the invasion of France—Operation Overlord—on 6 June, 1944. Although no aircraft carriers were involved in this campaign, four Fleet Air Arm Seafire squadrons were attached to the 2nd Allied Tactical Air Force, the Royal Air Force component supporting the Allied advance through France and the Low Countries towards Germany.

The United States Marine Corps also nearly became involved in this campaign, with a group equipped with Chance–Vought Corsair fighters trained in the use of 11·75-inch Tiny Tim rockets for use against the German 'V' weapon sites in the Netherlands and Belgium. However, the sites were overrun by Allied ground forces before the squadrons could be sent to Europe.

By this time, air-to-surface rockets had already been used on anti-submarine duties, as well as against enemy ground positions, vehicles and tanks. The first naval rocket success of the war had come in May, 1943, when Sub-Lieutenant Horrocks, RN, flying from the escort carrier HMS *Archer*, sank U–752.

ASW remained vital in the North Atlantic to the end of the war in Europe, but as the war progressed, so did the means of countering the submarine menace. Royal Air Force Coastal Command, which earlier had placed Wellington bombers on long-range maritime-reconnaissance duties, to help the Short Sunderlands and Consolidated Catalinas on the longer patrols while gradually phasing out the shorter-range Avro Ansons, eventually started to introduce Boeing B–17 Flying Fortress and Consolidated B–19 Liberators to operate alongside the Lockheed Hudsons that were employed in protecting convoys.

Although by this time the Luftwaffe was outnumbered and overstretched, it was still a formidable force. Out of well over 100 aircraft on long-range operations from northern Italy, more than fifty were Dornier Do217 and Heinkel He177 heavy bombers, with radar-controlled glider bombs available for anti-shipping operations. Some 200 anti-shipping aircraft were also available in the south of France, while in the north of France on 'D' day, there were fifty torpedo-equipped Junkers Ju88 bombers prepared for anti-shipping operations against the Allied invasion fleet; but such operations were not maintained for long due to a worsening shortage of fuel.

On the other side of the world, in the Pacific, the Japanese advance was stopped relatively quickly and then put into reverse. This did not mean that the Americans escaped further loss after Pearl Harbor, however, and an early casualty was the original American aircraft carrier, the USS *Langley*, sunk by Japanese aircraft in February, 1942, while delivering thirty-two Curtiss P–40E fighters from Australia to Java.

An early spectacular success, measured in terms of its effect on Japanese and American morale, was the daring raid on 18 April, 1942, by sixteen USAAF North American B–25 Mitchell bombers on the Japanese cities of Tokyo, Kobe, Yokohama and Nagaya. To achieve this token gesture, intended primarily to undermine Japanese confidence, the aircraft had to take off from the USS *Hornet*, America's newest carrier, fly 700 miles to make their raid, and then go on to land in China. *Hornet*'s sister ship, USS *Enterprise*, provided fighter cover for both vessels and for the bomber aircraft. One beneficial effect of the attack was to force the Japanese not only to strengthen their fighter defences, but also to divert bomber aircraft from the Pacific campaign to raiding the remaining airfields in China, so that they would not be available should the Americans plan a repeat raid.

The first tangible naval victory for the United States Navy in the Pacific, in

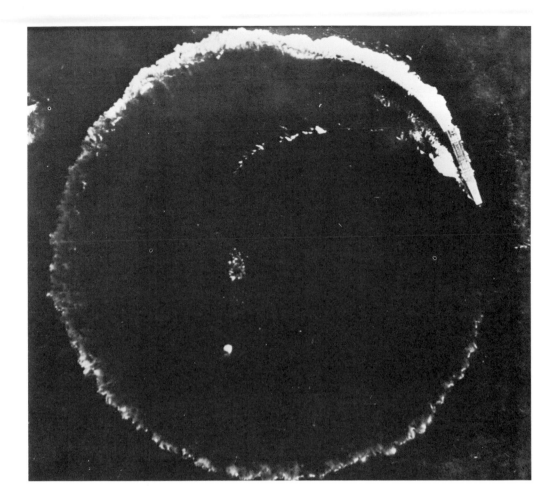

which carrier-borne aircraft played a major role, came in the Coral Sea, between New Guinea and the Solomon Islands in the early May of 1942. A Japanese fleet approached the area intent on invading Port Moresby in New Guinea, a convenient stepping stone for an attack on Australia. The Japanese warships included the aircraft carriers *Shoho*, *Zuikaku* and *Shokaku*, with a total of 125 aircraft, while the defending American Task Force 17 had the two carriers, USS *Yorktown* and USS *Lexington*, with 141 aircraft.

Aircraft from the USS *Yorktown* surprised the Japanese warships on 4 May, sinking a destroyer, but Task Force 17 spent the following day trailing the *Shoho* and her escorts, which were diverting the

The Japanese aircraft carrier *Shoho* circles to avoid American bombs during the Battle of the Coral Sea

Americans' attention while the main force slipped into the Coral Sea. On 6 May, the two main fleets, unaware of each other's proximity refuelled at sea while only some seventy miles apart! The Battle of the Coral Sea started in earnest on 7 May, with aircraft from TF17 attacking the *Shoho*, scoring as many as seven torpedo hits and eleven bomb hits with bombs of between 500lb and 1,000lbs, and sinking the vessel within ten minutes. Sixty Japanese aircraft from the *Zuikaku* and *Shokaku* meanwhile attacked TF17, sinking two vessels, but shaken by the early loss of the *Shoho* and the increasingly unfavourable odds, the Japanese High Command recalled the troopships. That night, the two opposing fleets were so close that six Japanese aircraft attempted to land on the USS *Yorktown*. Both fleets, by this time 200 miles apart, attacked each other simultaneously the following morning, with some ninety Japanese and eighty USN aircraft in the air. The *Zuikaku* sought refuge in a squall, but the *Shokaku* suffered serious damage and was forced to withdraw for repairs, while the USS *Lexington* was torpedoed in the Japanese attack, and some hours later was ripped apart by a petrol vapour explosion due to its fuel lines having been ruptured in the attack.

While the loss of the USS *Lexington* outweighed the loss of the *Shoho*, the effect on the respective fleets meant that the Americans had come off best. Not only had they foiled a Japanese invasion attempt, but they were also better placed to replace vessels, aircraft and aircrew. And strange as it may seem, the Japanese Naval Air Force was already beginning to feel the strain by this time, having lost a quarter of its front-line aircraft between December, 1941, and May, 1942. Futhermore, even at this early stage, the delivery of new Japanese aircraft and the training of new Japanese pilots was only just ahead of losses. The long time that Japan had had to prepare for war and the relatively easy success of the Chinese campaign, had meant that she had never built a training organisation capable of producing large numbers of pilots quickly; nor had she the industrial capacity of Britain or America, or possibly even of Canada. The Allies, who had had to expand quickly, created a vast training organisation, and kept it working.

It took a major effort by the Japanese aircraft industry to provide sufficient numbers of Mitsubishi A6M2 'Zeke' Zero-Sen fighters, Nakajima B5N2 'Kate' attack aircraft and Aichi D3A2 'Val' dive-bombers to bring the aircraft carriers *Akagi*, *Hiryu*, *Soryu* and *Kaga*, *Hosho* and *Zuiho*, *Ryujo* and *Junyo*, up to their full aircraft complement for two major opera-

tions Japan was about to launch. One of these was to be a raiding force destined for the Aleutians, and this was intended to draw Allied attention away from the other, and main, operation—an attack on the strategic Pacific island of Midway, in mid-Pacific between Japan and the United States. The USN commander in the Pacific, Admiral Nimitz, was alerted to the Japanese intention to invade Midway, and divided his available forces into two powerful Task Forces, 16 under Rear-Admiral Spruance, with the USS *Enterprise* and *Hornet*, and 17 under Rear-Admiral Fletcher, with the USS *Yorktown*.

On 3 June, the Aleutians raiding force under Vice-Admiral Hosogaya with the carriers *Ryujo* and *Junyo*, attacked Dutch Harbour in the Aleutians, off Alaska. The Americans were not fooled by this, and Midway-based USAAF Boeing B-17 Flying Fortress heavy bombers attempted to attack the Japanese Midway force, but without success. By this time, that force had been divided into three groups: Vice-Admiral Nagumo's carrier group, with carriers *Akagi*, *Kaga*, *Hiryu* and *Soryu*, and their 270 aircraft; Admiral Yamamoto's battle group, with the carrier *Hosho* and a strong force of capital ships; and Vice-Admiral Kondo's assault force, with the *Zuiho* and twelve transports.

The opposing fleets clashed on 4 June, using aircraft, and while more than 100 Japanese aircraft flew to attack Midway, some fifty USN and USAAF aircraft based on the island flew to attack the Japanese fleet, with both sides achieving little. Nagumo's reconnaissance aircraft had already warned him of the presence of US carriers in the area, and he had wisely held back more than half of his aircraft to counter the US air attack if it materialised, confident in the knowledge that the Americans had little available to match his Zero fighters. On the carriers of the day, however, it was necessary to clear most aircraft off the flight deck before other aircraft could land on it, and the Americans attacked as the Japanese carriers were returning their fighters

to their hangars, ready to receive the returning aircraft from the Midway raid. Spruance sent the entire force of Grumman Wildcat fighter, Douglas Dauntless dive-bomber and Devastator torpedo-bomber aircraft from the USS *Enterprise* and *Hornet*, while Fletcher sent half of the available aircraft from the USS *Yorktown*, making a grand total of 156 aircraft, although thirty-five out of the first forty-one torpedo-bombers were shot down by Japanese fighters or anti-aircraft fire. The second wave of US dive-bombers scored direct hits on *Kaga*, *Soryu* and *Akagi*, all of which sank later in the day! *Hiryu* escaped detection at first and her aircraft found the USS *Yorktown*, bombed and torpedoed her, and left her crippled. Later, aircraft from the USS *Enterprise* dive-bombed *Hiryu*, and after a long battle with the ensuing fires, she was abandoned the following day and finally sunk by Japanese destroyers using their torpedoes.

Hiryu on fire after being attacked during the Battle of Midway; the port-side island can be seen clearly

The USS *Yorktown* was finally sunk on 7 June, despite desperate efforts to save her, following a Japanese submarine attack.

The three Japanese carriers actually sunk by USN aircraft were lost largely due to fires spreading throughout the vessels and igniting aviation fuel—the result of poor armour protection and minimal damage-control training for Japanese naval personnel, the latter being a fault that the British and Americans always studiously avoided. The Japanese lost some 300 aircraft at Midway. Forty-two of them were lost in aerial combat, and most of the remainder with their ships, or to anti-aircraft fire!

The Battle of Midway left the Japanese carrier fleet in a decidedly depleted state, and thereafter the Japanese effort was to

The USS *Yorktown* on fire at the height of the Battle of Midway

be concentrated increasingly on defence rather than offence. Nevertheless, in July, 1942, the Imperial Japanese Navy amalgamated its forces into the Combined Fleet, in an attempt to regroup its shattered forces into a viable mobile attack force.

New aircraft carriers continued to enter service, and throughout the war, the Imperial Japanese Navy was to receive new aircraft carriers of one kind and another, even though there were no large classes such as the British Illustrious and Colossus, or the American Essex and Independence classes, and no escort carriers as such. Indeed, one might be excused for believing that the Japanese never really decided on a definitive carrier design, since some of the evidence suggests that they were inordinately fond of modification for its own sake, including, for example, the modification of the Chitose class seaplane carriers to handle midget submarines.

One of the new aircraft carriers had already entered service in time for the Midway and Aleutians operations, taking part in the latter. That vessel, the *Junyo*, had the distinction of being the largest serving aircraft carrier to have been converted from a merchant vessel, only the stillborn Italian *Aquila* having been larger. Designed to a standard displacement of 24,000 tons, *Junyo* was based on a passenger liner hull requisitioned in August, 1940, while still under construction. Although the conversion started at an early stage of construction and allowed both an upper and a lower hangar deck to be fitted (but with restricted headroom in both), the original liner machinery was retained, and this meant that the *Junyo*, despite her lack of armour protection, tended to be rather slow, with a speed of just 24 knots; and since she was without a catapult, some difficulty was found in flying off aircraft in light wind conditions.

The vessel was one of the more conventional Japanese carriers in appearance, with two lifts serving the hangars and a starboard side island incorporating a funnel, although this was angled outwards.

Junyo entered service in May, 1942, and was followed in late July by her sister ship, *Hiyo*.

The two seaplane carriers, *Chitose* and *Chiyoda*, were also converted into aircraft carriers after *Chitose* had been damaged in battle. The latter vessel reappeared as an aircraft carrier in November 1943, while her sister had returned to service with the same modifications just a month earlier. Both vessels had a standard tonnage as carriers of just over 11,000 tons, and conformed to the Japanese style of completely flat-topped aircraft carrier, with a starboard downward-pointing smokestack. The funnel for the diesel machinery, unique to this class of carrier, was positioned in the same way, but aft of that for the boilers. A reasonable 29 knots could be attained by the unusual diesel and steam machinery, and thirty aircraft could be accommodated aboard.

One of the most conventionally designed Japanese carriers, the *Taiho*, was also the last vessel to be laid down before the attack on Pearl Harbor, and had the war continued for longer than it did, she might have proved to be the lead ship of a class, since halfway through the war the Imperial Japanese Navy decided to mount a carrier construction programme based on the two most successful existing designs. However, the shortage of suitable shipyard accommodation prevented full implementation of the programme, and no further vessels of the Taiho class were ever constructed. A large, fast carrier of 29,000 tons, the *Taiho* was laid down in 1941 and completed in March, 1944, having a service speed of 33 knots and accommodation for more than sixty aircraft. She had a starboard side island incorporating a funnel which was still angled outwards in typical Japanese fashion, and her bow, plated up to the flight deck, gave her a very British appearance. However, armour plating of the flight deck extended only between the two lifts, and hangar floor; end and side armour was minimal, while the anti-torpedo protection was some ten feet inboard of the hull. Additional concrete protection was fitted around the fuel tanks. The total weight of armour gave the vessel a considerable draught for her tonnage—more than thirty-one feet—and put the lower hangar deck on the level of the waterline.

The other standard design, and the only one to have any number of vessels built to it, was the Unryu class, of which the nameship was laid down in 1942, together with two sister ships. Three more were laid down in 1943 and never completed, and plans were in hand for a further five. In essence, the class was almost identical to the *Hiryu* of 1939, but

Most Japanese aircraft carriers were one-off vessels, with *Unryu* being one of the few class leadships

the islands were all on the starboard side. *Unryu* entered service in August, 1944, and was followed within days by her identical sister, *Amagi* (originally the name of an ill-fated sister of *Akagi*), and in October, by *Katsuragi*, a close sister, but some two knots slower at 32 knots. Two more Unryu class vessels were building at the end of the war, the *Kasagi* and the *Ikoma*, while another of the almost identical Katsuragi class, the *Aso*, was also building.

To this day, the Japanese retain the distinction of building the largest aircraft carrier ever to enter service outside the United States—the *Shinano*, 65,000 tons, converted from the third and last giant battleship of the Yamato class. A large

starboard side island with an angled funnel to match gave the vessel a faint resemblance to the American USS *Saratoga* and *Lexington*, although on *Shinano* the battleship hull lines remained more in evidence. Some of the battleship hull armour was removed, however, and the armoured flight deck area was again confined, as on *Taiho*, to the areas between the two lifts. Speed was a poor 27 knots, but in fact *Shinano* never had an opportunity to prove herself. While she was completing near Tokyo in November, 1944, it was decided to move her to Kure to avoid the increasingly heavy and daring Allied air attack; and while on passage to Kure she was torpedoed by the submarine USS *Archerfish*. The combined result of

One of the first Essex-class vessels was a new USS *Yorktown*

four torpedo hits and poor damage control meant that the largest-ever non-American aircraft carrier sank within hours of her being attacked on 29 November!

There was less variety in the American wartime aircraft carrier programme, which concentrated on two classes, the large Essex class of 27,000 tons and the smaller, light fleet or CVL, Independence class of 14,000 tons. There were some individual variations within these classes, and all of the later Essex class vessels exceeded the original standard displacement by more than a thousand tons.

Design of the Essex class started in 1939, largely to provide an improved Yorktown class, and the entire class of thirty-two vessels was approved and laid down between 1940 and 1944, although the final seven were never built and many of the others were delayed as the war reached its end. A large and even pyramidal island on the starboard side incorporated the funnel, while three lifts, including one on the deck edge, and two catapults helped these large vessels handle more than a hundred aircraft. A maximum speed of 33 knots could be attained. Heavy defensive armament was provided, but relatively light flight-deck armour remained an American carrier characteristic, with the main armour on the hangar deck. The first of these vessels, the USS *Essex*, entered service on the last day of 1943, but before another year had passed another six vessels, the USS *Lexington, Yorktown, Bunker Hill, Intrepid,* a new *Wasp* and a new *Hornet,* had entered service. In common with the Royal Navy, the United States Navy has always tended to perpetuate warship names, as several other navies also do so to a lesser extent.

Yet even with a construction programme capable of completing six large aircraft carriers within a year and a further programme of escort carrier conversion, the United States Navy still required extra carriers quickly, and it was decided that conversion of some of the Cleveland class light cruisers would provide nine light fleet carriers with the right combination of speed and aircraft accommodation. The design had its limitations, with a wooden flight deck and poor hangar accommodation for the planned complement of aircraft; and aft of the small starboard island were four very small and low funnels, although these and the island were clear of the flight deck. The maximum speed of the vessels was a reasonable 31 knots. Two catapults helped in launching the heavier aircraft, but the original forty-five aircraft soon had to be reduced to nearer thirty, and whenever possible these vessels operated only with fighters—Grumman Wildcats or Hellcats, or Chance–Vought Corsairs—leaving off the dive-bomber or torpedo-bomber squadrons.

Sister ships of the British HMS *Illustrious* continued to enter service during the war years, with many modifications and improvements incorporated in the fifth and sixth vessels, HMS *Indefatigable* and HMS *Implacable.* In addition, a shortened, lower-powered version of the class was built in HMS *Unicorn,* intended primarily as a 'Fleet Air Arm Supply and Repair Ship', or fleet maintenance carrier. She had few aircraft of her own, but was intended to provide a full maintenance support for up to four Illustrious class vessels when operating far from shore bases for extended periods. Armour protection was still provided, but the service speed of the ship was just 24 knots. Completed in March, 1943, HMS *Unicorn*

spent her first few months as an operational fleet carrier before passing to her intended duties. There she proved to be a success, enabling the fleet carriers to operate at maximum pitch for longer than might otherwise have been possible under intensive warfare conditions.

Although the British planned a new large carrier design during the war, none of these vessels was completed until some time after World War II ended. However, the British interpretation of the light fleet concept was able to prove itself before hostilities ended, even though most of the many vessels built to this design were not completed until the post-war period. Rather than using a converted hull form, the British light fleets were built as carriers from the keel upwards, but merchant navy standards of construction were applied to permit construction in many more shipyards than might otherwise have been able to handle carrier work. To keep weight down, armour and armament was kept to the minimum, while a maximum speed of just 25 knots was considered sufficient, and machinery and equipment generally was also kept to a simple minimum. These differences apart, the vessels looked like smaller versions of conventional carriers, and followed British practice in having a starboard island incorporating a single large funnel, and hull and bows plated up to the flight deck. The first five vessels, HMS *Colossus, Venerable, Vengeance, Glory* and *Ocean,* together with another two built as maintenance carriers, were ready for service during late 1944 and early 1945. Altogether ten vessels were laid down to the original design and another six to a modified and slightly larger one. The latter vessels had 16,000 tons standard displacement against the original 13,000 tons, and after the war they operated in no less than seven navies apart from the Royal Navy! Aircraft accommodation, planned for twenty-four aircraft, could frequently be stretched on the original version to almost forty Corsairs and Fairey Barracudas.

While these massive carrier construction programmes were in hand, innova-

A Kawanishi H8K2 Type 2 'Emily' long-range reconnaissance and attack flying-boat

tion was also the order of the day for the Japanese Naval Air Force. On 4 March, 1943, Kawanishi H8K2 Type 'Emily' four-engined reconnaissance flying-boats, used for an attack on Hawaii, refuelled en route to their target from a submarine, using a secret rendezvous at French Frigate Shoals!

The Japanese were still licking their wounds from their ill-fated Midway attack when the United States, prompted by Japanese airfield construction on Guadalcanal, in the Solomons, which could have posed a threat to Australia–United States convoys, launched an invasion of this strategic island. As well as carrier-borne aircraft, the Guadalcanal campaign employed USN, USMC, USAAF and Royal New Zealand Air Force land-based aircraft, and before embarking on the invasion, the Allies hastily constructed an airfield on the island of Esperitu Sanctu. The campaign started in earnest on 7 August, 1942, with Rear-

Admiral Turner, USN, landing the 1st US Marine Division on the islands of Guadalcanal and Tulagi, while Rear-Admiral Crutchley, RN, headed a force of eight cruisers and fifteen destroyers to provide covering fire, and Vice-Admiral Fletcher, USN, commanded the main naval force of carriers and battleships, with escorts. The carriers were the USS *Saratoga*, *Enterprise* and *Wasp*. The invading Americans scored many early successes, and captured the newly-completed airfield. Renamed Henderson Field, it remained as the focal point for fierce fighting for some months afterwards.

The Japanese, who were naturally forced to respond quickly to this attack, sent fast troop transports and a strong naval force, including Vice-Admiral Nagumo's carriers, the *Shokaku* and

The Japanese carrier *Zuiho* hit by torpedoes

Zuikaku, with 137 aircraft aboard, while the small *Ryujo* operated in a diversionary role. On 24 August, aircraft from the USS *Saratoga* bombed and torpedoed the *Ryujo*, sinking her, while Japanese aircraft caused only slight damage to the USS *Enterprise*. A few weeks later, however, as the campaign dragged on, the Japanese submarine I-19 torpedoed and sank the USS *Wasp*—the original vessel of this name—and an escorting destroyer, but when the Japanese later landed troops on Guadalcanal, they did so without any carrier aircraft cover of their own!

Another battle in the area was not long in coming. Believing, wrongly, that Henderson Field had been recaptured and that the US forces on Guadalcanal were in retreat, the Japanese sent a strong carrier force to the area to wipe out the last remnants of the American invasion force. Vice-Admiral Kondo was in the van of the fleet with a strong battleship force and the carrier *Junyo* with fifty-five aircraft, while the main fleet was under Vice-Admiral Nagumo, with 160 aircraft spread over the carriers *Shokaku*, *Zuikaku* and *Zuiho*. Against this, the Americans, under Vice-Admirals Murray and Kinkaid, could only muster the USS *Enterprise* and *Hornet*, with 170 aircraft, although another sixty aircraft were based at Henderson Field. The two fleets met in the Battle of the Santa Cruz Islands on 26 October, when early damage was done to the *Zuiho* by American reconnaissance aircraft and the *Shokaku* was later seriously damaged and put out of action for several months. In addition, Japanese aircraft losses soared past the hundred mark, largely due to effective American anti-aircraft fire. Nevertheless, while the Japanese were forced to withdraw, the main loss in the battle was on the American side. The still new USS *Hornet* had to be abandoned after aircraft from the

Junyo and *Zuikaku* scored seven bomb and two torpedo hits within seven minutes, and two other Japanese aircraft crashed onto the carrier's deck. The vessel was later sunk by American destroyer torpedoes, although another Japanese attack was mounted on the sinking vessel after the destroyers had departed.

The loss of the USS *Wasp* and *Hornet* was soon made good with the new ships of the Essex class carrying these already honourable names.

A further major naval battle occurred off Guadalcanal on November 12, 13 and 14, with aircraft from the USS *Enterprise* sinking the crippled Japanese battleship *Hiei* on 13 November, and the cruiser *Kinugasa* the following day.

These battles showed the Zero-Sen to be finally outclassed by American aircraft, including the new Grumman Hellcat fighter which had replaced the Wildcat. An improved Zero, the Mitsubishi A6M3 Type O Model 32, had been rushed to the Solomons, along with a float-variant, the A6M2–N Type 2 'Rufe',

for operations in areas where airfields were either non-existent or untenable. In some cases, airfields were fast becoming a luxury, and Mitsubishi F1M2 Type O 'Pete' observation seaplanes had been used as fighters.

On the American side, with new aircraft and renewed confidence, the first USN fighter ace had appeared, Captain Joe Foss, USN, who shot down twenty-six aircraft in sixty-three days while flying a Hellcat in the Guadalcanal campaign.

One fundamental difference between the Japanese conduct of the war and that of the Allies, was the lack of protection the Japanese afforded to their convoys, and the lack of interest they took in convoy attack. They were always mainly interested in engaging the enemy fleet rather than in cutting off his supplies. While the first US convoy carrier escort group, centred around the CVE USS *Bogue* with nine Grumman F4F–4 Wildcats and twelve TBF Avengers, did not

A Fleet Air Arm Grumman Hellcat lands on an escort carrier

appear until April, 1943, the Americans had, in fact put considerable effort into convoy protection much earlier. The Avenger was one of the first real carrier-borne anti-submarine aircraft, but it was also available for torpedo-attack duties, and had established some notable achievements, as when twenty-two USMC TBM–1C Avengers flew 3,400 miles across the Pacific, from Esperitu Sanctu to Guam via four refuelling points, to provide additional portection against Japanese submarines in the area. The USN also provided eight squadrons of Consolidated PBY–5 Catalina flying-boats for anti-submarine duties in the North Atlantic, basing these in Britain under RAF control. It also had an airship detachment based on Brazil—once that country entered the war—for South Atlantic convoy protection, and land-planes and flying-boats on both coasts of the United States.

The growing numbers of escort carriers, intended mainly for convoy escort duties, training and aircraft transport, soon started to appear in the assault role, providing cover for invading marine and army units, and making a far more significant contribution to the war effort than their designers had ever anticipated. Escort carriers provided such cover for invasion forces in the Pacific and in the Mediterranean, although their short flight decks, coupled with the light breezes of the Mediterranean, meant that they were not as satisfactory in Mediterranean operations as in the Pacific, where heavily-armed aircraft could take-off more easily.

One of the more notable new aircraft on the Allied side to appear at this time was the Chance-Vought F4U Corsair, delivered to the US Navy, US Marine Corps, and the Fleet Air Arm, as well as to many air forces, including the Royal New Zealand Air Force in the Pacific. Less significantly, in 1943, the Fleet Air Arm started to replace its Albacores with Barracudas and Avengers.

Strangely, in view of the fact that one-third of the Guadalcanal campaign ground attack aircraft had been flown by USMC personnel, the US commander in the Pacific, Admiral Nimitz, decided in 1943 to omit carrier training from the training requirement for USMC pilots. This decision left the USMC aircraft on the sidelines in the campaigns of late 1943 and early 1944.

The USN took an increasingly offensive role as 1943 progressed. In May, a task force under Rear-Admiral Kinkaid retook Attu in the Aleutians, with the help of just one escort carrier, and CVEs were again much in evidence for the retaking of Rendova Island, near New Georgie, in early July. Then in the autumn, repeated USN attacks on Rabaul in New Britain —first on 5 November with the USS *Saratoga* and *Princeton* (one of the first Independence class light fleet carriers) and then on 11 November with the USS *Essex, Bunker Hill* and *Independence*— meant that Rabaul could no longer be regarded by the Japanese as a suitable naval base. The attack on Rabaul had been the operational debut not only of the light fleet carriers but also of the new Curtiss SB2C–1 Helldiver dive-bomber, which from this time on started to replace the older Douglas Dauntless on the attack carriers.

Other elements of naval air power were not being neglected, and in a war that still placed much importance on the battleship and cruiser, the Curtiss SC–1 Sea Hawk was replacing the older Vought–Sikorsky OS2U Kingfisher and Curtis SO3C Seamew aboard these ships.

A large part of the central Pacific was still under firm Japanese control, and on 19 November, 1943, a massive US effort was made to take the Japanese-held Gilbert Islands. The attack was under the command of Vice-Admiral Spruance with Rear-Admiral Pownall commanding the carrier force, which consisted of US carriers *Yorktown, Lexington, Enterprise, Essex, Bunker Hill*, and *Saratoga*, the light fleet carriers USS *Independence, Princeton, Monterey, Belleau Wood* and *Cowpens*, and the now inevitable CVEs, with seven hundred aircraft! Within twenty-four hours, this force gave the

Americans aerial supremacy. Nevertheless, the USS *Independence* suffered heavy damage from a torpedo attack by a Japanese submarine, while the escort carrier USS *Lipscombe Bay*, was sunk by the submarine I–175 on 24 November.

Attention was next turned to the comparatively nearby Marshall Islands, and starting on 29 January, 1944, US Task Force 58 under Vice-Admiral Mitscher attacked Japanese airfields in the area. At his disposal were more than seven hundred aircraft, operating from the aircraft carriers USS *Enterprise, Yorktown, Essex, Intrepid, Bunker Hill* and *Saratoga*, and the light fleet carriers USS *Belleau Wood, Princeton, Langley, Cowpens, Monterey* and *Cabot*. (Out of the nine Independence class vessels, the USS *Langley* and *Cabot* were the sixth and seventh to be completed, but the first two to have been laid down as carriers rather than converted from cruisers during construction.) The attack on the Japanese airfields was maintained into early February, and on 31 January American forces landed on the nearby Kwajalein Atoll.

Both Rabaul, in New Britain, and the Marshall Islands proved difficult areas for the advancing Allies, and generally the Japanese forces on the islands had to be neutralised by bombing, due to the difficulty of actually occupying the islands.

On 17 February, part of the US Fifth Fleet under Vice-Admiral Spruance led the assault on Truk Atoll, further west, using the USS *Essex, Enterprise, Yorktown, Intrepid, Bunker Hill, Belleau Wood, Cabot, Monterey* and *Cowpens*. Carrier aircraft sank the Japanese cruiser *Naka*, and in addition the Japanese lost twenty-six merchant vessels and 300 out of their strength of just under 400 aircraft based on Truk. Many of these losses were attributable to American aircraft, although a number were accounted for by surface vessels. A counter-attack by seven Japanese torpedo-bombers resulted in some damage to the USS *Intrepid*.

Before February was out, US carrier groups had also attacked the Marianas, midway between Truk and Japan.

The Allied position in the Pacific was strengthened during this period by the arrival of British aircraft carriers. During April, 1944, aircraft from HMS *Illustrious* and the USS *Saratoga* attacked Sabang on Sumatra, while HMS *Indomitable* was also in the region and HMS *Victorious* arrived shortly afterwards from her successful action against the *Tirpitz*, followed by HMS *Unicorn*. A fourth Illustrious class vessel arrived almost a year later, in March, 1945, enabling the four British carriers and their fleet maintenance carrier to form Task Force 57. Before this, in March, 1944, the fourth vessel, HMS *Indefatigable*, had created British naval aviation history, with the first landing of a twin-engined aircraft, a de Havilland Mosquito IV fighter-bomber flown by Lieutenant-Commander Eric Brown, RN, aboard a British carrier.

American landings on Hollandia, on the coast of New Guinea, on 22 April, were supported by the inevitable CVEs, while further attacks were made on Truk towards the end of the month, in preparation for the assault on the Marianas.

Task Force 58 remained busy, attacking the Marianas during early June and also the Bonin Islands, between the Marianas and Japan. In the latter attack, 300 Japanese aircraft were destroyed for the loss of just twenty-two USN aircraft. The first US landing on the Marianas came on 15 June at the island of Saipan, supported by aircraft from eight CVEs, which were also holding the reserve aircraft for the attack carriers.

The first Battle of the Philippine Sea, or 'Marianas Turkey Shoot', came on 19 and 20 June, with Mitscher back with the Fifth Fleet under the overall command of Spruance. Almost nine hundred aircraft were spread over the aircraft carriers USS *Hornet, Yorktown, Bunker Hill, Essex, Enterprise, Wasp* and *Lexington*, and the light fleet carriers USS *Belleau Wood, Cabot, Cowpens, Langley, Bataan, Monterey, Princeton*, and *San Jacinte*—all but one of the entire USN CVL strength. Against this the Japanese Vice-Admiral Ozawa could place just 430 aircraft, spread over the aircraft carriers *Taiho*, *Shokaku*, *Zuikaku*, *Hiyo*, *Junyo*, *Ryuho*, *Chitose*, *Chiyoda* and *Zuiho*.

The Japanese Fleet assembled east of the Philippines to relieve Saipan, while both fleets sent submarines into the Philippine Sea, and the Japanese hoped to position the Americans between their fleet and their bases in Guam. First sighting of the US Fifth Fleet by Japanese aircraft came on 18 June, and the following morning Mitscher, not certain of the Japanese position but expecting an attack, put his 450 fighters on standby. About midday, Japanese aircraft attacked from Guam, and the USN fighters were scrambled to intercept the attacking formation. By chance they also happened to intercept the attacking Japanese carrier-borne aircraft, which appeared in four waves, and those that managed to escape the American fighters suffered serious losses from the anti-aircraft fire of the American fleets. Only a hundred Japanese aircraft returned to their carriers

While the Japanese aircraft were away from their carriers attacking the Fifth Fleet, the submarine USS *Albacore* torpedoed the *Taiho*, which later blew up with the loss of more than half her crew as petrol fumes ignited. Later the USS *Cavalla* torpedoed the *Shokaku*, which sank three hours later, again as petrol vapour ignited. As the Japanese fleet retreated, it was followed by three Fifth Fleet carriers, while the rest remained covering the assault on Guam. The following day, late in the afternoon, Mitscher launched a dusk attack of more than 200 aircraft against the Japanese. With just thirty-five fighters left to fend off the attack, the carrier *Hiyo* was badly damaged and two hours later was destroyed by a petrol vapour explosion. Two oilers were also sunk, and the carriers *Zuikaku* and *Chiyoda* badly damaged. The final attack cost just twenty American aircraft, but on the homeward flight, another eighty ran out of fuel and crash-landed into the sea or onto carrier decks, with the loss of some fifty airmen, leading Spruance to refuse Mitscher per-

mission to pursue the Japanese fleet further.

During July and August, the British carriers HMS *Victorious*, *Illustrious* and *Indomitable* attacked strategic targets on Sumatra, and during September, Mitscher's force attacked targets in the Philippines.

The naval war was by this time moving steadily towards Japan, with heavy carrier-borne aircraft attacks on the Philippines, Okinawa and Formosa. From 10 to 16 October, Admiral Halsey took the US Fifth Fleet to attack first Okinawa, then the northern part of Luzon in the Philippines, followed by Formosa, off the Chinese mainland and an area with a concentration of strong Japanese forces. During this almost triumphal progress, the Japanese lost 600 aircraft against ninety lost from the USN. The operation was primarily a run-up to the US invasion of the Japanese-occupied Philippines, which were of vital strategic importance to Japan, since without control of these large islands, the main supply route for oil from Sumatra to Japan would be severed. The landing of US forces at Leyte on 20 October was the signal for the entire Japanese fleet to put to sea.

The Japanese had some new cards to play in this battle, with new versions of the older JNAF aircraft, and some new aircraft, including the Kawanishi N1K1–J Shiden 'George' land-based fighter, Nakajima P1Y1 Ginya 'Fances' shore-based attack aircraft and J1N1-S Gekko 'Irving' twin-engined night fighters and a few Aichi D4Y3 Suisi 'Judy' attack bombers. Perhaps more important, the ensuing Battle of Leyte Gulf was notable for one of the major developments of the war in the Pacific, the first kamikaze attacks. Meaning 'Divine Wind', the original Kamikaze had been a pre-war record-breaking aircraft, but the resuscitated name was now applied to suicide aircraft, utilising the Shinto philosophy, which decreed that death in combat was a certain way to heaven.

The Japanese could only muster four aircraft carriers, the *Zuikaku*, *Zuiho* and the two sisters, *Chitose* and *Chiyoda*, against strong American forces which included Mitscher's carrier force with the USS *Essex, Enterprise, Hornet, Hancock, Franklin, Wasp, Intrepid, Lexington, Cabot, Cowpens, Belleau Wood, Independence, Princeton, Langley, Monterey* and *San Jacinte*, plus some eighteen CVEs. The American Third Fleet could put no less than 1,400 aircraft into the air, against just 116 from Vice-Admiral Ozawa's small fleet, although another 300 Japanese aircraft were based ashore on the island of Luzon.

First encounters in the Battle of Leyte Gulf actually occurred in the Sibuyan Sea, between the Philippine Islands of Luzon and Mindoro, on 24 October. When aircraft from Luzon attacked the northernmost units of the Third Fleet, a bomb passed through the flight and hangar decks of the USS *Princeton*. It detonated explosives on armed and fuelled aircraft, starting a chain of explosions that finally blew up the vessel, seriously damaging the cruiser USS *Birmingham*, which lay alongside, ready to take off casualties. However, aircraft from the Japanese carriers failed to find the American ships and attempted to fly on to Luzon, but were intercepted while doing so, and most were shot down. Further naval battles took place between battleships and cruisers during the night, while the following day, Japanese battleships found four escort carriers and sank the USS *Gambier Bay*, also damaging the USS *Fenshaw Bay*, *Kalinin Bay* and *White Plains*. Later the USS *St. Lo*, a CVE, was also sunk, in one of the first kamikaze attacks.

Later, still on 25 October, Mitscher found the Japanese carrier fleet and flew off more than 500 aircraft to destroy it, quickly sinking the *Chitose*, while *Chiyoda*, *Zuiho* and *Zuikaku* were sunk later. *Chiyoda*, burning and abandoned, actually had to be despatched by US cruiser gunfire. During two days of battle, the Japanese had lost most of their battleships and cruisers.

However, the new Japanese suicide weapon was a force to be reckoned with, and during November, 1944 kamikaze attacks reached a peak, scoring direct hits on the USS *Intrepid, Franklin, Lexington, Essex, Hancock, Cabot* and *Belleau Wood*.

The kamikaze was born out of desperation, and the desperation is understandable. The *Shinano* was sunk even before she could enter service, while within weeks, on 15 December, another new carrier, the *Unryu*, was torpedoed and sunk by the submarine USS *Redfish*. The Royal Navy systematically destroyed the oil wells and refineries in Sumatra with Grumman Hellcats, Chance–Vought Corsairs and Supermarine Seafires providing cover for the Grumman Avengers from HMS *Victorious, Illustrious* and *Indefatigable*. The United States Navy meanwhile provided heavy aerial cover for further landings in the Philippines, with six CVEs supporting the landings on Mindoro and eighteen supporting the landings on Luzon, where strong kamikaze resistance was encountered and resulted in the sinking of the USS *Ommany Bay*.

During the preceding year or so, progressively fewer United States Marine squadrons had been available for carrier operations covering invasion forces—a role in which they had excelled, since they were capable of mounting strafing, bombing and rocket attacks on enemy positions only seventy-five yards away from those occupied by friendly troops. Early 1945 saw their welcome return to these all-important operations; and in the intervening period, in the Solomons, they had introduced an aerial observation post —AOP—role, with twenty-four ex-United States Army Piper O-1 Cub high-wing monoplanes, flown and maintained not by regular air and ground crews, but by USMC members with peacetime experience of private flying! The return to carrier operations now meant more than simply operating alongside USN units aboard attack carriers. For the first time, the USMC received carriers of its own, with four CVEs allocated to the assault role earmarked exclusively for marine air operations. The first of these

Above: A JNAF Kawanishi Ki–21 'Sally'
bomber limps home over the jungle

Opposite: A captured Yokosuka M4Y8 Oka
'Baka', designed to be delivered by Mitsubishi
G4M3 bombers

vessels, the USS *Block Island*, entered service in February, 1945, and was followed shortly afterwards by the USS *Gilbert Islands*, *Cape Gloucester* and *Vella Gulf*.

While British attacks on Palembang in Sumatra intensified during late January, Vice-Admiral Mitscher's Task Force 58 with sixteen aircraft carriers and light fleet carriers launched the first large USN attack on Japan itself, destroying more than 500 Japanese aircraft for the loss of eighty-eight USN aircraft. The USN's air element was becoming more effective all the time, with radar-equipped Grumman Hellcats and Chance-Vought Corsairs successfully countering Japanese night raiders, while radar-equipped Grumman Avengers were outstandingly successful in finding and destroying Japanese surface vessels and submarines. On 19 February, US forces landed on Iwo Jima, needed for airfields which could provide bases for the fighters that were used to cover air raids on Japan. Eleven CVEs from TF51 covered the landings, while long-range air support came from Mitscher's TF58. The determined kamikaze attacks mounted by the defending Japanese cost the USN the

CVE USS *Bismarck Sea*, while the USS *Saratoga* was also hit by six kamikaze aircraft, although the carrier was saved.

In March, TF58 renewed the assault on Japan itself, with the USS *Hornet*, *Enterprise*, *Essex*, *Bennington*, *Bunker Hill*, *Franklin*, *Intrepid*, *Hancock*, *Wasp* and *Yorktown*, with the CVLs USS *Cabot*, *Bataan*, *Belleau Wood*, *Langley*, *Independence* and *San Jacinte*, with some 1,200 aircraft. The strong kamikaze counter-attack caused serious damage to the USS *Wasp*, *Enterprise*, *Intrepid*, *Yorktown* and *Franklin*, with the last-named suffering more than 1,000 casualties amongst her crew. Nevertheless, most of this force was still available for the US landings on Okinawa on 1 April, while reinforcements from the British Pacific Fleet under Vice-Admiral Rawlings brought more than 200 aircraft aboard the carriers HMS *Illustrious*, *Victorious*, *Indomitable* and *Indefatigable*. The Allied advance was functioning so smoothly that after the Okinawa campaign, three of the eighteen CVEs used were redeployed to cover Australian forces advancing through Borneo.

A new variation on the kamikaze theme occurred during the Okinawa campaign,

when a number of Kawanishi Ki.21 Type 2 'Sally' bombers crash-landed on Yontam Airfield shortly after its capture by the Allies in May, to discharge fanatical Japanese commandos who destroyed nine aircraft, damaged twenty-nine others and set fire to a fuel dump before being eliminated by USAAF guards.

The kamikaze tag applied to many Japanese aircraft, and when Vice-Admiral Orida put his plan for concentrated kamikaze attacks on the 201st and 202nd Air Corps in October 1944, there was no shortage of 'volunteers', many pilots finally being chosen by roster than by strict test of merit. Many of the aircraft used were standard bombers, fighter-bombers and even Zero-Sen fighters, but weapons specifically designed for kamikaze operations included the Yokosuka M4Y8 Oka 'Baka' glider bombs, delivered by specially-modified Mitsubishi G4M3 bombers. (These weapons would have made their operational debut during the Philippines campaign, but for the sinking of a transport with the 'Oka' gliders onboard.) During the Okinawa campaign, there were some 900 kamikaze attacks, which resulted in some 280 hits on Allied warships, although by no means all resulted in serious damage. On one occasion, out of 360 kamikaze aircraft on a massed raid, some 300 were shot down by fighters and only twenty actually scored a hit. Part of the problem was that the suicide aircraft were either flown high, and had to make a shallow dive in order to retain control of the aircraft, during which time they were a sitting target for anti-aircraft fire, or else they were flown low, and risked being pounced upon by fighters. Either way, the net result was a high loss of experienced pilots and often good aircraft, both of which were hard to replace.

Few new aircraft types entered JNAF service at this stage, largely due to the policy of developing new versions of existing types rather than completely new aircraft, in complete contrast to JAAF policy. Some of the few new aircraft included the Aichi D4Y4 Susei, developed from the D4Y3 'Judy' ground-attack aircraft, the JAAF-developed Matsushito D5Y1 Myujo and Nakajima Kitsuk twin-jet fighter, based on the Messerschmitt Me262 fighter. Yet in spite of the appalling shortages of aircraft and pilots, waste occurred even at this late stage. As an example, both JNAF and JAAF squadrons were scrambled to counter Allied bombing raids, on the basis that over-water defence was a JNAF responsibility while the JAAF was responsible for countering overland aircraft. It was not until late spring that fuel shortages forced some degree of co-ordination onto the two rival air arms, by which time panic aircraft were being pressed, untried, into service, including the rocket-powered Mitsubishi J8M1 Shusui, similar to the Messerschmitt Me163 Komet.

Fuel shortages prevented the carriers *Amagi* and *Katsuragi* from leaving port, so on 24 July, 1945, both ships were bombed, with *Amagi* capsizing. The wrecked *Katsuragi* was later given temporary repairs so that she could act as a repatriation transport.

The USN and RN meanwhile prepared for the invasion of Japan— 'Operation Olympic'. A British 'Tiger' force was planned to have around fourteen aircraft carriers and light fleet carriers and eighteen escort carriers, with some 600 aircraft, while the Royal Air Force was to provide twenty heavy bomber squadrons. The United States Navy grouped together twenty-six CVs and CVLs with a staggering sixty-four CVEs. The Japanese, on their part, planned a final kamikaze onslaught of some 5,000 aircraft, many of them unsuitable and flown by pilots with the bare minimum of training considered necessary for their one and only solo flight.

However, the dropping of the first atomic bomb on Hiroshima on 6 August, followed by the second one, on Nagasaki on 11 August, brought Japanese surrender and a relatively merciful end to a war which would otherwise have had an even more bloody and savage conclusion —probably not least for the tens of thousands of Allied prisoners in Japanese prison camps, as well as for the attacking Allied and defending Japanese forces. The factors surrounding the decision to use the atomic bomb on Japanese cities are all too often forgotten.

The end of the war in the Pacific came as something of an anti-climax, but undoubtedly it was a war in which the aircraft carrier and naval aviation had proved itself. Even at the last, the combined British and American carrier fleet was a pistol held to the head of the defeated Japanese, who themselves had just one carrier still fit for operations—the small *Hosho*, their first carrier, which had spent much of the war as a training vessel. Yet sheer numbers alone did not decide the outcome. The war could have lasted longer, and been even more serious for the Allies, had the Japanese used their carrier forces more effectively from the beginning, or had they even designed their vessels better and paid more attention to crew training.

7 The Balance of Power Changes

The return of peace in 1945 saw naval aviation more firmly established as a vital and integral part of the fleet than ever before. If World War II had been a naval war, it had been so largely because of the frequent use of a still relatively new weapon, the aircraft carrier, which had enabled friend and foe alike to wage war beyond the range of aircraft operating from secure shore bases. Without the aid of carrier-borne aircraft, the Japanese advance through the Pacific and the American advance which followed, driving the Japanese back, would have been a more difficult, bloody and time-consuming business. Indeed, the war in the Pacific might not have happened at all had Japan not been able to strike a major pre-emptive blow at Pearl Harbor, using her carrier force.

Military air transport had become vitally important—and appreciated as such—during the war, but even if the USAAF or the RAF had deployed its whole air transport effort to move the equipment necessary to establish a new airfield, it could not have done so at anything like the speed with which an aircraft carrier—a fully equipped and sophisticated airfield with its own air traffic control, maintenance, accommodation and medical facilities—could move as desired. And as aircraft became more sophisticated, the carrier's advantages multiplied. The introduction of more sophisticated aircraft demanded more complex maintenance facilities, longer and better paved runways, and the aircraft carrier was able to meet all these demands, as well as to cope with the need for ever more sophisticated radar.

The end of the war found the Royal Navy with seven large aircraft carriers. They were mainly of the Illustrious class, but also included the by now elderly HMS *Furious*, used for training, and the maintenance carrier, HMS *Unicorn*. In addition, there were five light fleet carriers, with more building, and forty escort carriers, together with an aircraft strength which had increased from 232 aircraft in nineteen squadrons to 1,336 aircraft in seventy-eight squadrons, more than half of the 1945 total of aircraft having been built in the United States. Still more impressive was the United States Navy. It had twenty large or attack aircraft carriers, with five more building and an even larger type fitting out, together with eight light fleet carriers of the Independence class and sixty-nine escort carriers, while its aircraft total amounted to a staggering 41,000. Most of the large aircraft carriers in the USN were of the Essex class, although the USS *Enterprise* had survived the war, along with the USS *Ranger*, which was being used for training and aircraft transport duties.

In sharp contrast, the Japanese Navy had just one operational aircraft carrier, the *Hosho*, its first and smallest, although two others were made seaworthy to act as transports before going to the breakers.

The two main Allied navies had not developed alone, and apart from the vital contribution made by RAF Coastal Command, had also enjoyed the support of vastly strengthened RNZAF maritime-reconnaissance squadrons. These squadrons, with Lockheed PV–1 Venturas, developed from the Hudson, Grumman Avengers and Consolidated Catalina and Short Sunderland flying-boats, had played a vital role in the Solomons campaign and elsewhere in the Pacific. The RAAF, too, had been very much in the front line, with Consolidated Catalinas and Martin Mariners, as well as anti-ship Bristol Beauforts, a development of the Blenheim. RAAF Catalinas had, towards the end, mined harbours in mainland China and Formosa, denying these to the retreating Japanese. The British Empire air forces had often operated far from home, not only in the British Isles or in the Pacific, but also, in the case of the South African Air Force, in the Mediterranean, the Aegean and the Adriatic. South African Lockheed Venturas and Short Sunderlands and Catalinas had also operated in the Cape area, on home territory, attacking twenty-four U-boats, intercepting seventeen blockade runners and rescuing almost 500 survivors from Allied shipping losses in the Indian Ocean and South Atlantic.

At the end of the war, these air forces found themselves with maritime-reconnaissance elements which alone outnumbered their entire 1939 strength!

Amongst the Allies whose efforts have been accorded less recognition than might have been the case, were Mexico and Brazil. Both of these maintained anti-submarine patrols along their coasts in support of the anti-Axis cause, and were helped by the United States to modernise their small air arms for this purpose. USN units were also based in Brazil after that country declared war on Germany and Italy on 22 August, 1942.

Obviously, peace meant a reduction in fighting strengths, with servicemen conscripted for the war anxious to resume their civil occupations, governments anxious to repair war-battered economies, and the whole *raison d'être* for a massive level of defence expenditure suddenly removed. Yet, the post-war run-down was by no means as drastic as that at the end of World War I. This was partly because of the realisation that to return to the weak and undefended state of the inter-war period posed unacceptable risks to the democracies, and partly because of the necessity for large occupation forces in Germany, parts of Italy, Japan and Austria. But the main reason for the comparatively slow run-down was an awful awareness that the new peace was fragile and uneasy, with the Soviet Union, a wartime ally, intent upon territorial expansion, and a dangerous situation existing in post-war China.

The European countries, only just liberated from German occupation, had other problems of their own, with both France and the Netherlands finding difficulty in re-establishing authority over their colonies, in the wake of the departing Japanese. Britain, while granting independence to her largest and most troublesome overseas possession, India, and not having suffered occupation herself, nevertheless found grave difficulty in disentangling herself from the unwelcome League of Nations mandate for Palestine as the new state of Israel slowly came into being. She also faced problems with communist bandits in Malaya. Even without such problems, some 1,750 USN and USMC aircraft were deployed in the Far East at this time, including many in mainland China until the communist take-over in 1949 forced their withdrawal.

Post-war naval aviation was meanwhile being shaped, slowly at first, by two developments which had come to fruition during the war years—the jet aircraft and the helicopter.

Development of the jet engine had taken place in Germany and Britain between the wars, with Dr Hans von Ohain and Air Commodore Sir Frank Whittle, RAF, working independently of each other, their work leading to the experimental Heinkel He178—the world's

A Ryan Fireball compound piston and jet-engined aircraft, with both engines working!

First jet landing on an aircraft carrier; Eric Brown brings his Sea Vampire down onto the deck of HMS *Ocean*

first jet aircraft—and the Gloster E28/39 Whittle. Eventually, the Germans put the Messerschmitt Me262 jet fighter into production, although Hitler decreed that it be used initially as a bomber, while the British put their Gloster Meteor jet fighter into service in July, 1944. The Meteor was not a carrier-borne aircraft, but after World War II ended, the Fleet Air Arm received Meteors for evaluation, and eventually operated a number of these aircraft on second line duties.

The arrival of the jet aeroplane coincided with the peak of development for the piston-engined fighter, and in fact the fastest of these aircraft entered service as the war in the Pacific was ending. The piston-engined aircraft was still by no means obsolete, offering superior range and load-carrying performance against the early jets. Because of this, some manufacturers attempted to provide the best of both worlds with so-called compound aircraft—a mixture of jet and piston propulsion—largely to enable the pure piston aircraft to leap the still small performance gap created by the jet. One such aircraft, the Ryan FR–I Fireball,

A Focke–Achgelis Fa330 rotating wing observation kite, ready to be launched from a German U-boat

entered USN service in some numbers, and it was one of these aircraft that inadvertently made the first jet-powered landing on an aircraft carrier, on 6 November, 1945. Ensign Jake C. West, USN, was on final approach to land aboard the CVE USS *Wake Island*, using both the engine and the jet unit of his Fireball, since the jet was not really powerful enough to fly the aircraft. However, the piston engine failed, forcing him to complete his landing with the limited power of his jet engine.

There was certainly no lack of intent on the part of the Royal Navy in arranging for the first jet aircraft landing aboard a British ship, since the aircraft used was a pure jet, a modified version of the de Havilland Vampire jet fighter—Britain's second and highly successful jet design. On 3 December, 1945, Lieutenant-Commander Eric M. 'Winkle' Brown, RN, successfully landed his Sea Vampire aboard the new light fleet carrier, HMS

Igor Sikorsky flying his VS–300 helicopter prototype

Ocean, while the vessel was underway in the English Channel. Brown was, of course, the same Fleet Air Arm test pilot who had landed the Mosquito aboard HMS *Indefatigable.*

In common with the jet engine, the helicopter also owed much of its development to pioneering work in the Germany of the 1930s, and limited numbers of the Focke–Achgelis Fa223 helicopter were produced after 1940, while some U-boats used the Fa330 unpowered helicopter, or rotating wing kite, for observation purposes. However, the most significant developments took place in the United States, with the Russian emigre Igor Sikorsky conducting tethered trials of his famous VS–300 prototype. After extensive modifications, this machine made its first successful free flight on 13 May, 1940, although it required further modification to become a fully practical machine. The first production helicopter was the Sikorsky R–4, which entered USAAF service in 1943, although even before this, the USN and USCG were

both represented at the trials of the prototype. Eventually, on 7 May, 1943, Colonel Frank Gregory, USAAF, landed an XR–4 helicopter on the tanker *Bunker Hill,* while the vessel was off the coast of Connecticut, repeating this achievement while the vessel moved ahead at varying speeds!

The advantages of the helicopter as an anti-submarine weapon were almost immediately appreciated by the USN and USCG, whose reports to the Bureau of Aeronautics commented on its small size and on its ability to offer the advantages of the airship within a smaller airframe— one more easily handled on the ground or on deck, and with greater manouevrability in the air. It also seemed reasonable to expect that a helicopter could cover a wider area than could any escort vessel, and do so more quickly and with lower fuel consumption. To test the suitability of the helicopter as an anti-submarine aircraft, two vessels were fitted with landing platforms, the USCG vessel *Governor Cobb* and the British SS *Dagheston.* It was on the latter vessel that the first sea-going trials were made, starting on 28 November, 1943. USCG and USN pilots flying

specially modified R–4s with floats made 166 landings on the ship, while a further 162 landings were made with Royal Navy pilots at the controls. More trials took place on both vessels during 1943 and 1944, and in one of these two Sikorsky YR–4B helicopters were embarked aboard the SS *Daghestan* with five Royal Navy pilots from the Helicopter Service Trials Unit, together with four US Navy and one USCG pilots. After the war, trials continued separately, including the landing by Lieutenant Alan Bristow, RN, on a British destroyer in September, 1946, and the landing by Lieutenant K. Reed, RN, on the battleship HMS *Vanguard*, in February, 1947. In both cases a Sikorsky Hoverfly helicopter was used.

Essex class aircraft carriers with the United States Navy in the post-war period were USS *Essex, Lexington, Yorktown, Bunker Hill, Intrepid, Wasp, Hornet, Franklin, Hancock, Ticonderoga, Bennington, Shangri-La, Randolph, Bon Homme Richard, Antietam, Boxer, Lake Champlain, Princeton* and *Tarawa*, followed by the USS *Leyte, Kearsage, Valley Forge* and *Philippine Sea* in 1946, and by the USS *Oriskany* in 1950. These vessels

Shape of things to come—a Sikorsky Hoverfly lands on the battleship HMS *Vanguard*

were joined by three Midway class aircraft carriers in 1945 and 1946. These were the USS *Midway, Franklin D. Roosevelt* and *Coral Sea*, which were essentially larger, 45,000 ton, developments of the Essex class, having an aircraft complement of 120, slightly more than that of the *Essex*. (Most of the Independence class light fleet carriers were placed in reserve, with the escort carriers.) This large carrier fleet was divided between Atlantic and Pacific Fleets—a return to the practice of the inter-war years. And in all the US Navy had a fleet of just under 9,000 carrier-borne and shore-based aircraft, while an organised Air Reserve could provide some 6,000 USN and USMC pilots.

The formation of the long-awaited United States Air Force in 1947, leaving the United States Army free to concentrate on creating its own organic air power while the new service controlled strategic air operations, might have been expected to reduce the old inter-service rivalries. However, in a period of steadily

One of the planes which arrived too late for the war in the Pacific, the Grumman F7F Tigercat fighter

reducing defence budgets, the rivalries were heightened once more. Both the USAF and the USN claimed the right to operate shore-based maritime-reconnaissance operations, with the USAF using the Royal Air Force as an example. Both services also claimed the right to conduct strategic operations, with the USAF backing its new six-engined Convair B–36 strategic bombers and a new development of the Boeing Super Fortress, and the USN countering this with a plan for 60,000-ton super carriers able to operate jet bombers. The B–36 had been developed, rather pessimistically, to be able to bomb Germany, flying non-stop from the United States, if Britain had been invaded, while plans were already far advanced for the first super carrier, the USS *United States*. A conference attended by the Chiefs of Staff of the US services in August, 1948, left the USN with the responsibility for maritime-reconnaissance, while the USAF received full backing as the service for strategic aerial warfare, with Congress voting funds for the development of a Strategic Air Command. The planned super carrier programme was then immediately scrapped, along with plans for a further three Midway class vessels, while a number of Essex class carriers had already been deleted from the programme as the war ended.

There had by this time been some rationalisation of defence effort, with the decision in June, 1948, to form a Military Air Transport Service (MATS), absorbing the individual air transport components of all three services. The USN was less than completely enthusiastic, contributing only its four Douglas R5D (C–54) Skymaster long-range squadrons when MATS finally came into existence in May, 1949. By that time two of these squadrons were playing an active part in the Berlin Air Lift, supplying West Berlin during the Russian blockade of surface routes to that city. It was not until 1956 that the remaining USN and USMC transport squadrons were handed over to MATS following a prolonged rear-guard action, after twin-boom and twin-engined Fairchild R40 Packet 'Flying Boxcar' transports had entered service, joining Grumman Albatross amphibians.

Many of the new USN aircraft had been designed for operations against Japanese forces in the Pacific, but had arrived just a little too late. Two of the more notable post-war fighters were the twin piston-engined Grumman F7F Tigercat, in single and twin-seat versions, and the single piston-engined Grumman F8F Bearcat, while an extremely versatile addition to the USN's inventory was the Douglas AD Skyraider. This was a single-engined piston aircraft originally intended to be one of the first true airborne-early-warning (AEW) aircraft, carrying radar to give advance 'over the horizon' warning of attacking kamikaze aircraft; but most of the Skyraiders were delivered after August, 1945, and became better known as highly effective attack aircraft.

Shore-based patrol duties fell to a variety of aircraft, the Catalina, which remained in service, being joined by Consolidated PBY and PB4Y Privateers, Lockheed PV2 Harpoons and Boeing B–17G Flying Fortresses (known to the USN as the PB–1W) as well as Martin PBM–5 flying-boats. These aircraft were soon outclassed to some extent by the classic Lockheed P2V Neptune, a large and attractive twin-engined landplane, originally intended for operations from Midway class carriers but in actual service always shore-based. The Neptune was designed to offer a considerable endurance for effective anti-submarine patrol, and one aircraft soon justified the type's reputation for range. In late 1946, this particular Neptune, nicknamed 'Truculent Turtle' by its crew, flew 11,250 miles without refuelling on a $55\frac{1}{4}$ hour flight from Australia to the United States. Neptunes soon also appeared in the maritime-reconnaissance squadrons of a number of countries, including the Royal Australian Air Force and the Royal Netherlands Naval Air Service. They were also used for a short time by the Royal Air Force, while British-built aircraft were awaited during the early 1950s.

Other records also came to the United States Navy in the early post-war years. One of the more notable was set by the

Record breaker—the Lockheed P2V Neptune prototype, 'Truculent Turtle'

Martin Mars transport flying-boats, which entered service in 1946, linking the Pacific Fleet's main bases in California and Hawaii. One Mars established a distance record for flying-boats of 4,748 miles in twenty-four hours, as well as lift records of 68,282 lbs on one occasion and of 301 passengers plus seven crew on another. Only four Mars transport flying-boats entered service, but all of them operated without accident.

The United States Navy wasted little time in entering the jet age, the first USN pure jet aircraft being the McDonnell FD-1, later FH-1, Phantom jet fighters, which were delivered to the first USN jet squadron, VF-17a, in July, 1947. Unfortunately, difficulties over the development of reliable jet engines delayed other jet fighter types which would have followed the Phantom into service. New piston-engined fighters had also been cancelled, but in their case due to a severe shortage of funds. So to provide a larger pool of jet-experienced pilots, the USN ordered fifty Lockheed F-80C Shooting Star jet fighters, giving the type the naval designation of TO-1. Large numbers of jet fighter and attack aircraft did not become available until after 1948, with the arrival of the Grumman F9F Panther, McDonnell F2H Banshee, Chance–Vought F6U Pirate and the North American FJ-1 Fury—a naval derivative of the highly successful Sabre jet, although early naval versions lacked the swept-wing of the USAF aircraft. The first operational carrier-borne USN jet fighter squadron was VF-5A Fury Squadron, which joined the USS *Boxer* on 10 March, 1948.

Other new aircraft included the Martin P4M-1 Mercator, a compound (jet- and piston-engined) flying-boat, and the Sikorsky HO3S-1 helicopter, the naval version of the S-51 Dragonfly, for air-sea rescue and carrier plane-guard duties. The Sikorsky HO3S-1 released destroyer escorts from such duties, and also gave the unfortunate victim of an accident a faster rescue! The USN and USMC also experimented with Piasecki HRP-1 helicopters, introducing the famous Bell 47 or HTL in 1950 for casualty evacuation.

One exception to the flood of new technology was the airship or blimp, of which 139 had been in USN service at the end of World War II, and which, in reduced numbers, remained in service for some years after the war ended.

A similar picture was presented by the post-war Royal Navy and its Fleet Air Arm, which after the cessation of hostilities found itself receiving new aircraft originally intended for operations in the Pacific. Three aircraft that arrived too late were the Hawker Sea Fury fighter, one of the fastest, if not the fastest, piston-engined aircraft ever built; the sturdy Blackburn Firebrand attack aircraft; and the sleek, long-range, de Havilland Sea Hornet twin-engined night fighter, a development of the Mosquito which was superior to anything in RAF service for night fighter operations. Later versions of the Grumman Avenger, the Supermarine Seafire and the Fairey Firefly (a late-wartime carrier-borne fighter-bomber and anti-submarine aircraft) continued to enter service, complementing the Chance–Vought Corsairs and other wartime aircraft that soldiered on in the new peacetime Royal Navy.

The post-war run-down of the Royal Navy was faster and more drastic than that faced by its trans-Atlantic cousin, although neither the Fleet Air Arm nor the Royal Air Force suffered cuts on the scale of those imposed in 1919. The return to the United States of Lend-Lease Programme vessels, especially many escort carriers, accounted for much of the reduction, and in addition the Illustrious class carriers were quickly placed in reserve, although HMS *Illustrious* herself acted as a trials ship, while HMS *Implacable* spent a short period serving with the Home Fleet and HMS *Victorious* eventually started a long and drawn-out refit. HMS *Furious* was withdrawn and scrapped in 1948.

An RAF Coastal Command Short Shetland out of its element

The backbone of the immediate post-war fleet rapidly became the light fleet aircraft carriers of the Colossus class, as new vessels, including HMS *Triumph* and *Glory* were delivered from the builders. Two new classes of aircraft carrier were under construction at this time. The larger class consisted of two 40,000 ton vessels, HMS *Irresistible*, later renamed HMS *Eagle*, and HMS *Audacious*, later renamed HMS *Ark Royal*. It had originally been intended that there should be four ships in this class, but the other two, *Malta* and *Gibraltar*, were cancelled. The smaller class was a heavier and more powerful development of the original light fleet classes. It consisted of four ships, *Hermes*, *Albion*, *Bulwark*, and *Centaur*, although the nameship, *Hermes*, was being delayed by a series of stop-go decisions that interrupted her building. A number of light fleet carriers had been cancelled as the war ended. Soon many of the British-built escort carriers were being broken up, so that by the late 1940s only one—HMS *Campania*, in reserve—remained.

After the war, the Fleet Air Arm was intended eventually to account for a third of the Royal Navy's strength, but to emphasise that it was a part of the Royal Navy and dispel any notions of its becoming a service within a service, the title Naval Aviation was introduced in 1946. However, in regular useage the new appellation never completely replaced 'Fleet Air Arm', and the old title was readopted during the late 1950s. Some strengthening came with the formation of four Royal Naval Volunteer Reserve squadrons in September, 1947—one each with Supermarine Seafire 4s and 17s, one with Fairey Fireflies, and one with North American Harvard advanced trainers.

The introduction of jet aircraft for the Royal Navy was no faster than for the United States Navy, due almost entirely to the longer time taken to put British aircraft into production. The de Havilland Sea Vampire did not become a fully operational carrier-borne jet aircraft, and the Royal Navy's first carrier-borne jet air-craft designed as such, the Supermarine Attacker, made its first flight on 27 July, 1946, although it did not enter full service until 1949! The Attacker was followed shortly afterwards by the effective and popular Armstrong-Whitworth Sea Hawk—a near relation of the RAF's extremely successful Hawker Hunter—which first flew on 2 September, 1947, although it did not enter service until the early 1950s, when it was joined by the de Havilland Sea Venom, the carrier-borne development of the Venom jet fighter-bomber, itself basically an improved Vampire.

One unusual jet aircraft of this period deserves mention, although only three prototypes were built and the aircraft did not enter production. The world's first and only flying-boat jet fighter was developed by the British firm of Saunders-Roe. Designated the SR–A/1, it used two Metrovick Beryl turbojets, which gave it a maximum speed of 512 mph. The aircraft first flew on 16 July, 1947, and although it might have delighted Jacques Schneider, it soon became apparent that, in spite of successful trials, there could be no practical application for it.

The Royal Air Force's Coastal Command continued to develop during this period, with Avro Lincoln and the earlier Lancaster heavy bombers modified, and with Boeing B–17 Flying Fortresses for maritime-reconnaissance duties. And like the USN, the RAF could still find a place for the flying-boat. Its Short Shetland flying-boats, intended to replace the faithful Sunderland, failed to do so to any great extent, and left the later marks of the wartime aircraft in service throughout the late 1940s and well into the following decade.

All might have seemed well, but one indication of the troubled times ahead came with RAF participation in the Berlin Air Lift. The main aircraft used were Douglas C–47 Dakotas and Avro Yorks, but a small number of Short Sunderland flying-boats also operated from Hamburg to the Havel See, on the outskirts of the city. Another pointer lay in the need to

Royal Danish Air Force Consolidated Catalina amphibian

deploy the new light fleet carrier HMS *Triumph*, with her Supermarine Seafires and Fairey Fireflies, off the coast of Malaya, where she helped hard-pressed RAF units to support the army in a successful campaign against communist-backed bandits from 1949 onwards.

Action against communist guerillas also fell to the lot of other British aircraft carriers, after they had passed to new naval air arms.

In March, 1945, the French Navy, the Marine Nationale, obtained the loan of a British escort carrier, which joined the Fleet in September as the *Dixmude*, ready for the post-war reconstruction of French naval aviation, or the Aeronavale as it became. Although the old aircraft carrier *Bearn* was still available after the war, she was used only as a training carrier, and then as an accommodation ship, and before long another British carrier transferred to the French Navy, none other than the light fleet carrier HMS *Colossus*, which was renamed *Arromanches*. In November, 1946, fierce fighting broke out in French Indo-China, and the *Dixmude* was dispatched to the area with a full complement of Douglas SBD–5 Dauntless dive-bombers. At times during the years of fighting then ahead, she became the main source of air support for ground forces, especially when operations from bases ashore became difficult due to terrorist activity. At other times, the *Dixmude* and the *Arromanches* ferried aircraft from France to Indo-China, until in August, 1951, the *Arromanches* was stationed off the coast of Indo-China for the rest of the war. There she operated Grumman F6F Hellcat and Curtiss SB2C Helldiver dive-bombers, while a shore-based Aeronavale unit operated Convair PB4Y Privateer heavy bombers.

The post-war Royal Netherlands Naval Air Service was planned during the final stages of World War II, and after the Netherlands had been liberated, Dutch naval airmen were trained in Britain while Dutch airfields were cleared and rebuilt. Eventually, a base was established at Valkenburg for an initial force of thirty Fairey Firefly fighter-bombers, and a two year lease was taken on the escort carrier HMS *Nairana*, which joined the Dutch Fleet as the *Karel Doorman*, named after the World War II admiral.

The Dutch, too, were having difficulty in regaining possession of their territories in the Far East. The Dutch East Indies—Java, Sumatra, the Celebes and much of Borneo—had declared their independence as soon as the Japanese had departed, and fierce fighting soon developed. Dutch forces engaged in the encounter included shore-based RNNAS squadrons, operating Douglas C–47 Dakota transports and Consolidated PBY–5 Catalina flyingboats, while using training types in the counter-insurgency role. Intervention by the United Nations led to a peaceful settlement on 27 December, 1949, and Dutch forces withdrew from the area, leaving their aircraft behind to provide the nucleus for the future Indonesian Air Force, the AURI.

A Royal Canadian Navy Grumman Avenger flying over HMCS *Magnificent*

Meanwhile, HMS *Nairana*, alias *Karel Doorman*, had been returned to the Royal Navy in March, 1948, and eventually went to the breakers, while two months later the rather more practical light fleet carrier, HMS *Venerable*, joined the Royal Netherlands Navy. Ironically, since the very lack of carrier-borne air cover contributed in no small way to the poor Allied showing in the Battle of the Java Sea, she was promptly renamed *Karel Doorman*. The new ship also received new aircraft, including later marks of the Fairey Firefly for anti-submarine duties and twenty-four Hawker Sea Fury fighter-bombers, with additional Sea Furies built in the Netherlands under licence by Fokker. A small number of Supermarine Sea Otter aircraft were obtained for search and rescue—SAR—duties, along with the first Dutch helicopters, Sikorsky S-51 Dragonflies.

A more settled early existence awaited two other new air arms, in the Royal Canadian and Royal Australian Navies.

The Royal Canadian Navy's Naval

High and dry, a Royal Australian Air Force Short Sunderland

Aviation dated from World War II, when four Fleet Air Arm squadrons had been earmarked for manning by Canadian personnel, with plans for their eventual transfer to light fleet carriers. The war ended before these plans could take effect, but they were not abandoned, although the squadrons remained in the British Isles until March, 1946. Then the light fleet carrier HMCS *Warrior* arrived in Canada with Nos. 803 and 825 squadrons, operating Fairey Fireflies and Supermarine Seafires, the remaining two squadrons being temporarily disbanded. HMCS *Warrior* exercised and trained with the new Canadian naval aviators for the next two years, after which she passed into reserve when another light fleet carrier, HMCS *Magnificent*, arrived in Canada. A shore station had meanwhile been established at the Royal Canadian Air Force base at Dartmouth, Nova Scotia, and it was there that the remaining two Canadian squadrons were now reactivated and worked up. These two new squadrons were equipped with Fireflies and Seafires, while the original squadrons received improved marks of Firefly, and Sea Fury fighter-bombers.

Dartmouth itself was transferred completely to the Royal Canadian Navy on 1 December, 1948, becoming HMCS *Shearwater*, while 115 Grumman TBM–3E Avengers were acquired from the United States Navy and modernised for anti-submarine operations, replacing the Fireflies and further strengthening ASW operations of the RCN.

Similar plans were in hand for the Royal Australian Navy. Late in 1948, the Minister for the Navy announced that a Fleet Air Arm was to be formed, with two light fleet carriers purchased from the Royal Navy. The first, HMAS *Sydney*, formerly the Royal Navy's HMS *Terrible*, commissioned in the RAN in 1949, and the intention was that a second carrier, HMAS *Melbourne*, should follow a year or so later, but this ship was delayed by the decision to incorporate a number of improvements into her design. The RAN's Fleet Air Arm also established a shore station at Nowra, New South Wales, near Sydney, naming it HMAS *Albatross*, long after the withdrawal of the veteran seaplane of that name. Later, another shore station at Schofield was taken over from the Royal Australian Air Force.

HMAS *Sydney* arrived from Britain in June, 1949, carrying two squadrons, Nos 805 and 815, equipped with Fairey Fireflies and Hawker Sea Furies which were flown ashore to HMAS *Albatross*. The two squadrons had formed in the United Kingdom at HMS *Sea Eagle*, the Royal Naval Air Station at Eglinton, near Londonderry in Northern Ireland, in August, 1947.

However, after the formation of Australia's Fleet Air Arm, the Royal Australian Air Force still retained full responsibility for maritime-reconnaissance, using Catalina flying-boats for SAR, while Avro Lancaster and, later, Lincoln heavy bombers were used for long-range maritime-reconnaissance, a task in which they were helped by Short Sunderland flying-boats. The neighbouring Royal New Zealand Air Force also used Catalinas and Sunderlands.

A Royal Norwegian Air Force, which had been formed during the latter days of the war to replace the separate Army and Navy air arms, operated a small maritime-reconnaissance element with a single squadron of ten Catalinas.

In the late 1940s, the formation of post-war economic and military alliances was getting underway. In 1948, Belgium, France, Luxembourg, the Netherlands and the United Kingdom signed the Brussels Treaty, making a fifty year alliance for defence, including military and economic co-operation; and in 1955, when Italy and West Germany joined, this became the Western European Union, in which member states were pledged to provide assistance to each other in the event of aggression by an outside power. More important, in 1949 the North Atlantic Treaty Organisation came into being, embracing not only the Brussels Treaty organisation members but also the United States, Canada, Iceland, Norway, Denmark, Portugal, Greece and Turkey, with similar com-

mitments between all the member states. A unified command structure and deployment of forces within the NATO area evolved gradually during the 1950s. One other significant difference between NATO and the Brussels Treaty was the provision of military aid, primarily by the United States, for member nations.

Another regional defence organisation with economic overtones was the Organisation of American States. Formed in 1948, largely due to a United States initiative, it embraced almost all Latin American countries as well as the USA. Military aid flowed more quickly to members of the new Organisation, although of course it was formed almost a year before NATO, and much of the equipment its member-states received was secondhand, while later on NATO countries received mainly new equipment, and even help with new defence projects of their own. Brazil, with a long coastline to defend, received Lockheed PV2 Harpoon aircraft, while Chile, with another long coastline, received Catalina flying-boats. In addition, amphibian versions of the Catalina were supplied to Colombia and Ecuador, as well as to Peru, which also received Harpoons.

Such measures may have seemed alarmist, but although Soviet military power was still only at the outset of its massive growth and the Soviet Navy was still of relatively little consequence, the Soviet Union had occupied every nation in eastern Europe at the end of the war, with the exception of Greece. It had also failed to allow a return to normal political life in these countries after the defeat of Germany. An early indication of Soviet intentions came even at the height of the war, when USAAF Boeing B–29 Superfortresses which had force-landed on an airfield occupied by their supposed ally, were expropriated, copied by the USSR and entered service as the Tupolev Tu–4, backbone of both the early post-war Russian strategic bomber force and its long-range maritime-reconnaissance force.

Soviet Naval Aviation reorganised after the war, with the old VVS–VMF becoming the A–VMF, or Aviatsiza–Voenno Morsikh Flota, and receiving not only Tu–4s but also the Russian Beriev Be–6 twin-engined flying-boat, which entered service in 1949. By this time, the Soviet Union was also well on the way to forming the Warsaw Pact, and turning its new European empire into satellite states.

The return of peace was something of an illusion, since more than ever, 'peace' was simply to mean a lack of all-out global conflict. As the number of navies with air arms and aircraft carriers increased, the late 1940s saw the Royal Navy and the United States Navy weaker than at any time since the start of World War II, with large numbers of aircraft carriers refitting, in reserve or even sold or scrapped. Thus by 1950 the USN had just thirteen aircraft carriers in commission, and the USMC had just sixteen squadrons, four of which operated jet aircraft. Fortunately, newer, bigger and better ships and revitalised organisations were on the way for both navies. But so were heavy demands on them, and on their carrier forces.

8 Into the Jet Age

The 1950s marked a rennaissance for the aircraft carrier. With the run-down of the Royal Navy and the United States Navy ended, both fleets came to have their largest-ever peacetime number of carriers, and indeed of other ships as well. Allied to this, the jet aeroplane rapidly became the rule rather than the exception for operation aboard ship, and its widespread introduction was aided by radical changes in the operation of aircraft to and from ships. While the existing naval air arms continued to develop during the

A Martin P5M Marlin flying-boat refuelling from a ship

decade, other navies created new ones, introducing aircraft carriers of their own; and the helicopter steadily made seagoing naval aviation available to even the smallest navy.

However, at the outset, the Royal Navy had only HMS *Implacable*, the light fleet carriers HMS *Vengeance*, *Theseus*, *Glory* and *Triumph* and the maintenance carrier HMS *Unicorn* actually in service, although the sole remaining escort carrier, HMS *Campania*, survived in reserve. However, other vessels were building and HMS *Victorious* was undergoing a major refit. The United States Navy, meanwhile, had thirteen carriers in service.

But neither navy actually had carrier jet squadrons at combat readiness!

War broke out in Korea on 25 June, 1950, when the communist state of North Korea attacked South Korea, crossing the border between the two countries—the 38th Parallel. South Korea immediately appealed to the United Nations for help, and a fifteen-nation force entered the war on her side. On 13 September the Allies launched a counter-attack, and on 15 September the 1st US Marine Division landed at Inchon, on the west coast of Korea. Support for this operation was provided by the US Seventh Fleet under the command of Vice-Admiral Struble, with the aircraft carriers USS *Boxer*, *Philippine Sea*, *Valley Forge*, two escort carriers, and the British light fleet carrier HMS *Triumph*, which had been put at his disposal. The first aircraft carrier actually in Korean waters while the counter-attack was being mounted was the escort carrier USS *Sicily*, with just twenty-four aircraft. HMS *Triumph* was the sole aircraft carrier available to the British Far East Fleet at the time.

A Martin PBM–5 Mariner flying-boat being lifted aboard the seaplane carrier, USS *Salisbury Sound*, in Japanese waters during the Korean War

The United States played the leading Allied role in the war, and for the USN it was in certain respects reminiscent of World War II in the Pacific, with aircraft carriers operating in support of ground forces. However, anti-submarine patrols also had to be mounted, and the carrier-borne aircraft were joined in this work by Martin PBM–5 Mariner flying-boats based on Japan. The only real contribution the Royal Air Force made to the war was also in anti-submarine operations, for which they used two squadrons of Short Sunderland flying-boats, which also helped in the blockade of North Korean ports. To put operations into perspective, the USN provided 10 per cent of all Korean War air support operations, and the United States Marine Corps 26 per cent, with the bulk of the remainder coming from the USAF and other land-based air forces.

Royal Australian Navy Fairey Firefly and Hawker Sea Fury aircraft ranged on the flight deck of HMAS *Sydney* during the Korean War

Britain's effort largely centred around the Fleet Air Arm, although ground forces were also deployed ashore. HMS *Triumph*, with her Seafire 42s and Firefly Is, though first on the scene, was soon relieved by HMS *Theseus*, which strangely enough replaced her de Havilland Sea Vampire jet fighters with Hawker Sea Fury F.10 fighters and Fairey Firefly 5s before leaving Britain. HMS *Unicorn* operated in support of HMS *Theseus* and her reliefs, first HMS *Glory* and then HMS *Ocean*, while for two six-month stretches these vessels were joined by HMAS *Sydney*. In spite of the lack of jet fighter cover, which hampered operations against North Korean and Soviet Mikoyan MiG–15 jet fighters, HMS *Triumph* conducted 900 operational sorties, and HMS *Theseus* managed 4,500 sorties in a six-month period, for the loss of just five aircrew.

At the start of the war, the Chance–Vought F4U Corsair was the main USN and USMC ground-attack aircraft. Some of these also remained in Fleet Air Arm service, but before long the Douglas Sky-

raider was proving itself to be one of the most outstanding ground-attack aircraft of all time. Shore-based squadrons of Grumman F9F Panther jet fighters—one USMC and three USN squadrons—provided air cover, but early overall aerial superiority for the UN forces soon allowed piston-engine aircraft to operate freely, even over the front lines, with little interference, even though there were complaints afterwards from Royal Australian Air Force units about the effectiveness of their obsolete Gloster Meteor jets against the MiG–15s. Eventually, some USN jet fighters operated from the aircraft carrier, USS *Valley Forge*.

The first USN aircraft to destroy an enemy jet aircraft was a Panther, which on 9 November, 1950, shot down a MiG–15 in aerial combat, while USMC squadrons sometimes used Douglas F3D–2 Skyknight jet fighters on night operations. However, the only real USN fighter ace of the war, Lieutenant Guy Bordelon, USN, who shot down five enemy aircraft, flew a Corsair; and most night-fighter operations were still being conducted by piston-engined Grumman F7F–4N Tigercats. It was not until the end of the war, in 1953, that the USN and USMC were deploying large numbers of jet fighter aircraft over Korea, using the successful McDonnell F2H Banshee all-weather fighter. A twin piston-engined attack aircraft, the North American AJ–1 Savage, used jet boosters and had been designed to operate from the large Midway class aircraft carriers, but was soon diverted to reconnaissance duties and finally became a carrier-borne tanker aircraft, for in-flight refuelling.

One of the real innovations of the Korean War was the widespread use of helicopters, not only for plane-guard duties from aircraft carriers, including HMS *Glory* and *Ocean*, but also for troop-carrying and casualty evacuation, or CASEVAC. The early USMC experiments with Sikorsky HO3S and HRS, and Piasecki HRP–1 helicopters, led to the arrival in Korea of Squadron VMO–6, with HRS helicopters for observation duties, although casualty evacuation also fell to this unit. Later, Bell HTL helicopters—the USMC designation for the famous Bell 47—became the main type for observation duties, with the assistance of Stinson OY Sentinel light aircraft. Transport and troop-carrying operations were first carried out regularly by another USMC helicopter squadron, HMR–161, which arrived with Piasecki HRP–1s.

Further progress towards the eventual development of stand-off bombs, or air-to-ground missiles, came with the use of radar-equipped, pilotless, Grumman QF6F Hellcats to carry high explosive loads onto enemy targets in Korea.

In spite of the importance of land-based aircraft during the war, the value of the aircraft carrier with its high degree of mobility, relative immunity from the effects of a counter-attack by ground forces, and comprehensive support facilities, was brought home to the British and American governments. Plans for the further run-down of the USN and RN were firmly shelved, and a three-year expansion programme for the Fleet Air Arm was initiated. The programme included the re-starting of work on HMS *Hermes*, which had been stopped as an economy measure, and the development of specially-designed aircraft for the Royal Navy, to prevent it from relying too heavily on aircraft designed for the Royal Air Force.

The strength of the communist threat to South-East Asia also became more significant as a result of the Korean War, and countering it became an important part of British, American and Australian policy.

One of the other side-effects of the war was the inability of the occupying powers in Japan to maintain large forces there while the war was in progress. In 1950 this led to the creation of a para-military National Police Reserve by the US Military Commander. A decision to form a Japanese Maritime Self-Defence Force followed on 26 April, 1952, with the force formally coming into existence on 1 July, 1954. Preparations for the new JMSDF —the term 'navy' would have been politically and emotionally unacceptable so soon after the end of World War II— included the opening of a naval air station at Tateyame in September, 1953, and this was followed by other air stations at Kanoya and Omawa. Naturally, most of the early aircraft deliveries were of training types, to provide refresher training for veteran World War II Japanese pilots, many of whom in due course became instructors for a new generation of Japanese navy fliers. Typical of the early deliveries for training—and eventually for operations—were Bell 47 helicopters and obsolescent US types, the North American SNJ–6 and Beech SNB–4 trainers, Grumman JRF–5 and Convair (formerly Consolidated) PBY–6A Catalina amphibians for maritime-reconnaissance and SAR duties, Grumman TBM–3S and TBM–3W–2 Avenger and Lockheed PV2 Harpoon anti-submarine aircraft. These were followed by Bell H–13 and Sikorsky S–51 helicopters.

The new JMSDF developed steadily throughout the 1950s, and eventually extensive modernisation was put in hand. This started in 1957, with the arrival of Grumman S2F–1 Tracker and Lockheed

The only other operator of the Avro Shackleton maritime-reconnaissance aircraft, apart from the Royal Air Force, has been the South African Air Force

P2V–7 Neptune aircraft for ASW and maritime-reconnaissance duties, and was followed by licence-production of the Neptune in Japan by Kawasaki, while Sikorsky S–55 helicopters were also produced in Japan, by Mitsubishi. By late 1958, the total personnel strength of the JMSDF amounted to some 25,000 men, including those in the air arm.

Similar military pressures in Europe resulted in German re-armament, just a little behind that of Japan. The Treaty of Paris, on 10 April, 1955, established the British, American and French occupation zones of Germany as the German Federal Republic—West Germany—acknowledging the fact that the Russian zone had become a Soviet satellite, the German Democratic Republic. The new German Federal Republic immediately joined NATO, as Italy had already done, and a planning group was established to study the future German Federal Navy, or Kriegsmarine. This time, there was no doubting that the Kriegsmarine would have its own aircraft and aircrew firmly under its own control.

Aircrew for the Kriegsmarine squadrons were trained at the USN Flying School at Pensacola, Florida, and the Royal Naval Air Station at Culdrose, Cornwall. Orders for the first operational aircraft were placed in Britain for the most part, with an initial seventy Armstrong-Whitworth Sea Hawk Mk100 and 101 fighter-bombers and fifteen Fairey Gannet AS4 anti-submarine aircraft. The aircraft, supplied during the mid-1950s, were followed by American Grumman SA–16A Albatross amphibians and Sikorsky S–55 helicopters for SAR duties.

Meanwhile, the Soviet Union was formalising its relations with its satellite countries in Eastern Europe by means of the Warsaw Pact of 1955. Under its terms, the forces of all the member states were controlled directly by a Joint High Command in Moscow. The word 'joint' could effectively be disregarded, since everything, including standardised equipment production was under direct Soviet control; and even outside the Soviet Union, Soviet forces would not bow to national control by a satellite, in marked contrast to the normal NATO practice. All but one of the member nations were allowed their own high commands and general staffs, although subservient to Moscow, the exception being East Germany, which has had Soviet officers occupying the highest posts in its armed services since the formation of the Democratic Republic.

US aid to Japan, Germany and the new NATO members was generously provided under a number of different military aid programmes, of which the most important was the Mutual Defence Aid Programme, covering the provision or loan of equipment—not necessarily of US-manufacture. One example of MDAP at work was the loan of four squadrons of Lockheed P2V–5 Neptune maritime-reconaissance aircraft to the Royal Air Force Coastal Command between 1952 and 1956. These were loaned to bridge the gap while British Avro Shackleton four-engined long-range maritime-reconnaissance aircraft could enter service, to replace the Neptunes, Avro Lancasters and Short Sunderlands.

There was a sound purpose behind the American generosity. The United States on its own could not contain communist expansion worldwide. It needed the bases, territory, and manpower, which its allies were capable of providing so long as they were offered some assistance with equipment procurement. Today, however few NATO members receive or require US aid.

Major changes in the organisation of the USN took place in line with the commitment to NATO, and these changes also included some alterations to American strategy. The traditional Atlantic and Pacific Fleets disappeared. Instead there was a US First Fleet in the Pacific, a US Second Fleet in the Atlantic, a US Sixth Fleet in the Mediterranean and a US Seventh Fleet in the Far East, the last two being completely new, in line with the new US commitment. The Second and Sixth Fleets were committed entirely to NATO, operating alongside the national fleets of America's allies, of which only Britain and France endeavoured to maintain warships beyond

A Lockheed WV–2 airborne-early-warning Constellation

their own coastal and offshore waters. Each fleet operated as a carrier task force, with two or three carriers, and was expected to be able to work independently of shore bases if necessary.

Even before this radical change took effect in 1954, the United States Navy was establishing a strong presence in the Mediterranean. The first step was the move of USN squadrons into the Royal Naval Air Station at Hal Far in Malta in October, 1951, while the island was still a British possession. At first, Convair PB4Y Privateers were based at Malta, but before long these were replaced by Lockheed Neptunes and airborne-early-warning (AEW) Lockheed WV-2 Constellations. During the 1950s, the base moved from Malta to Naples. Another interim base was established in Morocco, before an agreement with Spain gave the United States Navy the use of facilities at Rota, in return for providing the equipment-starved non-NATO Spanish forces with modern aircraft and ships. Eventually the Sixth Fleet was also able to use Naples and Athens as major shore-bases.

The naval expansion of the period coincided with a spate of improved technology, for as aircraft became faster and carriers bigger, other developments also occurred to enhance the effectiveness of the carrier and its air group. Three inventions helped aircraft carriers and their aircraft to move efficiently and effectively into the jet age during the 1950s. They were the angled flight deck, the steam catapult and the mirror deck landing system; and all three happened to be British in their conception.

Probably the most important of these inventions was the angled flight deck, which allowed aircraft to land and take off at the same time, without interference between the two operations, even on small carriers. It also allowed the deck forward to be used as an aircraft park if the catapults were not in use, without any danger from aircraft overshooting. Not the least advantage, however, was not just that an aircraft could overshoot and make a second attempt to land, but

that one which failed on take off or landing and pancaked into the sea could do so without fear of being run down by the vessel—an important feature from the pilot's point of view!

The invention was the brainchild of Captain D. R. F. Cambell, DSO, RN, but ironically, the first aircraft carrier to have the interim half-angled flight deck was the USS *Antietam*, in 1952. The new Hermes class light fleet carrier, HMS *Centaur*, entered Royal Navy service in 1953 with a half-angled flight deck, which, unlike the fully angled deck, could be incorporated with minimal dockyard work. However, the fully angled deck was more effective and made better use of deck space. The first deck landing on a British half-angled deck came in May, 1954, when HMS *Centaur* finished her trials and joined the fleet, and Captain H. P. Sears, RN, landed on her.

Related to the angled deck development was the mirror deck landing system. This gave the pilot a clear indication that his landing approach was correct—neither too high nor too low—by reflecting the landing light of his aircraft on the glide path, thus replacing the batman and assisting in the landing of heavier and faster aircraft. The system, which was relatively easy to fit to existing aircraft carriers, first appeared in 1954, based on an idea by Commander H. C. N. Goodhart, RN.

The third development, the steam catapult, aimed at bridging the gap between higher aircraft take-off speeds and the relatively static maximum speeds of aircraft carriers, which had not been helped by the relatively slow initial acceleration of the un-reheated jet engine. Originally conceived by Commander C. C. Mitchell, OBE, RNVR, the steam catapult was developed by the Royal Navy and Brown Brothers of Edinburgh, and fourteen months of trials aboard the light fleet aircraft carrier HMS *Perseus* preceded the first live take-off by Lieutenant-Commander J. M. Glaser, in July, 1951. The steam catapult came into operational use two years later, replacing the pneumo-hydraulic catapults, or accelerators, which dated from the 1930s, although much improved in the interim. Even before the advent of the steam catapult, British catapults had been modified to American standard to use a strop, which towed the aircraft off in effect, rather than using the launching trolleys at first favoured by the British for both landplanes and seaplanes.

Initially, aircraft carriers placed steam catapults in place of the older type on the fore-deck, having one or two, depending on the size of the ship. But on larger vessels, waist catapults were also placed on the fully angled flight deck, with one of these on British carriers and two on the larger American aircraft carriers. With such a layout, British carriers would have two catapults and American carriers four.

At first, much was made of the reputed ability of the steam catapult to launch a jet aircraft even while the ship was at anchor in nil wind conditions. This was normally an impracticable proposition anyway, and increased take-off weights soon meant that forward speed became essential to help the catapult. The traditional practice of flying carrier air squadrons to shore bases on entering port if further flying was envisaged was therefore never dropped.

If all these developments had taken place before World War II, the situation might have been worse for the British and Americans in the Pacific, since at the Battle of Midway the Japanese commander could have launched his fighters while receiving his attack aircraft!

It was the need to incorporate these new developments into the new Australian aircraft carrier HMAS *Melbourne*, originally HMS *Majestic*, that had delayed delivery of the ship to her new owner. In the meantime, the Royal Australian Navy had borrowed another British light fleet carrier, HMS *Vengeance*, to act as a training carrier after her arrival in Australia in 1953. A little earlier, in 1952, the RAN introduced its first helicopters, Bristol Sycamores, and in 1953 it opened a new shore base at Schofield, named HMAS *Nirimba*. Progress continued with the delivery of de Havilland Sea Vampires

A Royal Australian Navy Fairey Gannet anti-submarine aircraft about to be catapulted from HMAS *Melbourne*

for carrier jet training in 1954. HMAS *Melbourne*'s arrival in Australia in May, 1956, also brought new de Havilland Sea Venom FAW53 all-weather fighters and Fairey Gannet ASW aircraft to the Royal Australian Navy. These together with the ship herself, meant that the Australian Fleet Air Arm was amongst the most modern and well-equipped in the world at the time.

Following the arrival of HMAS *Melbourne*, HMS *Vengeance* returned to the Royal Navy, although her stay in Britain was to be short, while HMAS *Sydney* became the training aircraft carrier and fast troop transport.

Modernisation of Australia's armed forces had not been confined to the Royal Australian Navy, however, even though that force had also received new Daring class destroyers and other vessels at the same time. The Royal Australian Air Force was meanwhile introducing a squadron of Lockheed P2V-5 Neptunes, replacing Harpoons and Lancasters, although some specially modified Lincolns remained in service.

Concern at communist expansion and its threat to stability was not an exclusively British or American preoccupation, and in 1955 the South-East Asia Treaty Organisation (SEATO) was formed. This was a multilateral alliance including Australia, France, New Zealand, Pakistan, the Philippines, the United Kingdom and the United States, although, unlike NATO, it lacked a formalised command structure. In part, SEATO was the answer to Australia's and New Zealand's request for membership of NATO, but other treaties also covered the relationship between these countries and the United Kingdom and United States, notably ANZUK and ANZUS.

Just as the RAN had to face delays while waiting for HMAS *Melbourne*, so did the Royal Canadian Navy while waiting for its light fleet carrier, HMCS *Bonaventure*. In 1952, the RCN Naval Aviation was operating four squadrons, two each of Avengers and Sea Furies, with some Bell HTL-4 and Sikorsky

HO4S-1 helicopters, delivered a year earlier. The trend towards US aircraft meant the adoption of US-style squadron designations, with VF, VS and VH prefixes denoting fighter, ASW and helicopter squadrons respectively. Hampered by the lack of an operational aircraft carrier, the RCN had no direct role in the Korean War, although some of its pilots flew with USN squadrons. However, the RCN was one of the first navies to place helicopters aboard a ship normally too small for regular aircraft operation, when three Bell HTL-4s were deployed aboard the Arctic patrol vessel HMCS *Labrador* in 1953. Later on, Vertol HUP-3 Retriever twin-rotor helicopters operated from this ship.

HMCS *Magnificent* was on loan from the Royal Navy while HMCS *Bonaventure* was awaited, and Sikorsky HO4S-1s were operated from this ship on planeguard duties. In the interim, no time was wasted in attaining an operational standard for the RCN squadrons, which had the first of thirty-nine McDonnell F2H-3 Banshee jet fighters delivered during 1955, along with the first of sixty-six Grumman S2F-1 Tracker antisubmarine aircraft, built under licence by de Havilland Canada. Dunking sonar Sikorsky HO4S-3 helicopters were introduced for ASW operation from aircraft carriers, and in preparation for the arrival of HMCS *Bonaventure* in mid-1957— complete with angled flight deck and the other innovations—pilots went ahead with jet training, using Canadair T-33 Silver Stars. Conversion training of Banshee and Tracker pilots also went ahead, aboard the USS *Wasp*.

Expansion of the Royal Navy's Fleet Air Arm, or Naval Aviation, included a fairly rapid introduction of jet aircraft from 1951 onwards, when the Supermarine Attacker was fully operational. Up-to-date piston-engined aircraft, such as the Sea Furies, could then be transferred to the RNVR squadrons. In November, 1951, the Royal Navy's last piston-engined type, the fifty Douglas AD-4W Skyraiders, were introduced for airborne-

A flight of Armstrong-Whitworth Sea Hawks from HMS *Eagle*

early-warning duties. The first of a large number of Fairey Gannet turboprop anti-submarine aircraft entered service in March, 1954. Another anti-submarine aircraft, the Short Seamew, designed for operations from smaller aircraft carriers, was soon discarded in the interests of standardisation and carrier modernisation. It also soon became clear that dunking sonar ASW helicopters could operate successfully and effectively from vessels too small for the Gannet. The Fleet Air Arm's first dunking sonar helicopters, Sikorsky HO4S–3s for No. 845 Squadron based on Malta, had been delivered under the Mutual Defence Aid Programme, and followed the earlier delivery of Sikorsky HRS–2 helicopters in January, 1953, for use against terrorists in Malaya, and twenty Hiller HTO–1s for pilot training. Generally, however, Sikorsky helicopters for the Royal Navy and Royal Air Force were built under licence in Britain by Westland, who also obtained rights to build them for naval use in Europe and much of the British Commonwealth.

HMS *Eagle*, the first large aircraft carrier for the Royal Navy, entered service in 1952, and in March, 1953 the Fleet Air Arm received Armstrong-Whitworth Sea Hawk jet fighters, which entered service just in time to take part in the Coronation Flypast for Queen Elizabeth II later that year. Altogether, 300 Royal Navy aircraft took part in the flypast, including the other new Fleet Air Arm jet fighter, the de Havilland Sea Venom, and the turboprop Westland Wyvern carrier-borne attack aircraft.

Eventually having a standard displacement of 41,000 tons—rather more than that projected at the time of ordering—HMS *Eagle* possessed only a traditional flight deck at first, though she later received a half-angled flight deck. She also had two steam catapults forward and mirror landing systems. A half-angled flight deck was incorporated in the *Eagle*'s

Hellcats and Helldivers aboard the ex-American Independence-class light fleet carrier *La Fayette*, off French Indo-China

sister ship, HMS *Ark Royal*, when she joined the fleet in 1955. Well armoured, each of these vessels could take some sixty aircraft of the types then in service, had two hangar decks, two lifts, and a service speed of more than 33 knots.

In spite of the delay to the nameship, which eventually set a rather sad record for the time taken in her construction, the three remaining vessels of the Hermes class entered service in 1954, with HMS *Centaur*, *Albion* and *Bulwark*. In effect smaller versions of HMS *Eagle* and *Ark Royal*, these vessels only had half-angled decks, and a rather smaller aircraft capacity of around forty machines, including the comparatively large Fairey Gannet, with its twin turboprop unit driving a contra-rotating propeller system. All three vessels had two steam catapults forward.

The Aeronavale had not been standing still either, and while the Royal Navy received much overdue but welcome additions to its fleet, the Marine Nationale obtained two American Independence class aircraft carriers on loan while awaiting the construction of two new French aircraft carriers. Named in French service the *La Fayette* and *Bois Belleau*—USS *Belleau Wood*, of course—these two vessels complemented the *Arromanches* during the 1950s. They initially operated with piston-engined aircraft before the 1954 French withdrawal from Indo-China, where they were deployed.

New aircraft for the Aeronavale included the Sud Aquilan carrier-borne fighter—licence-built versions of the de Havilland Sea Venom—and Vertol H–21 and HUP–2, Bell 47 and Sikorsky S–55 helicopters. In addition, Grumman TBM–3 Avengers remained in service along with Short Sunderlands and Avro Lancasters ashore, which provided the

The first super carrier, the USS *Forrestal*, with Phantom and Hawkeye aircraft prominent amongst the types ranged on the flight deck

bulk of the Aeronavale's long-range maritime-reconnaissance effort. However, French replacements for the first generation of jet fighters were put in hand during the late 1950s, with development of the Dassault Etendard jet fighter-bomber and the Breguet Br.1050 Alize turboprop anti-submarine aircraft. Both types were timed to enter service ready for the arrival in the early 1960s of *Clemenceau* and *Foch*. Ashore, a French long-range maritime-reconnaissance aircraft was to be some way off, and the Lancasters and Sunderlands were replaced with Lockheed P2V–6 and 7 Neptunes.

The United States Navy, besides receiving new aircraft carriers, modernised its existing fleet, fitting first half-angled and then fully-angled flight decks, and quickly incorporating the other developments as well. The original decision to cancel the 60,000 ton super carrier, USS *United States*, although not rescinded, was effectively reversed when in October, 1955, the USS *Forrestal*, 60,000 tons, joined the fleet, since she was built to a design that owed more than a little to that of the USS *United States*. Able to carry some seventy or eighty of the larger aircraft entering service with the USN during the 1950s, the USS *Forrestal* had four deck-edge lifts which left the maximum amount of free hanger and flight deck space. In addition to having a fully angled flight deck she also had four steam catapults, two forward and two waist catapults on the flight deck angle. She was later joined by three sister ships—USS *Saratoga*, in April, 1956, USS *Ranger* in August, 1957, and USS *Independence*, in January, 1959.

New jet aircraft for these vessels included the Douglas F4D–1 Skyray, McDonnell F3H Demon, Grumman F9F Cougar and F11F Tiger, North American

A USN McDonnell Demon, while on a visit to a British aircraft carrier

FJ–2 Fury and Chance–Vought F7U Cutlass, as well as the supersonic Chance–Vought—later known as Ling–Temco–Vought or LTV—F-8 Crusader, with the unusual features of variable-incidence wings to correct a nose-down tendency on the approach. Grumman S–2 Tracker twin piston-engined anti-submarine aircraft also joined the American carriers, and in common with the Gannet and Alize, these aircraft were an improvement over the Avenger in that a single aircraft could carry anti-submarine detection equipment and also depth charges or bombs, while the Avenger had had to divide these duties. Another aircraft with features in common with the Gannet was the E–1 Tracer airborne-early-warning development of the Tracker, using basically the same airframe, which made its first appearance in the same year as the Tracer.

An innovation in the delivery of supplies to aircraft carriers at sea was carrier-onboard-delivery, or COD, again with a Tracker development, the TF–1, which

appeared in 1955, although in 1962 the designation C–1 Trader was adopted, along with a general move to common aircraft designations through the USN and USAF.

The new generation of carrier-borne jet fighters was the first to use air-to-air guided missiles, including the Sparrow and Sidewinder, introduced in 1955.

Altogether, the USN and USMC had some 15,000 aircraft at this time, and the deliveries of new aircraft they received would have made any air arm or air force envious. However, the lack of standardisation must have created some problems, even if it did act as a safeguard against weakness or failure in any one aircraft type! Trader and Albatross transport aircraft were not transferred to the Military Air Transport Service.

Later versions of the Lockheed Neptune and the introduction of the new Martin P5M–1 Marlin brought a new anti-submarine device into service. This was the magnetic anomaly detector, developed to detect the local disturbance to the earth's magnetic field created by the presence of a submerged submarine. The device protruded beyond the tailplane in a housing which was sometimes referred

to as the MAD 'stinger'. Such changes to the structure of the aircraft were minor compared to those on the Lockheed WV–2 Constellations operated by the USN in the Mediterranean and over the North Atlantic. These aircraft had a large under-belly bulge and a large fin, or conning-tower-like structure, above the fuselage, giving the impression of a flying submarine!

With the dawn of the age of the nuclear-powered submarine, with no need to surface to recharge its batteries and with a high underwater speed, anti-submarine operations became at once more difficult and more important. The helicopter with its dunking sonar and, later, its torpedoes, was proving successful, with the Sikorsky HO4S–1 and then HSS–1. However, a purpose-built type, the Bell HSL–1 tandem-rotor helicopter, was disappointing. For other tasks, Piasecki and Kaman helicopters were also obtained, operating on plane-guard and SAR duties.

One failure amidst the stream of successes was the Convair XF–2Y Sea Dart, a delta-wing ski-fighter, intended to operate from snow, ice, water, mud or even sand. This aircraft flew on its trials throughout 1952 and 1953, until the project was abandoned after a prototype disintegrated in mid-air.

Considerably more successful was the Douglas F4D–1 Skyray prototype, which was prepared for an American attempt on the World Air Speed record. Trials with Lieutenant-Commander James B. Verdin, USN, as pilot, started over the Salton Sea, in California, on 25 September, 1953, although an early attempt at the record had to be abandoned due to a faulty fuel gauge. However, on 3 October, 1953, Verdin established a record of 753.4 mph (Mach 0·964) flying just a hundred feet or so above the lake level. This very low altitude made high transonic speed more difficult to achieve, due to atmospheric pressure, and it is not surprising that this was the last low-altitude attempt on the record.

A jubilant Verdin managed to say: 'The plane behaved perfectly. Turbulence didn't bother me a bit. I feel very fortunate to have been able to make the run.'

He might possibly have been even more jubilant a little later when the

USAF's first supersonic aircraft, the North American F–100 Super Sabre, failed to break his record.

Strangely, at a time of substantial arms expenditure and naval expansion, the USN chose to close its Naval Aircraft Factory at Philadelphia on 1 January, 1956, on the grounds of economy. This came at a time when the largest carrier-borne aircraft up to that date entered USN service aboard the new Forrestal class vessels. The Douglas A3D–1 Skymaster twin-jet bomber and jet flying-boats, Martin P6M Seamasters, were meanwhile joining shore-based units. Yet, the all-important role of the fighter was also being challenged, with the Terrier and Tartar anti-aircraft ship-borne guided missiles, which joined USN vessels for trials during 1956 and 1957.

Just a little standardisation and sub-merging of USN–USAF rivalry occurred with both services taking the same basic trainer, the North American T–28 Trojan, the naval T–28C version of which was fitted with an arrester hook.

Events were soon to prove that American support for her European allies, though generous, had its bounds!

A flight of Douglas Skymaster jet bombers from the USS *Forrestal*

On 31 October, 1956, British, French and Israeli forces invaded the Suez Canal Zone following Egyptian nationalisation of the international waterway without compensation. The action was response to worldwide fears that right of passage through the canal might be refused to ships of certain nationalities, including Israel. Planning for this successful attack started in August, 1956, and no less than fourteen squadrons of Fleet Air Arm aircraft embarked aboard the aircraft carriers HMS *Eagle*, *Albion* and *Bulwark* and the light fleet carriers HMS *Ocean* and *Theseus*, assembled in the Mediterranean for an exercise, with *La Fayette* and *Arromanches*. Meanwhile aircraft from other Fleet Air Arm squadrons, the Royal Air Force, Armée de l'Air and Aeronavale assembled at RAF bases on the British colony of Cyprus. Israeli land forces invaded the Canal Zone, attacking overland, while Britain and France launched an amphibious assault with air cover. The Egyptian Air Force possessed twice as many aircraft as the three countries combined could muster in the area, but the three allies attained aerial superiority within forty-eight hours —an achievement in no small part due to the use of carrier-borne aircraft, with aircraft based on Cyprus and Israel only

able to spend some ten minutes over the target area.

The most spectacular part of the whole operation was a surprise attack on Gamil Airfield, at Port Said. For this attack some 600 men of No. 45 Commando, Royal Marines, were ferried ashore in just ninety minutes by Westland S–55 Whirlwind helicopters from HMS *Theseus* and *Ocean*.

The Suez operation was called off on 7 November, as the result of an American threat to withdraw support for the currencies of the three nations, which were not unnaturally suffering a run due to what some regarded as an open-ended and costly commitment to Middle East operations. By that time, Fleet Air Arm aircraft alone had carried out some 2,500 sorties.

If the Suez operation, to this day a point of political controversy in the United Kingdom, proved that Britain and France were more vulnerable to outside pressures than had hitherto been suspected, it nevertheless amply demonstrated the worth of the aircraft carrier and its developing role. The lesson was not ignored, and shortly afterwards the two Hermes class carriers, HMS *Albion* and *Bulwark*, were withdrawn to be refitted as commando carriers. After the refit they were able to carry comfortably up to sixteen helicopters each, together with the vehicles and equipment required by a commando force of 800 men, or twice this number in an emergency. The two vessels would have needed refitting anyway, even as aircraft carriers, to incorporate an angled flight deck.

Another lesson of Suez was that the rising complexity and cost of defence called for highly trained and well-equipped professional forces, rather than for conscripts, who in two years could often learn little of value in an increasingly technological navy, army or air force. During the late 1950s and early 1960s, Britain thus became the first major power to create all-professional armed forces, backing these forces with volunteer reservists. One immediate loss, however,

was the Royal Auxiliary Air Force, reduced to the size of a token force. Later the RNVR squadrons also disappeared. A wrong decision at the same time was to declare that the future of the manned aircraft was at an end. This meant that Britain's aircraft industry devoted less attention to developing new aircraft for the Royal Navy and Royal Air Force than it otherwise would have done.

Some reduction in regular forces also took place, while the Royal Naval Reserve absorbed the Royal Naval Volunteer Reserve. Most of the vast reserve fleet was scrapped, including the last escort carrier, HMS *Campania*. While this has since been a sore point in some quarters, it has to be recognised that many of the vessels concerned were obsolete, and had not been maintained since withdrawal from service. Many of the light fleet carriers were also scrapped or sold, which was admittedly wasteful. However, HMS *Triumph* was used for training duties for a short period before undergoing a lengthy refit and conversion to a heavy maintenance ship, to support the fleet as a whole—a role different from that of the fleet maintenance carrier.

Nevertheless, on the basis of having a modern well-equipped Royal Navy manned by professionals, what was done was right for the second half of the twentieth century. It only became doubtful afterwards, when successive governments failed to maintain the original regular size and also proved reluctant to invest adequately in new equipment, or to support an effective if small reserve force, which in the Royal Navy tends to specialise in mine counter-measures.

The post-Suez Royal Navy and its Fleet Air Arm were in fine form, with two big modern aircraft carriers, HMS *Eagle* and *Ark Royal*, and two fairly new carriers undergoing conversion to commando carriers. One sister ship, HMS *Centaur*, remained as an aircraft carrier and in 1959 was finally joined in this role by the nameship of the class, HMS *Hermes*, complete with fully-angled flight deck, steam catapults, mirror landing aids, three dimensional radar, and provision for the fitting of anti-aircraft guided missile systems. Before this, HMS *Victorious* had rejoined the fleet in 1958, bringing the same high standard of equipment to the Royal Navy as the smaller HMS *Hermes* did a year later, but with a waist catapult and only one catapult forward, as against the smaller vessel's two catapults forward.

Ideally, something rather more imaginative might have been done with HMS *Theseus*, *Glory*, *Ocean* and *Perseus* than sending them to the breakers. They might, for example have been converted as commando carriers, while HMS *Albion* and *Bulwark* might have been refitted to *Hermes* standard. Nevertheless the Royal Navy and the Fleet Air Arm were in their best-ever peacetime condition, and this was helped still further by the arrival in service of a new generation of purpose-built carrier aircraft. These included the

Supermarine Scimitar jet fighter, the de Havilland D.H.110 Sea Vixen transonic fighter-bomber and the Blackburn, later Hawker Siddeley, NA.39 Buccaneer, a low-level transonic carrier-borne bomber capable of delivering nuclear weapons and stand-off missiles. Later versions of the last-mentioned aircraft not only further up-dated the Fleet Air Arm's capability, but also replaced most of the Royal Air Force's Canberra light bombers. The main feature of the Buccaneer was its ability to escape detection by flying below the enemy's defending radar net.

Westland-built versions of the Sikorsky S–58 helicopter, the Wessex, were also introduced for troop-carrying and anti-submarine duties, while a British helicopter, the Westland Wasp, was developed as the first helicopter specifically designed to operate from small warships. The Tribal class frigates one of the first warship classes specifically built to operate helicopters, were already on order, while plans were also in hand to put helicopters aboard the Royal Navy's Whitby and

Sea Venom and Scimitar aircraft aboard the rebuilt HMS *Victorious*

Rothesay class frigates as well as on the County class guided missile destroyers which were then being built. Such moves as these meant that even the smallest navy would soon be able to take aircraft to sea.

Other navies had also developed and modernised their air arms in the meantime. The Royal Netherlands Naval Air Service was left intact in March, 1953, when a Royal Netherlands Air Force was finally created; and with the introduction of MDAP, eighteen Lockheed PV2 Harpoons were delivered, to be replaced soon afterwards by a squadron of Lockheed P2V–5 Neptunes, supplemented with a small number of Martin PBM–5A Mariner amphibians. The carrier-borne squadrons were not neglected either, having fifty Grumman TBM–3S and TBM–3W Avengers delivered under the same programme. These were replaced later in the decade by Grumman Trackers and twenty-two Armstrong–Whitworth Sea Hawk fighter-bombers. The inevitable helicopters for plane-guard and SAR duties were also introduced, in the form of Sikorsky HO4S, or S–55, machines.

Still more significant were the developments taking place in India and in Latin America.

There had been a lull in development for Argentina's Aviacion Navale until 1956, when its Consolidated Catalinas were suddenly augmented by Chance–Vought F4U Corsair fighter-bombers. Then in 1957 the Catalinas were largely replaced by Lockheed P2V–5 Neptunes and Martin PBM–5 Mariners, together with a few Grumman F6F–5 Hellcat fighters and Goose and J2F–2 amphibians. This was in readiness for the arrival in 1958 of the light fleet carrier HMS *Warrior*, renamed *Independencia* before joining the Argentinian Navy.

Support for this rapid development of the Argentinian Navy came from the United States Navy, which also prepared the Brazilian Navy, or Marinha, for carrier operations. At first, Bell 47 and Westland Wigeon helicopters were introduced, but on the arrival in 1957 of the light fleet carrier HMS *Vengeance* (renamed *Minas Gerais*), North American T–28C Trojan armed-trainers and Grumman S–2A Tracker anti-submarine aircraft were also obtained for carrier operation. Yet in 1965, the operation of fixed-wing aircraft from the *Minas Gerais* passed to the Forca Aerea Brasileira, in spite of experience gained elsewhere.

The Indian Navy had decided to form a small Fleet Air Arm shortly after India gained independence, and the first positive step towards this aim came in 1953, with the opening in May of a naval air station, INS *Garuda*, at Cochin in southern India. This became the home of a Fleet Requirements Unit which initially operated Short Sealand amphibians and Hindustan HT-2 basic trainers these later being joined by Fairey Firefly target tugs. In 1957, another of the Royal Navy's diminishing band of light fleet carriers, HMS *Hercules*, was taken out of reserve and underwent a four-year refit, ready to join the Indian Navy in 1961 as the INS *Vikrant*. Aircraft ordered for the new ship were an interesting Anglo–French assortment, with Armstrong–Whitworth Sea Hawk fighter-bombers and Breguet Br.1050 Alize ASW aircraft.

In sharp contrast, Italy, a founder-member of NATO in 1949 and a country which had been deeply concerned with effective maritime-reconnaissance between the wars, at first contented itself with simply equipping the Aeronautica Militaire Italiano with a small number of Piaggio P–56 amphibians, until these were replaced by Lockheed PV2 Harpoons. This was something of an interim measure, since in 1957, US assistance meant that the AMI's maritime-reconnaissance squadrons were re-equipped with Grumman S–2A Trackers and Grumman SA–16A amphibians.

The Italian Navy, the Marinavia, started to take an active interest in the potential of the helicopter during the late 1950s, and with the AMI received Bell helicopters built under licence in Italy by Agusta. Indeed, the interest in helicopters

Attack TBM–3W and search TBM–3S
Avengers of the Royal Netherlands Naval Air
Service during the mid-1950s

amongst navies was becoming almost universal, with the Royal Swedish Navy, as another example, introducing Vertol 44K helicopters for ASW.

Towards the end of the decade, Admiral Gorshkov became Commander-in-Chief of the Soviet Navy, marking the end of the period in which the West could almost afford to ignore the Soviet Navy. Some development had taken place during the 1950s, but the main push forward was still to come. The A–VMF was divided into five regions, with a separate air force in effect for the Soviet Baltic, Northern Seas, North Pacific, Pacific and Black Seas Fleets. Equipment largely followed that for the Soviet Air Force, with Mikoyan MiG–15, MiG–17 and MiG–19 fighters entering service in succession, side by side with Tupolev Tu–16 and Ilyushin Il–28 twin-jet bombers,

versions of the piston-engined Tu-4, and —not in line with Soviet Air Force practice—Beriev Be–10 flying-boats. Generally, the link with the Air Force was so close that A–VMF units actually fought in Korea alongside Air Force units.

The A–VMF was spreading its wings further by the end of the decade, however, with the giant Myasischev Mya–4 four-engined jet bomber and Tupolev Tu–20 turboprop patrol bombers in service, while from 1950 onwards the force received vast quantities of the Mil Mi–1 and Mi–4—similar to the S–55—helicopters. Gorshkov's task was to convert the Soviet Navy from what Khrushchev described as 'metal-eaters' into an effective fighting force. In just a decade he was to achieve just that, in no uncertain measure.

9 The Nuclear Navy

The 1960s saw naval aviation and the aircraft carrier move into the nuclear age, with the commissioning of the world's first nuclear-powered aircraft carrier, the USS *Enterprise*. At the other end of the scale, naval aviation was at the same time also becoming firmly associated with far smaller vessels, such as frigates and destroyers, which themselves often used gas turbine propulsion, developed from the jet aircraft engine.

Designers of surface warships and of aircraft carriers had not delayed overlong in attempting to apply the benefits of nuclear power to a new generation of vessels, for obvious reasons. Nuclear-powered vessels have an infinitely superior unrefuelled range to that of conventionally-powered ones, and are therefore free from the need to refuel at sea or at a shore base. This not only reduces the number of auxiliary vessels a navy

requires, but also the number of warships it has to tie down to protecting them in a crisis. It also grants the freedom of the seas to navies, without their having to depend on a world-wide string of shore bases. These advantages apply almost as much to surface ships as to submarines, which had pioneered nuclear power at sea out of the very real necessity to eliminate the time spent re-charging batteries. However, widespread adoption of nuclear power did not come immediately, because of the very high cost of constructing nuclear vessels and the expense involved in providing shore facilities for refuelling when it did eventually become necessary —once every few years. Furthermore,

The first nuclear carrier, the USS *Enterprise*, in the Pacific some fifteen years after commissioning, with Corsair II, Intruder and Hawkeye aircraft well to the fore

during the early 1960s, fuel oil remained cheap and plentiful, thus offering little incentive to change to nuclear power.

In her design, the USS *Enterprise* broke no new ground other than in her large size—75,700 tons standard displacement—and in her power source, and even this provided propulsion through steam turbines. The new vessel, which commissioned in November, 1961, followed the pattern already established by earlier aircraft carriers. She had a starboard island superstructure, obviously unencumbered by a funnel, and a fully angled flight deck, with two steam catapults on the angled deck and another two forward, while four deck-edge lifts left the maximum amount of usable deck and hangar space available, helping the ship to cope with her load of more than eighty large jet aircraft. In spite of her size, she had a maximum speed of 35 knots, and was the fastest new aircraft carrier for many years.

The most telling comparisons came not with the smaller aircraft carriers still

Flying delivery van: a Grumman Greyhound COD aircraft lands on USS *John F. Kennedy*, a Kitty Hawk-class conventional carrier

favoured by other navies, which could not afford the high cost of nuclear power, but with the last class of conventional aircraft carriers ordered by the United States, the Kitty Hawk class. In many respects, the USS *Kitty Hawk* was simply a slightly smaller version of the USS *Enterprise*, commissioned in April, 1961; she had the same deck layout and number of lifts, and the now almost mandatory starboard island, but in spite of her lower tonnage—just over 60,000 tons standard displacement—she was able to accommodate the same number of aircraft. One reason for this was that the USS *Kitty Hawk*, without the weight of a large nuclear reactor, offered a lower standard displacement than the USS *Enterprise*, although full load displacements, with the conventional vessel carrying large quantities of fuel oil for her boilers, were far more closely matched, being 85,000 tons for the USS *Enterprise* and 77,000 tons for the USS *Kitty Hawk*.

The USS *Enterprise* was the sole vessel of her class, but the USS *Kitty Hawk* was joined by three sister ships, the USS *Constellation*, in October, 1961, the USS *America* in January, 1965, and the USS *John F. Kennedy* in September, 1968. A

clear indication of the capabilities of a nuclear-powered aircraft carrier (or CVN, to use the US Navy designation) came in 1964, when the nuclear-powered cruisers USS *Long Beach* and *Bainbridge*, joined the USS *Enterprise* to form a nuclear-powered battle group which sailed around the world in sixty-four days without once refuelling.

If the aircraft capacity of the new aircraft carriers seemed low in comparison with the hundred or more aircraft carried by the Essex and Midway classes, the figures were in fact deceptive, since the comparatively recent massive growth in aircraft sizes masked the real growth in aircraft accommodation aboard the new ships. Throughout the 1950s and 1960s, the Essex class aircraft carriers started to change roles, being found less often in the attack role and more often reclassified as CVS, or anti-submarine carriers, with some forty-five aircraft, including many helicopters as well as ASW Grumman Trackers and a fighter squadron for protection from anti-ship aircraft.

The 1960s saw the USN undergo a period of modernisation of its carrier and shore-based aircraft, and, with far fewer new types, improving standardisation. Some older aircraft did, indeed, survive in service throughout the decade, but these were few, the only really notable example being the Douglas Skyraider, which by this time operated exclusively in the ground-attack role. The achievement of standardisation, with all the benefits of simplified spares support, reduced costs and minimised conversion training, was helped by the introduction of a number of excellent aircraft, each of which effectively eliminated any possible competitor for its chosen task.

The first and most successful of these aircraft was undoubtedly the McDonnell F–4 Phantom II jet fighter-bomber, which was first flown in 1958 and entered service with the USN as the F–4B in December, 1960. This carrier-borne Mach 2.2 aircraft proved to be so successful that it was also ordered by the USAF, entering service with them in 1963. Outside the United States, Phantoms were ordered first by the Royal Navy and the Royal Air Force, and then by a few more very safe and carefully selected allies, before being sold more widely. As so often happened with successful USN aircraft types, many Phantoms also entered USMC service.

Another successful fighter-bomber or attack aircraft of the period was the Douglas A–4 Skyhawk, a slower, lighter aircraft which had entered USN and USMC service during the late 1950s, but which continued to play an important part for more than a decade afterwards, until gradually replaced by the larger and more powerful Grumman A–6 Intruder after 1960. An idea of the importance of reconnaissance and of electronic countermeasures, in an attempt to fox an enemy's defences, can be gathered from the inclusion of RF–4B reconnaissance Phantoms and EA–6A electronics countermeasures Intruders in USMC squadrons.

Probably one of the hardest-hitting of all USN aircraft came with the Chance–Vought A–7 Corsair II, a large single-seat, single-engined, carrier-borne attack aircraft, which first entered service in 1965. Bearing a strong resemblance to the earlier F–8 Crusader, the A–7 lacked the supersonic speed and variable-incidence wing of the earlier aircraft, while repeating the Phantom's success with the United States Air Force.

Although these aircraft helped ease the problems of air forces and air arms by their superb suitability for their purpose, the higher cost of development and the continued overall reduction in defence budgets which had once again become part of the international scene amongst the democracies forced changes on the aircraft industry. Chance–Vought was acquired by Ling–Temco in 1961, becoming Ling–Temco–Vought, or more usually, LTV, while McDonnell, with a highly successful product in the Phantom, found itself able to take over the ailing Douglas (suffering from a much reduced share of the defence budget and a temporary shortage in demand for civil aircraft), creating McDonnell Douglas in 1967.

In an attempt to use the new large carriers to the best advantage, an all-purpose carrier-borne bomber, the North American Rockwell A–5 Vigilante, was developed and entered service aboard the USS *Enterprise* in 1962, giving the vessel's air group a Mach 2·0 nuclear strike capability. However, before long this aircraft, and later marks, were converted for reconnaissance operations, and did not share the success of the Phantom and the Corsair.

To some extent, the role of the bomber was reduced when Polaris submarine-launched intercontinental ballistic missiles entered service with the United States and Royal Navies during the 1960s. The gun was also facing strong competition, with the contemporary of the *Enterprise*, the USS *Long Beach*, being equipped with Terrier and Tartar ship-to-air guided missiles and few guns for anti-aircraft defence!

Not all of the new aircraft were carrier-borne types, and a successor to the Lockheed Neptune appeared with the first flight of the Lockheed P–3 Orion, developed from the four turboprop-engined Electra airliner, in August, 1958. Deliveries of the first production variant, the P–3A, to the United States Navy started in August, 1962, replacing not only the P2V Neptunes, but also the still-numerous flying-boats in USN service, with the exception of a few that were replaced by Lockheed C–130 aircraft, a modified version of the MATS transport.

Like most decades in mankind's chequered history, the 1960s were anything but peaceful. The most serious and far-reaching of the many conflicts that contributed to a troubled international scene was that in Vietnam. Formed out of part of the former French Indo-China after the end of World War II, Vietnam was, in 1954, divided into a northern zone and a southern zone, with the former communist-dominated and the latter pro-Western. Other parts of what had been

French Indo-China—Cambodia and Laos—attempted a vague neutrality. After 1957, communist-backed guerillas started to mount increasingly strong attacks on towns, villages and highways in the south, while also attempting to impose their will on Cambodia and Laos. Initially, the United States provided equipment and advisers to strengthen and assist South Vietnamese forces, but as the situation deteriorated, the number of advisers grew, until eventually they were more akin to regular US troops in rank, numbers and individual experience. Eventually, America's President, John Kennedy, fully committed US forces to the war in Vietnam. These included USMC as well as United States Army units, with USN and USMC aircraft joining USAF and United States Army squadrons in providing support for American and Vietnamese ground forces. Sometimes Australian and New Zealand troops were also involved.

In its early stages, the war was not notable for naval engagements, although there was mining of North Vietnamese ports by American aircraft, while carrier-borne aircraft helped in providing air support for troops and in attacking Viet Cong-held positions and supply routes from the north. However, on 2 August, 1964, the destroyer USS *Maddox* was attacked by North Vietnamese torpedo-boats, and three days later, on 5 August, aircraft from the USS *Ticonderoga* and *Constellation*, wiped out the bases the torpedo-boats had used. Full involvement of the US Seventh Fleet started on 7 February, 1965, and except for brief lulls, from this time onwards an average of three aircraft carriers provided support for ground forces, as well as bombing North Vietnam.

There were other problems for the United States, almost as if set by fate, to test the courage and nerve of its leadership. The fall of the Batista dictatorship in a long-drawn-out Cuban revolution or civil war, which ended on 1 January, 1959, resulted in another dictatorship, under the communist leader Fidel Castro.

A Lockheed P–3B Orion of the RNZAF

A Sikorsky HH–52A (S–61) of the USCG

The island republic changed quickly from having been the recipient of reluctant US aid to a recipient of massive and willing Soviet aid—primarily military—in return for the use of bases close to the United States, and incidentally, cheap agricultural produce. The United States could do little to stop this, although it did hold on to its base at Cantallimo Bay for several years after the take-over by Castro. Positive action was called for in 1962, however, when the Soviet Union started to construct missile launching sites in Cuba, far too close to the coast of the United States for comfort. These bases completely negated the value of a United States defensive system based on the threat of major aerial attack over the North Pole or North Pacific, with the only real outside threat at the time being an attack across the North Atlantic, which could almost certainly be countered first by American forces in Europe or by America's European allies.

The United States warned, in October, 1962, that Soviet vessels approaching Cuba would be stopped and searched, and if found to be carrying military equipment, would be arrested or turned back by the United States Navy. Normally, such action would have amounted to a declaration of war, but the brinkmanship, enforced by deployment of massive naval forces in the Caribbean, worked, successfully calling the Soviet bluff!

An undoubted victory for the West, and one which maintained the balance of power and gave world peace another chance, the exercise nevertheless strengthened Admiral Gorshkov's hand in his efforts to obtain support from the Kremlin for his plans to rebuild the Soviet Navy. The lesson of the Cuban Crisis, as it became known, remains that the determined and effective deployment of force can be instrumental in resolving a crisis and preventing war, which tends to occur when one party believes that the other is bluffing and can be safely ignored, only to discover that the bluff was a real threat after all! The flexibility of sea power, and

the sovereign territory position of a ship in international law, could perhaps be considered other lessons of the crisis, and it was these that Gorshkov and his political masters took to heart.

Meanwhile, yet another anti-communist campaign was being conducted with strong naval support, this time in Malaya and Indonesia, the Royal Navy, with Australian assistance playing a major role.

Britain had granted independence to Malaya in 1958, to a government which was both democratic and reasonably pro-Western in attitude. In 1963, Britain created the Federation of Malaysia, incorporating the city state of Singapore, Malaya, and a number of small yet prosperous territories in Borneo, including Sarawak and Sabah, in the belief that such small states could only achieve and maintain their independence if federally linked together. It was also thought that a strong federation would allow a substantial reduction in the size of British forces deployed in the area. Singapore was later to leave the Federation of Malaysia, due to disagreements between the Malay and Chinese communities, but these disagreements were minor by the standard of international and even domestic affairs, and both Malasia and Singapore remained within the British Commonwealth afterwards.

At the outset, the only threat to the security and stability of the Federation was external, coming in the form of strong opposition from Indonesia, which had Soviet support for the regime headed by Achmed Soekarno. Indonesian policy was aimed at destroying the Federation and absorbing some of its territory. Once the threat became apparent, with infiltration by Indonesian forces, British forces in the area were reinforced with additional Army, Royal Air Force and Royal Navy units, including at various times the commando carriers HMS *Albion* and *Bulwark*, and the aircraft carriers HMS *Ark Royal* and *Victorious*. The naval and air force units countered the infiltrators by supporting troops fighting in the jungle

or by using helicopters and small naval craft to search for intruders attempting to reach the Malaysian coast, rather than by bombing and strafing Indonesian bases or supposed enemy-held territory. This operation successfully thwarted the Indonesian policy of confrontation, and finally ended with the downfall and overthrow of the Soekarno regime during the mid-1960s, after which a marked reduction in the size of British forces started in the area.

Indonesia received massive military aid from the Soviet Union, on a scale far in excess of that granted to China at the time, and even in some ways far superior to that provided for Russia's Warsaw Pact allies. The Indonesian Air Force, the Angatan Udera Republik Indonesia or AURI, was developed to a ludicrous degree, with the only strategic jet bomber fleet outside of Britain, the United States and the Soviet Union. The AURI had Tupolev Tu–16 long-range jet bombers, supplemented by Ilyushin Il–28s, which

A Russian Kamov Ka–25 Hormone shipborne helicopter flies past HMS *Ark Royal*

were comparable with the Canberra jet bombers operated by the Royal Air Force and Royal Australian Air Force in the area. The main threat to shipping came from the Kennel air-to-surface missiles which Tu–16s carried when operating on anti-shipping strike duties. The main resistance to Indonesia came at first from British, Australian, New Zealand and Malaysian forces in the area, but in 1962 Indonesia invaded Dutch West Irian, the sole remaining Dutch territory in the area, bringing Dutch and Indonesian forces into conflict again.

Some of the Indonesian equipment compared favourably with that in service with the British Commonwealth forces in the area, for it was not until 1966 that the Royal New Zealand Air Force could replace its Short Sunderlands with Lockheed P–3B Orions for maritime-reconnaissance. Two years later the Royal

Australian Air Force replaced the Neptunes in one of its two maritime-reconnaissance squadrons with these same aircraft.

One reason for the lack of the best Soviet equipment for the Chinese air arms was the start of the long and widening rift between the two communist ideologies during the early 1960s. The Soviet Union itself was developing strong maritime-reconnaissance forces with new aircraft, including the large Tupolev Tu–20 turboprop long-range reconnaissance aircraft, and as the decade progressed, Tupolev Tu–22 Blinder supersonic trijet bombers also joined the A–VMF. These aircraft were normally equipped with Kennel air-to-surface missiles or some similar weapon, while unlike many other naval air arms, attention was still paid by the Soviets to mine-laying as well as anti-submarine capability. The earlier Beriev Be–6 and Be–10 flying-boats were replaced from 1965 onwards with the Be–12 'Mail' flying-boat, with two turboprop engines and an advanced hull form to assist take-off.

The Soviet Union was also keeping pace with other navies, which were by this time developing a widening range of shipboard helicopters for operation from warships of all but the smallest sizes. However, at the time the Soviet Navy tended to keep its helicopter-carrying warships on the large size, as with the two sister ships, *Moskva* and *Leningrad*, which entered service in 1967 and 1968 respectively. These two vessels were completed as heavy cruisers forward, but with a large flight deck aft, from which up to thirty Kamov Ka–20 (or its successor Ka–25 'Hormone') helicopters could be operated, with different versions for anti-submarine or missile-guidance duties. Large broad-beamed vessels of 18,000 tons, these were the first Russian attempts at aircraft-carrying ships.

The mighty Soviet Union was by now moved by the need to rationalise its defences, and during the early 1960s, the A–VMF lost its fighter aircraft to the other two air arms, mainly the IA–PVO,

or National Air Defence. Even so, it was still left with a staggering thousand or so aircraft, of which about half were helicopters.

Another navy shared the Soviet's confidence in the value of the flying-boats—the Japanese Maritime Self-Defence Force. During the early 1960s, this rapidly growing force had some forty-eight Kawasaki-built and fifteen Lockheed-built P–2H Neptune maritime-reconnaissance aircraft, and sixty Grumman S–2A Trackers. First, Kawasaki produced a turboprop development of the Neptune, the P–2J Turbo-Neptune, with a modified fuselage and other improvements to the original design and equipment, with the first of fifty-four such aircraft entering service in 1968. The next year, the first of a large number of Shin Meiwa PS–1 turboprop maritime-reconnaissance flying-boats followed them, incorporating several decades of flying-boat development in this modern four-engined design.

The JMSDF was not attempting to move against the tide, however, and large numbers of helicopters were also introduced. These included Sikorsky SH–34G or HSS–1 and SH–3A or HSS–2 helicopters, better known as the Sea King, built under licence by Mitsubishi. The Sea King, with its anti-submarine torpedoes and dunking sonar, has often been regarded as having the electronics of a small frigate.

If the flying-boat was suffering mixed fortunes, so too was the aircraft carrier, in spite of the successful use of these vessels off Vietnam and Malaya.

Doubts about the value of the aircraft carrier obviously did not bother the Indian Navy, which finally commissioned the INS *Vikrant* in November, 1961, complete with her full complement of Armstrong–Whitworth Sea Hawks and Breguet Br.1050 Alize anti-submarine aircraft, plus Sud Alouette II helicopters —a type not commonly used aboard ships. In 1964, a second shore station was opened at Dabola, INS *Hansa*. Yet, the Indian Navy's one aircraft carrier was in

海上自衛隊

A Shin Meiwa PS–1 turboprop flying-boat of the JMSDF takes off

the middle of a refit during the twenty-two day Indo–Pakistan war of 1965, and played no part in the conflict between the opposing air forces, which ended in an Indian victory.

During the Vietnam war, HMAS *Sydney*, the veteran Australian carrier, found a new role as aircraft transport and fast troop transport, although Australian air involvement in the war was largely limited to providing helicopters to support Australian and New Zealand ground forces. Meanwhile, HMAS *Melbourne*'s strike capability was much enhanced by replacing her Sea Venoms with the small but effective Douglas A–4 Skyhawks. These aircraft, in spite of having been developed for the big-ship United States Navy, fitted perfectly onto smaller carriers.

Probably most impressive of all was the progress made by the Aeronavale, which received two magnificent new light fleet aircraft carriers, the *Clemenceau* and *Foch*, commissioned in 1961 and 1963 respectively. In addition to the squadrons of Dassault Etendard carrier-borne fighter-bombers and Breguet Br.1050 Alize ASW aircraft, ready and waiting for the new ships, the Aeronavale also obtained two squadrons of Chance–Vought F–8 Crusader transonic fighters. However, with such large aircraft embarked, the claimed maximum aircraft capacity of fifty for these two ships of just 27,000 tons standard displacement seems over-optimistic. The new carriers conformed to the by-then well-established idea of exactly how a carrier should look, with some superficial resemblance to HMS *Hermes*.

Ashore, the Aeronavale replaced its four squadrons of Lockheed P–2F and P–2H Neptunes with Breguet Br.1150 Atlantique twin-engined turboprop maritime-reconnaissance aircraft, with the first deliveries taking place during 1965.

The Marine Nationale also introduced a helicopter-carrying cruiser in 1967, with the *Jeanne d'Arc*, 11,000 tons—originally laid down as *La Resolue*, the change of

175

Dassault Etendard fighter-bombers of the Aeronavale

name being made when the French Navy's training cruiser, *Jeanne d'Arc*, was withdrawn. To a great extent, the new ship has herself acted as a training vessel, although with her capacity of up to eight large Sud Super Frelon troop-carrying helicopters she does have a strategic role as well, and is equipped with a range of guided missiles.

The Royal Navy meanwhile suffered a decade of uncertainty over the future of its Fleet Air Arm, though it is difficult to understand why this should have been so at a time when the Royal Navy was becoming more, rather than less, important, with the gradual transfer of responsibility for the British nuclear deterrent from the Royal Air Force's manned strategic bombers to the Royal Navy's Polaris missile-equipped nuclear submarines.

To be fair, the Royal Air Force also suffered certain difficulties at this time,

in spite of an overall impression of modernisation. To the RAF went the distinction of having the world's first jet-powered maritime-reconnaissance aircraft, the Hawker Siddeley Nimrod, developed from the de Havilland Comet IV airliner but with Rolls-Royce Spey turbofans replacing the Comet's Avon turbojets. The first Nimrods entered RAF service in 1969, joining RAF Strike Command, which had replaced the former Fighter, Bomber and Coastal Commands. The original intention was that the Nimrods should serve alongside the later Shackletons rather than replace them, but before long the Nimrod's superior speed became an excuse for first not replacing Shackletons on anything like a one for one basis, and then for prematurely phasing them out altogether. Just twelve Shackletons survived, in a new role, extending the range of Britain's shore-based defences after being fitted with

A Breguet Bn.1050 Alize anti-submarine aircraft on the catapult ready for take-off

Phantom fighters and Buccaneer bombers aboard HMS *Ark Royal*

radar taken from the airborne-early warning versions of the Royal Navy's AEW Fairey Gannets.

This obviously raises the question as to why the Gannets, or at least their radar, happened to be available in this way. The explanation is quite simple. A British Labour Government had decided to scrap the Royal Navy's aircraft carriers!

The decision came at a time of strength and confidence for the Fleet Air Arm. Five aircraft carriers, HMS *Eagle, Ark Royal, Victorious, Hermes* and *Centaur*, and two commando carriers, HMS *Albion* and *Bulwark*, were in service, operating some splendid aircraft. These included the first of more than sixty Westland S–61 Sea King helicopters with dunking sonar (replacing both the earlier dunking-sonar-equipped Westland S–58 Wessex helicopters and ASW versions of the Gannet, many of which were converted

for target-towing, training, or carrier-onboard-delivery duties). The de Havilland Sea Vixen and Supermarine Scimitar fighters aboard the carriers had been fitted with Red Top and Firestreak air-to-air missiles, while S.2 versions of the Buccaneer, with more powerful engines, were equipped with Bullpup air-to-surface guided missiles. More than this, the Royal Navy was looking forward to delivery of McDonnell Douglas F–4M Phantom interceptors—an Anglicised version with Rolls-Royce Spey engines—to give the larger carriers a Mach 2·2 air defence capability, and plans were far advanced for the ordering of at least two 60,000 ton super carriers!

Strangely, the period was one which had shown the Fleet Air Arm, its ships and aircraft, in a favourable light. Apart from the confrontation with Indonesia over Malaysia, the Fleet Air Arm had been called upon for assistance in three other separate incidents. Growing tension between Iraq and Kuwait in 1961 was quickly dispelled by the rapid deployment of Royal Marine Commandos from HMS *Bulwark*, with the arrival shortly afterwards of HMS *Victorious*. The latter vessel provided air defence radar and fighter control not only for her own aircraft but also for Royal Air Force aircraft in the area. Just three years later, a local crisis in East Africa, with unrest in the newly independent former British colonies, was brought to an end with the arrival of HMS *Albion* and *Centaur*, while HMS *Victorious* stood by. Finally, from 1965, the year of Rhodesia's famed unilateral declaration of independence in opposition to British proposals for independence which were supported by the United Nations, HMS *Eagle* and later HMS *Ark Royal* maintained a patrol off the Mozambique port of Beira, in an attempt to block oil supplies to Rhodesia.

Despite all this, HMS *Centaur* was withdrawn shortly after the decision to phase out the aircraft carriers was taken in 1965, with HMS *Victorious* following.

The move was linked with a political decision—to withdraw British forces completely from east of Suez, that is, from Aden, the Trucial States, Malaysia and Singapore, and one or two other smaller bases, excepting only Hong Kong. This was a decision made in spite of strong local opposition to the withdrawals from all the places concerned except Aden, and to the dismay of all anti-communist governments in the Pacific and Indian Ocean areas. Supporters of the aircraft carrier argued fiercely that the lack of bases would make the carrier more important than ever, in view of the time it would take for Royal Air Force bases to be re-established, and their vulnerability while this was in hand. They further argued that a naval task force moving into an area could, if necessary, remain relatively unobtrusive, and avoid inflaming any delicate situation that might arise.

Unfortunately, the situation was further complicated by what amounted to an ultimatum to the armed forces. This proposed either reducing the Fleet Air Arm to just a helicopter force, or else cutting out a large section of the Royal Air Force. Such a proposal, intentionally or otherwise, inevitably resulted in setting the two services at each other's throats, even though many RAF officers accepted that they needed the support of carrier-borne aircraft in the first instance to secure shore bases in any assault on enemy-held territory, and that only a Fleet Air Arm could produce senior naval officers with an appreciation of the value of air power.

It was finally decided to phase out the carriers at the end of their active lives. HMS *Victorious* was eventually scrapped in 1969, by which time the extensively refitted HMS *Ark Royal* and HMS *Eagle* were operating Phantoms. Refitting of these two ships was carried out in rather a haphazard and miserly fashion. Both received waist catapults and fully-angled flight decks, but HMS *Ark Royal* received an extended deck area and HMS *Eagle* took the three-dimensional radar from HMS *Victorious*. Neither ship received the full set of aids, and HMS *Eagle* was to operate Phantom fighters with greater difficulty than her sister.

The arrival of the Phantoms was also fraught with political problems. One of Britain's leading aircraft manufacturers, Hawker Siddeley, had successfully developed a vertical take-off fighter and ground attack aircraft, the HS 1127, later designated the Kestrel, during the mid-1960s, the intention being that it should act as a development prototype for a supersonic vertical take-off jet fighter, the HS 1184, for the Royal Air Force and the Royal Navy. The Royal Navy turned the aircraft down, preferring the Phantom, and the HS 1184 was cancelled by the British Government. Eventually, therefore, both the Royal Navy, and the Royal Air Force received Phantoms, with just two squadrons planned for the Royal Navy, which had hoped for more than a hundred, and a far larger number entering RAF service. Hawker Siddeley promptly brought the HS 1127 up to production status, renamed it the Harrier, and received a Royal Air Force order for it as a ground-attack fighter; and this was followed by an order from the United States Marine Corps!

Hawker Siddeley had been formed as part of a major reorganisation of the British aircraft industry during the early 1960s. This saw Hawker, Avro, Blackburn, de Havilland and Armstrong-Whitworth incorporated in Hawker Siddeley Aviation, while Vickers, Supermarine, Percival and Bristol became the British Aircraft Corporation. Fairey's airframe interests in Britain were absorbed by Westland, and only Short and Handley Page remained unaffected. BAC, Hawker Siddeley Dynamics and Shorts remained active in guided missile production and development.

Fresh hope came for the Fleet Air Arm with the development of the Harrier, which entered service with the Royal Air Force in 1969, making it the world's first operational vertical take-off combat aircraft. A new class of ship, the through-deck cruiser was mooted, planned to cost just half the price of a 60,000 ton super carrier, and able to operate a mixture of Harriers and Sea King helicopters. In truth, such a vessel was intended to be a light fleet carrier without catapults or arrester wires, and design work on the concept continued even though an order was some way ahead.

While the Fleet Air Arm was suffering this period of crisis over the future of its fixed-wing element, its helicopter operation went from strength to strength. In 1961, the Royal Navy had introduced a new class of seven frigates, the Type 81 Tribal class. The first of these, HMS *Ashanti*, 2,700 tons, had the dual distinction of being the first purpose-built frigate in the world to have been designed to operate a helicopter for anti-submarine operations, and also the first with combined steam and gas turbine propulsion. Conversion of the Royal Navy's Type 12 Rothesay and Whitby class frigates to handle helicopters followed, while the next major class of Royal Navy frigates, the Leander class, 2,860 tons, was also designed to operate helicopters. No less than twenty-six of these highly successful and attractive frigates were built for the Royal Navy, while additional vessels were built in Britain for New Zealand and Chile. Other vessels of the design were built under licence in Australia (as the later versions of the River class), in the Netherlands (as the Van Speijk class), and in India. All of these warships used the Westland Wasp helicopter, which carried an anti-submarine torpedo and was specifically designed for operations from small warships. The same aircraft entered service with the Argentinian and Brazilian Navies as well. All Leander, Van Speijk and River-class frigates, plus the Rothesays, Whitbys and Tribals, were equipped with Short Seacat short-range anti-aircraft missiles, with a secondary anti-ship capability, while Chilean Leanders—amongst the last of the vessels to be delivered, during the early 1970s—were fitted with Exocet surface-to-surface missiles.

The Royal Navy's County class guided missile destroyers, the other Royal Navy class at this time to use steam and gas turbine propulsion, were equipped with Seacats and the longer range Seaslug missile, as well as a single Westland S–58 Wessex helicopter. Indeed, many Royal Navy support vessels, the Royal Fleet Auxiliary, were equipped with hangars and landing platforms for helicopters, mainly to accelerate replenishment of stores at sea; and one such vessel, the *Engadine*, was equipped as a helicopter support vessel, able to handle six large helicopters. The three Tiger class cruisers, HMS *Tiger*, *Lion* and *Blake*, were also earmarked for conversion to command cruisers, with hangar and landing platform for four Sea King helicopters, but only two of these ships were converted, while HMS *Lion* went to the breakers in 1972.

One significant development in both the Royal Navy and the United States Navy at this time was the introduction of assault ships, or amphibious transport

The new generation: the superb Italian cruiser, *Vittorio Veneto*, carries up to nine helicopters and is equipped with guided missiles

dock vessels. These vessels acted as troop transports, carrying landing craft in a stern dock which flooded and allowed them to float in or out, while a large landing platform was provided for troop-carrying helicopters. The USN introduced the first vessel of this type, the USS *Raleigh*, in 1962, following it with two others of the same 13,900 ton class before introducing twelve vessels of the larger USS Austin class in 1965. The Royal Navy introduced its first amphibious transport dock vessel, HMS *Fearless*, in 1965, and followed it with a second, HMS *Intrepid*, two years later. In addition, the USN had introduced the USS *Iwo Jima*, 18,300 tons, and six other ships of this class, in 1961, as purpose-built commando carriers, able to accommodate up to thirty assault helicopters.

This was completely in line with trends elsewhere, for although the Americans and Russians were a little slow to put helicopters aboard frigates or destroyers, other navies were faster. One of these was the Italian Navy, which in 1964 introduced helicopters aboard its Impavido class destroyers, using mainly Bell 47 and 204B helicopters built under licence in Italy by Agusta. These were followed by the first of two highly successful and effective helicopter-carrying

light cruisers, armed with guided missiles—the 6,500 ton *Andrea Doria*, later followed by a sister ship, *Caio Duilo*. These vessels could carry up to four Agusta-built Sikorsky SH–34J ASW helicopters, or a larger number of Agusta–Bell 204Bs, complementing the efforts of forty-eight shore-based Grumman S–2A Trackers which were also employed by the Italian Navy. Later, in 1969, a new class of cruiser joined the Italian Fleet, the *Vittorio Veneto*, 8,850 tons, with accommodation for up to nine 204B helicopters. A sister ship, the *Triest*, was planned but eventually cancelled.

Another supporter of the helicopter-carrying frigate was the Royal Canadian Navy, which introduced frigates reconstructed to accommodate a single large helicopter, usually a Sea King. The RCN itself disappeared in 1967, becoming part of Maritime Command of an integrated Canadian defence structure—the Canadian Armed Forces. Three years later, HMCS *Bonaventure* was scrapped after a comparatively short life of just thirteen years! The other part of Maritime Command was the maritime-reconnaissance

A flight of Royal Canadian Navy Grumman
Trackers, shore-based after the withdrawal of
HMCS *Bonaventure*

Royal Netherlands Naval Air Service Breguet
Br.1150 Atlantique

element of the former Royal Canadian Air
Force, operating Canadair CP–107 Argus
aircraft, a licence-built but piston-
engined development of the Bristol
Britannia four turbo-prop engined airliner, which had replaced the RCAF's
Avro Lancasters in 1957.

Unhappily, the Royal Netherlands
Navy had withdrawn the *Karel Doorman*
just a year earlier, leaving this service with
helicopters aboard its frigates. Breguet
Br.1150 Atlantiques replaced the RNN's
shore-based Neptunes in 1970.

However, the *Karel Doorman* was not
scrapped, but instead sold to Argentina
as a replacement for the *Independencia*.
After extensive refitting she joined the
Argentine Navy as the *Veinticino de
Mayo* (25th May), ending a period of
neglect of this service. Indeed, the fortunes of the Argentine Navy and the
Comando de Aviacion had been mixed.
Twenty Grumman F–9F Panther jet
fighters introduced in 1961 were largely
wiped out by Fuerza Aerea d'Argentina
units in April, 1963, when naval units
rebelled. Re-equipment followed, with
Grumman Trackers and Aermacchi
MB.326 armed-trainers as the usual
carrier-borne equipment, together with
the inevitable helicopters and a small
number of shore-based Lockheed P–2V
Neptune maritime-reconnaissance aircraft.

The ex-Royal Navy light fleet carriers
still in service were rebuilt throughout
the late 1960s, with the exception of the
Indian Navy's *Vikrant*, but including
HMAS *Melbourne* (almost continually
modernised) and the *Minas Gerais*. The
Royal Navy's remaining light fleet carrier,
HMS *Triumph*, after a spell as a cadet
training vessel, was refitted as a fleet
heavy repair ship.

An Armada Argentina Aermacchi MB.326 for operations from the aircraft carrier, *Veinticino de Mayo*

The real question at issue in the 1960s was not whether or not naval aviation remained a good idea in the nuclear age, with guided missiles gaining in importance. It was whether or not governments anxious to win votes, cut taxes and increase social expenditure could be convinced that defence was politically worthwhile. And if they could, a further question arose: could they justify expenditure on one of the most costly weapon systems, the aircraft carrier, even though it might also be one of the most cost-effective!

10 Challenge and Change

Today it takes five years or more to build an aircraft carrier or develop a new aircraft, and more than three years to train the pilot of a naval aircraft. Thus when we look back on a decade from its closing years the changes seem to be few. This has not always been so, for during World War II, CVLs or light fleet carriers could be produced in eighteen months or so, and during the 1920s and 1930s aircraft often remained in production for only two or three years, against the ten or twenty years of a good design today—which, incidentally, may remain in service for a good many years after production stops. Once too, the training period for an aspiring pilot could be measured in weeks, and before that in days. This creates the paradox of an age of accelerating technical progress actually seeing a slowing down of change in operational practice.

So, the start of the 1970s tended to be an extrapolation of trends established during the previous decade. The proliferation of small warships fitted to carry helicopters continued, along with the less far-sighted run-down of the Royal Navy's Fleet Air Arm; so, unhappily, did the war in Vietnam.

In spite of this, one significant development did occur within the decade, showing all the signs of being the most significant one since the first attempts to

The two seat training version of the Harrier V/STOL fighter, aboard the French aircraft carrier, *Foch*. Note the civilian markings of this demonstration aircraft

First operational V/STOL jet aircraft to go to sea were the Hawker Siddeley AV–8A Harriers of the USMC

match ships and aircraft together—the availability of operational vertical take-off and landing jet aircraft. The first of these to be used by a naval air arm, the British Hawker Siddeley Harrier, were delivered to the United States Marine Corps in 1970, and became operational shortly afterwards from assault ships of the Iwo Jima class. Designated the AV–8A attack aircraft, vertical take-off in USMC service, the Harrier was originally intended to be built under licence in the United States by McDonnell Douglas. Had this happened, the Harrier would have been the first non-American combat aircraft to receive such treatment since Martin produced the English Electric Canberra jet bomber during the early 1950s. However, the small size of the initial order—about a hundred aircraft—meant that direct purchase was cheaper, although an up-rated version, the AV–8B, has been developed by McDonnell Douglas for the 1980s.

The Harrier quickly proved itself to be a better aircraft than either the USMC or the RAF had expected. Far from being a novel attack aeroplane, it soon proved itself to have exceptional manoeuvrability, particularly when its vectored thrust, for vertical take-off, was applied in flight, producing an effect known as 'viffing', By 'viffing' an experienced Harrier pilot could outmatch a Mach 2·2 Phantom fighter in a low-level dog fight, in spite of the Harrier's much slower maximum speed, which meant that the aircraft was barely transonic. Given a short take-off run into the wind, using STOL rather than VTOL, the Harrier's weapon load or range could also be increased considerably. A later development by the manufacturer, the brainchild of Lieu-tenant-Commander R. D. Taylor, RN, soon proved that a low angled ramp, or 'ski-jump', towards the end of the take-off run could also improve warload and rate of climb.

While the British progressed with their through-deck cruiser design, the Americans also designed a new class of vessel, the low-cost sea control ship, intended to operate helicopters and Harriers or other vertical take-off aircraft, even though American and French attempts to rival the Harrier were not successful. The Americans, however, soon showed themselves to be in no real hurry to press ahead with such a vessel, and since they had large aircraft carriers able to take a variety of aircraft to sea there was little need for them to do so. Indeed, the average size of American carriers was rising as the older units started to be phased out gradually, and replaced by new and even larger vessels.

The world's largest warships have for many years been the largest of the American carrier fleet, and this tradition was maintained by the introduction in May, 1975, of the first of a new class of at least three nuclear-powered aircraft carriers, the USS *Nimitz*, named after the US naval commander in the Pacific during World War II. This 81,600 ton standard displacement vessel followed the general style of the earlier USS *Enterprise*, although its aircraft capacity was increased to almost 100 large warplanes. A second vessel, the USS *Dwight D. Eisenhower*, entered service in 1977, and a third, the USS *Carl Vinson*, is scheduled for 1981. The third vessel is named after a former Representative for Georgia and Chairman of both the House of Representatives Naval Affairs Committee and Armed Services Committee, and is probably the first US warship to be named after a living person. A fourth as yet unnamed, vessel is planned.

Such large vessels naturally allowed the USN the freedom to operate large or very fast aircraft, but unfortunately the USN and USAF requirements for the next generation of interceptors, or air superiority fighters, differed. The USAF opted for the McDonnell Douglas F–15 Eagle as a Mach 3·0 Phantom replacement, while the USN chose the Grumman F–14A Tomcat, a variable-geometry or swing-wing fighter with a two-man crew. (Variable geometry offers a low angle of sweep for the wing leading edge during take-off or landing, and a higher angle of sweep for high speed flight, thus reducing drag.) The first prototype, conceived as the USN's VFX air superiority fighter, flew in 1971, with entry into service during 1975. The second air arm to operate variable-geometry aircraft was the Kriegsmarine, with the first of Anglo–German–Italian shore-based Panavia Tornado strike aircraft in 1979.

The high cost of such aircraft coupled with the high cost of nuclear-powered warships—some fifty per cent higher than conventional steam-powered vessels—has meant that the USN cannot hope to replace its Phantoms on a one-for-one

Officially a frigate, the USS *California*, 10,150 tons, is larger than most cruisers. The nuclear-powered vessel is missile-armed and has a helicopter landing platform

World's largest warship, the USS *Nimitz*, with
Corsair IIs

USN frontline fighters for the eighties, the
Grumman F–14A Tomcat

basis with Tomcats. As a result
McDonnell Douglas and Northrop are
developing a new lightweight Mach 2·0
plus air superiority fighter, the F–18, for
service during the early 1980s. This aircraft also differs from the USAF requirement, an air force version, the F–17,
having been rejected in favour of the
General Dynamics F–16.

To see these differences in perspective,
one must remember that air force and
naval requirements do sometimes differ,
and the choice of different types of aircraft is sometimes inevitable, even though
it leads to the doubling of development
costs, higher unit costs due to lower production runs, and lack of standardisation.
The need for a two-crew arrangement
and the advantages to carrier operation
of variable-geometry convinced the USN
that the Tomcat was the better naval aircraft. The need for twin-engined aircraft
for safe and reliable carrier operation also
made the USN reluctant to accept the
cheaper single-engined F–16. This was
also a factor in the Royal Navy's preference for Phantoms rather than
HS1184s.

The second of these requirements is
often under-estimated. At various times,
the Harrier loss-rate has been the subject
of criticism, but if an aircraft has just
one engine, its loss rate is likely to be
some three times that of a twin-engined
aircraft. Low-flying attack aircraft, which
in today's military conditions are forced
to fly as low as possible to avoid anti-
aircraft defences, also suffer a high loss
rate, due in no small part to a high
incidence of bird strikes. The Harrier
suffers from both problems, but there
would be difficulty over control in a twin-
engined V/STOL aircraft using vectored thrust for take-off and landing,
while an aircraft using a combination of
ordinary jets and lift jets would carry an
unacceptably heavy load in its mixture of
power plants.

More mundane new aircraft for the
USN included the Grumman E–2A
Hawkeye AEW aircraft, with twin-turbo-
prop engines, which actually entered
service during the mid-1960s, and the
Grumman C–2 Greyhound development
for COD which followed it. Both aircraft
tend to be confined to the larger attack
carriers rather than the surviving anti-
submarine carriers of the Essex class.
Further redundancy amongst aircraft of

Tracker-replacement, the Lockheed S–3A
Viking and anti-submarine aircraft

USS *Spruance*, one of the new generation of
helicopter-carrying guided missile destroyers

Helicopters and assault craft—the amphibious assault ship USS *Tarawa*, showing the floodable stern dock

the Tracker generation came during the mid–1970s, with the entry into service in 1973 of the first Lockheed S–3A Viking ASW aircraft. This aircraft uses turbofan propulsion, and has the considerable range, for a carrier-borne aircraft, of 2,000 miles, carrying depth charges, anti-submarine torpedoes or missiles, and sonar buoys. After many years of delay, the Canadian Armed Forces eventually ordered licence-built Lockheed P–3C Orions—designated as Canadair CP–140 Aurora—late in the 1970s, and in spite of the PS–1 and Turbo-Neptune developments, so has the JMSDF.

The effectiveness of the helicopters carried by many warships also increased during the 1970s. In addition to the dunking sonar carried by the Sea King and other large helicopters, other ASW sys-

tems also appeared, including 'Jezebel'. In this system a pattern of sonar buoys is dropped into the sea and signals are transmitted back to the helicopter, and these signals can if necessary be relayed to a warship equipped with Ikara or Asroc anti-submarine missiles. One advantage of the 'Jezebel' system is that the sonar is passive, that is it effectively 'listens' for a submarine. Other systems use active sonar, transmitting a signal and working on the resultant echo, which is effective except that the submarine is immediately alerted to the fact that it is being hunted, and can take evasive or defensive action.

A large proportion of the USN's destroyer force during the decade dated from the end of World War II, although many had been extensively modified or rebuilt, and a few even fitted with helicopter landing platforms. With a few exceptions, US cruisers and destroyers or frigates did not generally come to carry a helicopter until the appearance of the

Spruance class of thirty guided missile destroyers in 1974. These were joined later by the first of the smaller Oliver Hazard Perry class of fifty-six guided missile frigates in 1977. The 6,900 tons of the USS *Spruance* and the 3,500 tons of the USS *Oliver Hazard Perry* may seem high for vessels of their class, but the USN has in recent years shown itself quite capable of describing such vessels as the USS *Virginia*—of 11,000 tons and fitted with two helicopters—as destroyer leaders, even though this nuclear-powered vessel is larger than a pre-World War II cruiser!

New helicopters, including the Sikorsky LAMPs, have been ordered for these vessels, with two helicopters to be carried by the USS *Oliver Hazard Perry* and her sisters.

The USN has also recognised the importance of amphibious assault ships. Five large amphibious assault ships with docking facilities and a through flight deck were introduced from 1975 onwards, the first being USS *Tarawa*, 35,000 tons standard displacement. The introduction of larger helicopters, such as the Sikorsky SH–53 Sea Stallion, of the USMC, has meant that faster, heavier and more effective assaults on enemy shores can be mounted if necessary.

The Vietnam war rumbled on during the first half of the 1970s, in spite of a pause in the bombing of North Vietnam at the start of the decade. Later the main Northern ports were mined in an attempt to reduce the supply of war materials to the communists. At the end of 1972, the USS *Midway, America, Saratoga, Kitty Hawk, Oriskany* and *Enterprise* were all in action against targets in Vietnam at the same time, as part of the US Seventh Fleet. This final burst of pressure by the USN helped in bringing the North Vietnamese to sign a cease-fire with the Americans, allowing the US forces to pull out of Vietnam in response to internal political pressures in the United States. Although neither the North nor the South was supposed to receive further massive military aid under the terms of the cease-fire, this part of the agreement was openly ignored by the Soviet Union, which supported a massive offensive that led to a complete communist take-over of Vietnam during April, 1975. The US Seventh Fleet found itself in action again at this time, evacuating almost 20,000 Americans and South Vietnamese, although many more of the latter were forced to find their own hazardous way to freedom.

Just over a year later, after the fall of Cambodia to an exceptionally severe communist regime, three Cambodian fast patrol boats captured an American merchantman, the MV *Mayaguez*, in the Gulf of Siam, with her crew. The patrol boats

Sikorsky Sea Stallion and Boeing Chinook helicopters aboard the USS *Iwo Jima*

were promptly sunk by aircraft from the USS *Coral Sea*, and a day later a helicopter-borne assault released the ship and its crew!

Other battles were being fought meanwhile, although mostly without the help of naval aviation. An exception was another of the recurring wars between India and Pakistan, which in December, 1971, saw Armstrong–Whitworth Sea Hawk aircraft from the INS *Vikrant* attacking Chittagong and Cox's Bazaar in East Pakistan. It was this war that ended in East Pakistan gaining its independence from West Pakistan, and becoming the new state of Bangladesh.

The rundown of the Fleet Air Arm continued, with first HMS *Albion* and then HMS *Eagle* being withdrawn in 1972, while HMS *Hermes* was refitting as a commando carrier, to be recommissioned as such during August, 1973, so that HMS *Bulwark* could be placed in reserve. HMS *Bulwark* rejoined the fleet in early 1979, however, after the withdrawal of HMS *Ark Royal*, while HMS *Hermes* became an ASW carrier before this, ready to receive the first Hawker Sea Harrier V/STOL aircraft during late 1979 or 1980. HMS *Bulwark* was destined for a return to the reserve fleet in 1980, with the commissioning of the Royal Navy's first through-deck cruiser, HMS *Invincible*.

Laid down in 1973, HMS *Invincible* marked the British Government's recognition of the importance to the fleet of its own integral airpower; and in spite of earlier proposals that the vessel's Harriers would be flown by RAF personnel, it now seems that most, if not all, will be handled by naval aircrew. Lightly armoured and of 16,000 tons standard displacement, the ship conforms to the now-traditional carrier design, but has certain unusual features. Its twin funnels, vaguely similar to those of the first HMS *Eagle*, are dictated by the needs of gas turbine

engines, while its flight deck, which is only slightly angled, stops just short of the f'o'scle, with a 'ski-jump'. Earlier figures indicating an aircraft complement of ten Westland S-61 Sea King helicopters and five Harriers can be discounted. Each vessel of this class will in fact have eight Harriers out of the Fleet Air Arm's total of thirty-four, and a true complement is nearer to a dozen Sea Kings and the same number of Sea Harriers. The figures have been underestimated by the Royal Navy to minimise RAF opposition to a rebirth of the Fleet Air Arm. Two more ships of this class will enter service during the 1980s, HMS *Illustrious* being due for 1982 and a new HMS *Ark Royal* for 1984.

The Sea Harrier is a naval development of the Harrier, with the up-rated engines of the USMC and later RAF Harriers, plus Ferranti Sea Spray radar for the over-water attack role in a lengthened nose.

Criticisms of the poor aircraft complement of the Invincible class, together with the need by smaller navies for cheap aircraft carriers, persuaded Vosper–Thorneycroft, now part of the nationalised British Shipbuilders, to design a 'Harrier Carrier' of just 6,000 tons standard displacement and able to carry four Harriers and four Sea Kings. The impression this vessel gives of being a miniature light fleet carrier is only dispelled by two unusual features—the provision of a turntable aft on the flight deck, so that the slightly ungainly Harrier can be turned easily on a pitching and rolling deck, and the grill on which a Harrier can be positioned for quick fighter response. The grill is based on the discovery that the Harrier gains the maximum lift from its thrust once it is twenty feet above the ground; and since the grill has a twenty-foot deep well below it, it artificially gives the Harrier that height at the moment of take-off.

Westland-built Sea King SAR helicopters of the Royal Norwegian Air Force

HMS *Sheffield*, one of the Royal Navy's newest
classes of warship

In marked contrast to the Nimrod, the Embraer
EMB–111 Bandeirante is a Brazilian attempt
to provide maritime-reconnaissance at reasonable cost in coastal waters

Vickers, another part of British Ship-builders, followed with a 13,000 ton 'MAC' ship, able to carry twice as many aircraft as the 'Harrier Carrier'. All of these vessels, including the Invincible class, have a ramp forward to give Harriers assistance during STOL take-off.

By the 1970s, the Royal Navy was concentrating on all gas turbine propulsion for its new warships, apart from nuclear submarines and mine countermeasures vessels or offshore patrol vessels. In 1971, the Type 21 Amazon class frigates, the first post-war commercial shipyard design accepted by the Royal Navy, started to enter service. They were initially equipped with Westland Wasp helicopters, but these were replaced after 1975 with Westland–Aerospatiale Lynx helicopters. The superior performance of the Lynx—which in Aeronavale service has a dunking sonar—in ASW duties will eventually be extended to air-to-surface warfare, with the introduction of BAC Sea Skua missiles, aimed to provide warships with protection against fast missile-armed patrol boats. The Amazon class vessels are also currently equipped with Short Seacat and Exocet surface-to-surface surface skimming missiles. The Seacats, however, are gradually being replaced with Sea Wolf missiles, so accurate that they can defend the warship against missile attack as well as aircraft strike, and even track and destroy a 4·5-inch gun-shell!

The eight vessels of the Amazon class were joined by the Royal Navy's last combined steam and gas turbine vessel, the destroyer HMS *Bristol*, 6,000 tons, originally intended to be lead ship of a class of vessels designed to defend the Royal Navy's ill-fated 60,000 ton carriers. However, while there may have been only one HMS *Bristol*, the Type 42 Sheffield class guided missile destroyers which followed are still being ordered, with already more than a dozen in service, under construction or planned. Equipped with Westland Lynx helicopters, these ships, of which two have also been built for the Argentinian Navy, use Sea Dart missiles for area air defence. They are being joined eventually by the Broad-

197

Trials for the British Hawker Siddeley Harrier
aboard the French helicopter carrier *Jeanne
d'Arc*

sword Type 22 guided missile frigates, with Lynx helicopters, Exocet and Sea Wolf missiles, and this class will replace the Leander-class frigates.

Meanwhile, frigates of the Rothesay and Whitby classes have been withdrawn from service, and so has one more cruiser, HMS *Tiger*, in June, 1978.

While some small addition to the RAF's Nimrod maritime-reconnaissance force was made during the early 1970s, the most significant development took the form of an order for eleven of an airborne-early-warning version of this aircraft to replace the Shackletons, starting in 1979. Originally, the Shackleton replacement was to have been on a NATO-scale, with some twenty Boeing 707 E–3A AEW aircraft, but delay by the other European partners in NATO encouraged the British Government to press ahead with its own system, although this will be compatible with the NATO system. In addition to its AEW role, the AEW Nimrod has a secondary maritime-reconnaissance capability.

Ardito, the Italian interpretation of the modern destroyer, but able to carry two helicopters

Seldom do developments occur in isolation, so it was only natural that the Italian Navy should order, in late 1977, a 12,000 ton helicopter cruiser. But unlike the Andrea Doria and Vittorio Veneto classes, this vessel, the *Guiseppe Garibaldi*, will have a through flight deck. The French also planned a helicopter carrier with a through deck, but this vessel, the PA75, was intended to be nuclear-powered and more of a commando carrier than an ASW helicopter carrier. At the time of writing, the order for it has been postponed for budgetary reasons. Both navies introduced helicopter-carrying warships, including the Italian Audace class 4,400 ton destroyer in 1971, with two helicopters, and the smaller Lupo class light frigate, of which the first of four for the Italian Navy was delivered in 1977. The Lupo class is also on order for Peru, and an improved version able to carry two helicopters is being

A busy flight deck aboard the much modernised and still highly-effective HMAS *Melbourne*, shown here with Douglas A–4 Skyhawks and Westland-built S–61 Sea King ASW helicopters

Niteroi, one of the most recent Brazilian warships, follows the trend towards guided missiles and helicopters.

built for the Italian Navy, which will probably have eight. The three French Tourville class 5,000 ton guided missile frigates, which first entered service in 1974, carry two Lynx helicopters, as do the more recent Georges Leygues class. Ships of the latter class are 4,000 ton guided missile frigates, which should enter service from 1979 onwards, and which the French hope to build in quantity, finance permitting.

Some attempt at standardisation is also in hand, with the Royal Netherlands Navy's Standaart (Standard) frigates and the West German Type 122 frigates. These vessels conform to the same dimensions and are standardised in other areas as well, although equipment is varied to allow for the German 'brown water' and the Netherlands 'blue water' navies. The German vessels, in common with the French, are combined diesel and gas turbine-powered, with gas turbines for high speed dash only, while the Dutch vessels are all-gas turbine. Italian vessels, are normally steam or diesel, although the *Guiseppe Garibaldi* will be all-gas turbine-powered.

The Royal Australian and the Spanish navies are basing their destroyer or frigate requirements on American designs. The Royal Australian Navy, however, is planning eventually to replace HMAS *Melbourne* with some form of carrier able to operate Hawkey Siddeley Sea Harrier fighters and helicopters. These carriers will most probably be the Vickers MAC ship or the *Invincible* class, but possibly Harrier Carriers or even an Italian type. HMAS *Sydney* went to the breakers in 1975.

An exception is the Canadian Armed Forces, with their Iroquois class destroyers, first introduced in 1972, and able to carry two large Sea King helicopters each.

While ex-British light fleet carriers survive in the Brazilian, Argentinian, Indian and Australian navies (all except for the *Vikrant* having been extensively modernised), the only Independence class vessel still used as an aircraft carrier is the former USS *Cabot*, now the Spanish Navy's *Daedalo*. The *Daedalo* operates

The Japanese destroyer *Murakumo* with a flight of Mitsubishi-built HSS–2 helicopters

helicopters and Hawker Siddeley AV–8As, delivered via the USMC, making the Spanish Navy the second in the world to take vertical take-off jet aircraft to sea. The Indian Navy also hopes to be able to operate Harriers in due course.

The Soviet Navy created a stir in 1976 with its first through-deck cruiser, the *Kiev*, 40,000 tons standard displacement. This strange vessel, the first of at least four with the second, *Minsk*, completed in 1978, has an extremely large island superstructure on the starboard side, and an angled flight deck. The through deck stops well short of the fo'c'sle, which is packed with missile and gun systems for surface-to-surface, surface-to-air and anti-submarine warfare. In addition to the inevitable Kamov Ka–25 helicopters for missile guidance and ASW duties, the Yakovlev 'Forger A' vertical take-off fighter is deployed aboard these ships. The Yakovlev 'Forger A' is similar in appearance to the Harrier, although rather less neat, and it seems to be far less developed and not nearly as potent as the Harrier. Developed from the un-designated 'Freehand' fighter, 'Forger A'

has two lift jets to augment its single main turbojet engine, and can only, reportedly, take off vertically, lacking Harrier's option of short take-off.

It is not completely clear to what extent the Soviet Navy understands carrier operations, but there is no doubt that it intends to do so. It should certainly have some idea, after twenty years and more of shadowing British, American and French warships, often at far closer range than good seamanship would consider wise.

While most warships of 2,000 tons and over now carry a helicopter, more recent developments have been centred on allowing vessels of around 1,000 tons, such as the Vickers Vedette offshore patrol vessel, to carry one. The fact is that in the late 1970s, a helicopter is an indispensible aid to surface warships, extending their range and, most important, their anti-submarine capability. In the Royal Navy, every frigate or destroyer has this capability. In this way, just over three-quarters of a century after the first tentative controlled heavier-than-air flights by the Wright brothers, the aeroplane has in one form at least become inseparable from the effective exercise of sea power.

11 The V/STOL Ship

The future can but be the subject for speculation, and perhaps the wisest way to speculate is to look at existing and projected developments and attempt to assess what factors will be likely to work for and against their realisation.

A submariner will quite rightly point out that in an age of manpower shortages in the armed forces of the democracies, the submarine is the naval weapons system that uses manpower most economically. He will also add that in another decade or two, satellite reconnaissance will be able to hold every surface vessel hostage to missile attack in any conflict, and in this he may be right. The problem is that submarines, whether patrol or ballistic missile carrying, conventional or nuclear, tend to be weapons for all-out warfare. You cannot defend a country's territorial limit, its fisheries, or its oil rigs with a submarine unless you are content to sink any vessel coming into the protected area. Still less can you show the flag effectively, fire a warning shot across bows, land troops for the evacuation of innocent civilians, or protect a convoy, particularly during an uncertain period when a threat of war might just be avoided. Yet submarines are admittedly vital. The only trouble is that the Soviet Union has 400 of them—ten times the number deployed by Nazi Germany in 1939—and some 40 per cent are nuclear-powered and far more difficult to find and destroy than World War II submarines, in spite of improved detection techniques.

There are those who would put their faith in small ships. Fine. Small ships are important and will always be so. It just happens that the modern defensive missile systems with their sophisticated radar equipment, will not fit into the smallest frigates or corvettes.

On the other hand, many naval purists insist that only a big aircraft carrier is effective, and that the limited number of aircraft which can be deployed aboard a small carrier, coupled with their limited range and warload, makes such vessels useless. Others would say that a big carrier could be eliminated quickly by a single nuclear-warhead, whether delivered by plane or missile. Another argument is that cheaper and smaller carriers, with their helicopters and vertical take-off aircraft, allow many more vessels to be ordered; thus such vessels can be present in so many more places at once, and if the worst comes to the worst, present many more targets for the enemy to have to cope with.

There is something in all of these arguments, but an even more important consideration is whether we need, and whether we will commit ourselves to providing, defence of a reasonable standard.

Pacifism is an attractive philosophy. It is rather pleasant to consider that we are all brothers under the skin, and just one big family. The sad fact, however, is that no one country has ever escaped war by adopting pacifism as a national policy! Sweden and Switzerland have remained neutral for more than a century through maintaining strong defence forces and a degree of conscription and military commitment seldom found in free democratic countries. In addition, the grace of God has provided them with terrain so

The first of a new Soviet-class, *Kiev*, on trials, being trailed by the Leander-class frigate, HMS *Danae*

Opposite above: Kiev's vertical take-off jets, Yakovlev Yak–25 'Forger A' strike aircraft

Opposite below: Most navies have accepted the helicopter-carrying destroyer. This is the Japanese Maritime Self-Defence Force's *Hiei*

HMS *Invincible*, the first of three through deck cruisers or light fleet aircraft carriers, entering Royal Navy service in 1979

daunting that prospective enemies have turned their attention elsewhere, and have generally been overcome by the rest of Europe, helped by the New World!

Is there a threat to the democracies? The record of the Soviet Union since World War II—perhaps one should really say since 1939—has not been good, and in spite of detente, most of eastern and central Europe languishes under the Russian jackboot while Soviet-backed Cuban forces have rampaged across the Horn of Africa and the former Portuguese colonies of Angola and Mozambique. If one asks what the Soviet intentions towards the West might be, it is difficult to provide a certain answer, although one can speculate wisely. However, that no good will is intended can be gathered from the attitude of the Soviets towards their own people. Love of mankind, like charity, begins at home.

Through the ages, the countries most determined on war and destruction have been those which have also inflicted injustice upon their own people, in Napoleonic France, Nazi Germany, Fascist Italy, Imperial Japan, and Soviet Russia.

For as long as a reasonable nuclear balance can be maintained, the Soviet Union is unlikely to risk an all out nuclear war, and the real threats come on the so-called 'central front' of Europe, on Europe's flanks in Scandinavia and the Mediterranean, on the main sea routes of the world, and in those countries supplying scarce but vital raw material. On all but the first, naval power is vitally important, and even there, reinforcements from North America will only reach Europe in time if the North Atlantic can be controlled. This is because of Russia's superiority in conventional forces in Europe, the importance of which has been increased by America's decision to delay deployment of the so-called neutron bomb in Europe. The neutron bomb is, in effect, not a bomb, but an anti-tank weapon able to deplete Soviet superiority on the ground with the minimum of risk to civilian populations near the war zone.

In short, naval power is essential to patrol the oceans of the world and to ensure that reinforcements can be rushed to wherever they may be needed, and also to mount an amphibious landing on NATO's flanks or on the shores of other pro-Western and non-aligned nations under Soviet threat. Only control of the seas can provide all this; and only control of the seas allows influence to be exercised in more subtle ways, such as showing the flag, and so creating a presence because of the strategic nature of a warship, which is national territory in a way which no aircraft can match.

Where does the aircraft carrier enter into this? The carrier's great advantage is that it is probably the most cost-effective of all weapons systems. This is because it can be used at all times and any time, regardless of the level of crisis, and is capable of landing troops or conducting an evacuation far more easily than can smaller warships, or ever larger vessels such as cruisers. In a battle, its aircraft, each of which can carry a variety of ordnance, can attack repeatedly, each offering a range of options, unlike some missile systems, which are single shot without a reload facility whilst the vessel remains at sea. Another virtue of the carrier lies in the way in which it can call an aircraft back!

The USN view of its future carriers (after the fourth Nimitz has been delivered): the Sea Control Ship, to operate McDonnell Douglas-built AV–8B Harriers and Sikorsky Sea King helicopters

Many of the Oliver Hazard Perry-class frigates are already in service, but here one is joined by two of the planned Sikorsky Mk.III LAMPS helicopters

But what size of carrier is needed?

While it is true that small carrier's have their limitations, it is also true that giant carriers offer too tempting a target, and cannot use certain waterways. In fact, since even the largest carrier aircraft can use carriers of the Midway class, it is in many ways a pity that the Americans did not order larger numbers of vessels of this size, rather than a few very large carriers. On the other hand, politicians do not always think in this way. The British Government cancelled large carriers costing an estimated £100 million apiece in 1965, and later ordered vessels planned to cost half as much at 1965 prices; but it did not think of ordering twice as many!

Even the Americans are becoming dubious about the cost and effectiveness of the giant carrier, although growing concern over Soviet intentions may effectively counter this. However, for the United States Navy, it is unlikely that small carriers will be ordered for some time, at least not in large numbers, because all of the nuclear-powered carriers, of which there will soon be four, as well

Artist's impression of an AV–8B ashore

as many of the large conventional carriers and assault ships, are new enough to remain in service for some years, particularly since the USN tends to give its vessels a long life.

In Europe, the small carrier has already found acceptance in Britain, France and Italy, and doubtless all three, plus Australia, and possibly later Argentina, Brazil and India, will eventually operate vessels of this type, choosing one or another of several classes which will be built. The Japanese and the Germans may possibly follow suit, although German naval aviation is largely shore-based, using Tornado and Atlantique aircraft for operations in the Baltic. However, it would take a severe fright to arouse Canada from its indifference to world events.

Just how effective these small vessels will remain in the future will depend on the development of a successor to the Harrier. If, out of the various designs proposed to replace the Harrier and Jaguar aircraft under AST 403 (Air Staff Target, 403), the Royal Air Force decides to accept an aircraft with V/STOL capability, then all will be well, since the AST 403 will have supersonic and light fighter capability—provided the British Admiralty can accept the position and take this aircraft. The RAF is concerned that in the future, the Royal Navy may press for its own purpose-built fighter, in which case the available funds for new aircraft development might be over-stretched. However, if the Air Staff does not entirely forget the Royal Navy's needs, the situation may never arise.

Smaller and lighter is better—high cost F–14As will have to be supplemented by the cheaper McDonnell Douglas F–18 carrier-borne fighter

Guiseppe Garibaldi, the new Italian through deck cruiser, now being built

The Vosper-Thorneycroft private venture Harrier Carrier would have a displacement of just 6,000 tons, yet could take four Harriers and four Sea Kings, although here a Westland Lynx is in evidence

The prototype Hawker Siddeley Sea Harrier
shows its paces taking off from an improvised
'ski jump'

HARRIER SKI-JUMP USING MEDIUM GIRDER BRIDGE

Helicopter carrier of the future? In spite of stop-start development, it may simply be a matter of time before large surface effect ships or hovercraft supplement conventional frigates and destroyers

An alternative to the hovercraft, the hydrofoil uses foils with an aerodynamic shape, but helicopter-carrying versions have not yet been mooted

There is an old saying, 'When poverty walks in through the door, love flies out of the window.' Naval and air force relationships exemplify it admirably. If both services can have what they want, or most of it, they realise their need for each other; but make funds scarce, and inter-service rivalry ceases to be healthy, forgets the end results of the conflict, and causes immense damage. Politicians should never forget this. However, some rivalry is inevitable, since pride in service contributes to efficiency and effectiveness. And no one would suggest unification of the armed forces in any country after the disastrous effect on morale of Canadian unification, even though the demoralising effect was in that case accentuated by the cuts which accompanied unification.

It is unlikely that much will come of plans for hovercraft or hydrofoils equipped to carry helicopters, following the USN's cancellation of the SES 2000 hovercraft frigate, which would have carried two large helicopters. The cost of running such vessels, together with their uncertain poor-weather performance, makes them a poor buy compared with the conventional ship. It is true that they offer greater speed, but extra aircraft can to some extent compensate for low speed in a ship. So if anything, the trend is towards putting helicopters in even-smaller warships, or carrying more small helicopters in full-sized frigates and destroyers.

Thus the future is increasingly one for small carriers operating V/STOL jet aircraft and helicopters, with perhaps a V/STOL airliner design developed to provide longer-range carrier-borne ASW and AEW operations. The exception to this will be in the two large navies, the USN and the Soviet Navy, both of which can afford to build and man large ships. However, it is unlikely that the next generation of American carriers will be bigger than the present generation; they may well be at least a little smaller.

Long-range maritime-reconnaissance from shore bases will remain important, and will continue to use modified civilian designs, as it has done, more or less, for the past fifty years or so, although the aircraft types include many conversions of smaller airliners and feeder-liner aircraft.

Index

222